HELLACIOUS CALIFORNIA!

HELLACIOUS CALIFORNIA!

TALES OF RASCALITY! REVELRY! DISSIPATION! AND DEPRAVITY! AND THE Birth of the GOLDEN STATE

GARY NOY

HEYDAY, BERKELEY, CALIFORNIA
SIERRA COLLEGE PRESS, ROCKLIN, CALIFORNIA

SIERRA COLLEGE PRESS

Library of Congress Cataloging-in-Publication Data is available.

Cover Art: "Portrait of Soldier," photograph by Jacob Shew, c. 1865.
   Image courtesy of the California State Library, Sacramento;
   California History Section, Digital ID: 2008-0327.
Cover Design: Ashley Ingram
Interior Design/Typesetting: Rebecca LeGates

Published by Heyday in collaboration with Sierra College Press
P.O. Box 9145, Berkeley, California 94709
(510) 549-3564
heydaybooks.com

Printed in East Peoria, Illinois, by Versa Press, Inc.

10 9 8 7 6 5 4 3 2 1

For my Grandma, Mary Ethel Lewis Winkle, who sparked my fascination with nineteenth-century American history

"It is my unbiased opinion that California can and does furnish the best bad things that are obtainable in America."

—Hinton Rowan Helper,
The Land of Gold: Reality versus Fiction, 1855

CONTENTS

Hinton Rowan Helper, c. 1860. From Helper, *The Impending Crisis of the South* (New York: A.D. Burdick, 1860), frontispiece. Image from a volume in the author's personal collection.

INTRODUCTION

I n May 1851, San Francisco was a city in recovery. On May 3 and 4, a massive conflagration had swept through the bustling city, and for ten hours the fire raged, swallowing everything in its path. When finally quenched, the flames had destroyed two thousand buildings, representing about three-quarters of the city, and at least nine lives were lost. It was "as if the God of Destruction had seated himself in our midst, and was gorging himself and all his ministers of devastation upon the ruin of our doomed city and its people," reported San Francisco's *Daily Alta California*. Most of the city was uninsured, and conservative estimates placed the damages at roughly $12 million (about $400 million today).

But San Franciscans were resilient. French argonaut Ernest de Massey, who had repeatedly witnessed both the destructive power of fire in Gold Rush San Francisco and the buoyant resurgence of the city, admiringly commented in a letter to his cousin in France: "One calamity more or less seems to make no difference to these Californians." Rebuilding began immediately, and a chorus of hammers and saws filled the air for weeks. In the hyper-accelerated Gold Rush society, however, construction was often rapid, slapdash, and dodgy. On Sunday, May 25, 1851, the *Alta California* noted that "a new building, recently erected on Central Wharf, was blown down by the force of the wind yesterday."

The weather that day was a great source of amusement in the paper:

> There was great sport yesterday not withstanding it was Sunday, the streets being converted into race courses, and races being run between men and their hats. The weather was highly favorable, being gloriously windy, and tiles [hats] of all descriptions blew off the heads of their owners and filling with the breeze galloped off, making much better time than those in pursuit.

But the fierce gale and precarious edifices meant little to a hardy band of travelers on the sleek clipper ship *Stag Hound*, which dropped anchor in the harbor that breezy Sunday. This moment marked the beginning of their grand Gold Rush adventure and what they devoutly wished would be the dawn of a new life. They were intensely optimistic, expectant and energized, and inspired by the seemingly irresistible compulsion known as gold fever. The seven paying passengers aboard the *Stag Hound* had arrived that morning after an eventful journey of 113 days from New York to San Francisco via Cape Horn, a voyage that included both high adventure (they had deftly rescued a shipwreck survivor off the coast of Brazil) and deep discomfort (most of the passengers had endured weeks-long bouts of seasickness, due in part to a terrifying storm near Bermuda and seven days and nights of ferocious weather rounding the cape).

Among their number was a confident twenty-one-year-old from North Carolina—sinewy, bearded, and possessed of a resolute gaze and a steely demeanor. His name was Hinton Rowan Helper and he was excited to begin his quest for golden glory, charged with the determination that animated the many hundreds of thousands of people who experienced the California Gold Rush. Helper presumed success and trusted that his stay in California would be brief, pleasant, and lucrative.

It was not. Hinton Rowan Helper hated California.

The young explorer spent three long, frustrating, tiring years in California. As did most, he failed miserably as a miner. Helper unhappily recalled that during one season, he realized a net profit of "ninety-three and a quarter cents in three months . . . or a fraction over a cent a day." He hungered to escape from this private hell and longed to return to his romanticized vision of North Carolina, a world of gentility, grace, and agrarian virtues.

Broke and disillusioned, Hinton Rowan Helper returned home in 1854 and vowed to persuade others to shun California and avoid the appalling Gold Rush torment he had endured. To that end, he put his nose to the grindstone, weaponized the alphabet, and swiftly produced a vitriolic diatribe entitled *The Land of Gold: Reality versus Fiction*, published in 1855. Helper's venomous broadside had elements of truth, but the best-selling book was also hyperbolic, full of overstated statistics and dubious anecdotes, not to mention laden with the blatant bigotry and casual racism characteristic of the era. It is best remembered for his caustic commentary on nineteenth-century California culture.

While Hinton Rowan Helper found most of California reprehensible, he did tender this backhanded compliment:

> I will say, that I have seen purer liquors, better segars [cigars], finer tobacco, truer guns and pistols, larger dirks and bowie knives, and prettier courtezans here, than in any other place I have ever visited; and it is my unbiased opinion that California can and does furnish the best bad things that are obtainable in America.

It is this Helper observation that provided the initial stimulus for the book you now hold: *Hellacious California!: Tales of Rascality, Revelry, Dissipation, and Depravity, and the Birth of the Golden State*. This book is designed to investigate the range of problematic pursuits that contributed to the California we recognize today—some frightening, some amusing, some mystifying, all impactful. Old California was, in a word, hellacious, but even in that single word we find more than one meaning. It can, both separately or simultaneously, connote something (or someone) that is, on the one hand, astonishing or, on the other, appalling. In embodying that duality, it is a word that perfectly reflects the impressive and astounding yet disconcerting, disappointing, and, perhaps above all, complicated nature of nineteenth-century California. *Hellacious California* presents but a snapshot of the questionable undertakings and, by turns, colorful and disreputable personalities of Old California, defined here as the period from the 1820s—when California came under Mexican control following Mexico's successful eleven-year war of independence from Spain—to the turn of the twentieth century.

The primary source material for our story is the rich trove of letters and letter sheets, diaries, journals, and newspaper articles chronicling the peccadilloes, embarrassments, failures, unorthodox desires, eccentricities, and other misbehaviors that befell or were perpetrated by the range of intriguing personalities who navigated the hazards of Old California. Some of the documents referenced in this book have been buried in archives for decades, and many have never before been published. Often, these sources are loaded with the prejudices of the participants, and, as with much historical documentation on any subject, the content is frequently rife with vulgarity, misogyny, racism, and cruelty that is especially repellant to our present-day sensibilities. *Hellacious California* attempts to avoid republishing the most offensive of these materials, instead presenting equally valuable alternatives. At times, however, the most informative window into the cultural attitudes of the period is through these odious passages, and some have been included here unvarnished, as any other approach would be dishonest.

o   o   o

The saga of nineteenth-century California reflects an ardent embrace of the things that made it at once both exciting and chaotic: the roiling mix of ethnicities and nationalities, the physical, political, and commercial isolation from established centers of power, the sheer number of eccentrics and outliers among its inhabitants, and the simultaneous endorsement of and reaction against the coarsest, most dissolute aspects of human behavior. Old California honored tradition but also revered change, and it was the setting for successive waves of societal invention, reinvention, and retrenchment. In short, Old California was a paradox—part romantic legend, part unforgiving reality. It is this unique legacy that animates the Golden State to this day, perpetuating a most fascinating and frustrating *continuum sui generis.*

Humans have long held competing visions of this stretch of land along the west side of the continent, and in Old California their descriptions ranged from those who agreed with Hinton Rowan Helper's assessment of the region as an abysm, perdition in the worldly plane, and a waking nightmare, all the way to those who saw California as Arcadia, a blissful wonderland, an unspoiled vision of humble pleasures and tranquil existence, what the prominent Californio doyen Mariano Guadalupe Vallejo characterized as "the true Eden, the land of promise."

For centuries before either of those men were born, however, the area that would become California was the exclusive domain of splendidly diverse Native cultures. With a pre-contact population estimated at three hundred thousand people, the region was the most densely inhabited part of Native America north of Mexico and was home to dozens of distinctive nations, all with their own languages and traditions. But that would change dramatically with the arrival of the Europeans.

Spanish explorers had briefly visited the region in the sixteenth century but had shown little interest in this distant holding of imperial New Spain. Similar indifference was also evident among other Europeans, and for more than a hundred years the future state of California existed as a private, and mostly ignored, Spanish outpost. It wasn't until the mid-eighteenth century that Spanish California began to attract attention from the global European market. English, French, and Russian explorers meandered along the oceanic rim of New Spain's northern province called Alta California, searching for trading possibilities and exploitable resources. Concerned that it might lose its monopoly on the territory, Spain responded in the 1760s by authorizing expeditions to gather intelligence and establish pueblos in the largely alien landscape. Spain had always preferred a minimalist approach to colonizing, and that seemed ideal for a geography that made California essentially a landlocked island—a remote landscape ringed by a forbidding fog-draped coastline, harsh deserts, and snowy, often impassable mountain ranges. As a result of this somewhat lackluster settlement effort over a period of fifty years, California was still only sparsely populated by Mexican citizens when Mexico gained independence from Spain in 1821. Only a few thousand Californios—the Spanish-speaking descendants of Spanish and Mexican colonists—had established a footprint along the Pacific shore and on the snaking pathway of the Spanish presidios and the Franciscan mission chain. Their economy was insular, primarily based on self-reliant cattle ranching centered on large estates that frequently used forced labor of the Native population.

Upon establishing hegemony, Mexico reversed the restrictive trade and immigration policies that had stagnated California's economy. The new Mexican government allowed free access to seaports, relaxed immigration procedures, and redistributed mission lands. California's cattle herds were now open to *Norte Americano* merchants seeking shoe leather and tallow for candles. American maritime trading vessels and whaling ships soon became common sights. And within a decade the American presence was manifest in Old California. By the 1830s, merchants and artisans from the United States were familiar figures in coastal cities like Monterey, and as California became more dependent on American shipping and trade goods, the society changed from self-sufficient agriculture to a ranching economy based on trade and exports.

The region began to prosper economically, and that lured more settlers, some of whom ventured into the interior valleys to establish agricultural dominions. A few of the newcomers received land grants (including John Sutter, who later became central to Gold Rush history), but hundreds made their way independently, establishing communities with little regard for Mexican law or authority. The United States government took note of the faraway domain and its improving prospects and, on several occasions, unsuccessfully negotiated to buy California or larger swaths of the Southwest. In 1835, the federal government even attempted to purchase San Francisco alone.

Even as the region's global reputation grew along with its economy, the Californio, European, and American populations of California remained small, totaling around ten thousand in the early 1840s. By this time, throughout the entire region that would become California, Californios numbered roughly eight thousand, while the American contingent was about eight hundred, but a major shift was about to take place. In 1846, tensions between Mexico and the United States boiled over, mostly because of boundary disputes in Texas, a clash that eventually led to the Mexican War of 1846–48. The conflict ended with the establishment of the short-lived independent Bear Flag Republic, but it was quickly replaced by United States occupation. The ultimate American victory was codified on February 2, 1848, by the Treaty of Guadalupe Hidalgo, which specified that Mexico would cede territory that includes the present-day states of Nevada and Utah, most of Arizona, half of New Mexico, a quarter of Colorado, a sliver of Wyoming, and *all* of California.

This transfer of land was a major turning point, but what almost no one knew was that two weeks earlier, on a crisp January morning in 1848, California had already changed forever.

o   o   o

On January 24, 1848, while inspecting work on a sawmill being constructed in the Sierra Nevada foothills, a surprised James Marshall spied gold nuggets gleaming in the early-morning sun. His discovery ushered in the California Gold Rush, the single largest migration to one spot for a single purpose since the Crusades. It was the pivot point of California history.

Within five years of Marshall's find, nearly three hundred thousand people had migrated to seek their fortunes in California, most of them coming to the San Francisco Bay Area and points east into Gold Country. They came from around the world, drawn by the incurable contagion of gold fever and by the promise that riches were abundant and "free for all," as the United States government had officially proclaimed. Argonauts came in all sizes and shapes, all ages, all races, and from all economic backgrounds, and they came with a full range of ambitions, affectations, prejudices, virtues, and vices. Within a matter of months, California became the most culturally diverse place on Earth.

It was an explosion that instantly altered the region's demographics, economy, and behaviors; virtually every aspect of the community was affected by the surge. The state population increased 1,400 percent in 1850 alone. The government transitioned from self-governing dominion to military governorship to statehood by 1850, and the legal system erratically converted from Mexican to American law, including a months-long period when, as forty-niner and California state senator Elisha Crosby observed, "there was very little law." The Californios were inundated by the human tsunami of the Gold Rush and lost power, influence, land, and personal property. The Native population was decimated through disease, violence, and the official validation of extermination policies, and within a generation, an estimated 94 percent of the California Indian population was wiped out.

The rapid transformation of the region led to the predictable repercussions, and tensions brewed and boiled over between members of different races, nationalities, and economic classes. Racism, exclusion, and xenophobia were openly exhibited in the turbulent politics of the era, and harassment of and violence toward Chinese people, Latinxs, people of African descent, and Native Californians was not only the norm but was reinforced by official bodies and policies, including, for instance, the anti-Chinese Workingmen's Party in the 1870s and the Chinese Exclusion Act of 1882.

Another marginalized group was women of all races; the new population was overwhelmingly young and male, with women and girls making up only about 8 percent of the population statewide. In some ways, the Gold Rush economy offered greater opportunities for women than they might find elsewhere, and yet the chauvinism of the male majority continued to relegate women to second-class status. Some women found success as entrepreneurs and made their fortunes during this era. Several gained social prominence and exerted cultural influence, particularly in larger cities. Many struggled but persevered against the harsh conditions and unfair social restrictions of the times. Life was challenging for all women, but non-white women had it particularly hard.

As diverse as they were, many of the newcomers to California had something in common: the audacious and resourceful attitude of individuals out to improve their circumstances. The first iteration of American California was governed by this spirit, and even as the Gold Rush intensity declined as the placers petered out, the attitudes of personal and entrepreneurial risk-taking remained strong. In the second phase of Americanization, the state was the site of related booms in both agriculture and transportation, particularly after the construction and completion of the Transcontinental Railroad in 1869. No longer was California an isolated land apart; it was now accessible to all who could afford a ticket—and for those who couldn't, they might at least be able to afford some California-grown produce. California increasingly became a part of the national and global economy, and individuals continued to amass impressive fortunes through mining, timber, and the railroad.

As the railroad helped the state ship products out, it also brought new waves of immigrants in, including agricultural workers, especially from the Midwest farming regions. Skillful advertising touted the extraordinary richness of California soils, the easy access to irrigated water, and the support of a state-of-the-art transportation network featuring railroads, steamboats, sailing ships, and stagecoaches. The call was answered by farmers from agricultural havens such as Iowa, Ohio, and Illinois who pulled up roots and relocated to California's inland valleys, where they produced a bounty of wheat, fruits, and row crops.

The tentacles of the railroad also brought new settlers and new opportunities to other regions of the state. In 1880, Southern California harbored only 6 percent of the state's population, but the balance was starting to shift. In Los Angeles County, the population skyrocketed 550 percent between 1880 and 1900, and the county went from representing 3.8 percent of the state population to 11.5 percent.

With this new type of immigrant came new attitudes into the fray. As conservative, family-oriented farmers began to supplant the younger, more freewheeling forty-niners, momentum built up in various efforts to harness what the Midwesterners in particular considered to be immoral behavior. They criticized the "anything goes" ethos of Gold Rush California, and they added support to existing or nascent reform movements that soon led to a plethora of legal limitations and prohibitions—or at least *attempted* limitations and prohibitions. The overwhelming atmosphere was of deep contradiction, with California serving as a battleground for the forces of light and dark. Old California was still proud of being on the cutting edge, but it was frequently fearful of what that edge represented. As always, some California and national observers felt that the state was a transcendent nirvana populated by stalwart adventurers, independent visionaries, and calculatingly brilliant speculators, but they, in equal measure, were challenged by the naysayers, an entire cadre of critics who maintained that California was a squalid sump of corruption and immorality—the troubled habitat of Hinton Rowan Helper's "best bad things."

By the end of the nineteenth century, a California-bred attitude had emerged: a swaggering self-assurance energized by a passionate but appreciably romanticized historical tale of toil, sacrifice, pride, and arrogance. In 1948, one hundred years after James Marshall's discovery of gold at Sutter's Fort in Coloma, historian John Walton Caughey summarized this viewpoint: "Californians . . . have a confidence that sometimes alarms strangers. They are in the habit of having great expectations, of entertaining roseate hopes and seeing them come true."

Stephen Birmingham, author of *California Rich: The Lives, the Times, the Scandals and the Fortunes of the Men and Women Who Made and Kept California's Wealth* (1980), a social history of the moneyed elite during California's formative years following statehood, echoed this assertion. By 1900, Birmingham wrote, the state's restive residents

> displayed a spirit and a character that would become typically Californian. The California élan involved a special doughtiness, a certain daring, a refusal to be fazed or put off by bad luck or circumstances, an unwillingness to give up . . . . But there is still more to the California spirit than a willingness to gamble and accept dares . . . . The Californians promptly acquired rather large chips on their shoulders, and, in addition to a certain hauteur, the California character became notably disputatious and competitive.

As Californians continued to earn their reputations as bold individualists with what-the-hell, live-for-the-moment attitudes, the negative perceptions persisted as well. For instance, in 1918, historian William Elsey Connelley linked the carnage of World War I to what he saw as California's historically dysfunctional and profligate ethos. The shamelessness of California culture, Connelley asserted, was "a disease that spread to all the world," and he traced back to the Gold Rush "the advent of character decadence and . . . moral degeneracy" that had infected Europe, which had then descended into "savagery for slim strips of barren territory." The contradictory image of the state as both a dream and a warning was profound and wide-reaching. Who knew California had such power?

o   o   o

Experimentation. Traditionalism. New blood. Old conflicts. Persistent transformation. Reinvention. Terrestrial paradise. Hellhole. Contradiction upon contradiction, Old California was a curious concoction. It sought stability but celebrated the untried idea, and it yearned for the trappings of the conventional even as it followed an unconventional path. Nineteenth-century California was quick on its feet and could turn on a dime, and that legacy persists to this day. It was (and still is) reckless, rambunctious, competitive, bohemian, and trail-blazing, but also cautious, skeptical, and callous. And just as the unique mix of people made California what it was in the nineteenth century, so does the ever-changing population contour the state today. As historian James N. Gregory wrote in his superb 1993 essay "The Shaping of California History":

> Continuous repopulation is the critical drama of California's history and the source of some of its unique cultural claims. Wave after wave of newcomers from an ever changing list of places have remade California again and again over the years, each time adding something new even while they allow the state to retain its most paradoxical tradition, the tradition of change.

Hellacious California!: Tales of Rascality, Revelry, Dissipation, and Depravity, and the Birth of the Golden State reaches back into the nineteenth century to shine a spotlight on the origins of the state's reputation as the home of a diverse collection of boundary-pushing, rule-flouting, big-dreaming individuals. It is not designed to be a comprehensive compendium of dubious conduct, an encyclopedia of crime, or to offer justifications for questionable behavior. There is much to choose from and too much to cover in the pages of one book, and so this offering will focus on just a handful of the unique, problematic, quirky, and downright unsavory markers along the route to modern California.

On this tour, we start by examining gambling, the widespread activity that J. Linville Hall, the first chronicler of Gold Rush California, called the "principal amusement" of the era. We will then contemplate Old California's penchant for producing and consuming alcohol beverages, and on the heels of drinking, we will reflect on the multiplicity of dining choices in the Golden State of the nineteenth century, ranging from injurious culinary choices to luxurious dining to unappetizing excess. *Hellacious California* will walk us through the astonishing use and abuse of tobacco, and then our path will survey the omnipresent, almost routine forms of fighting throughout the century, focusing on gun and animal duels, knife fights, and the development of professional prizefighting. From there the text moves the spotlight to sexual mores, courtship practices, and divorce, and then to a showcase of the astonishingly varied, idiosyncratic, and eccentric forms of entertainment in Old California. And, finally, as we reach the end of this expedition, *Hellacious California* will introduce us to the proliferation of scoundrels and con artists in nineteenth-century California.

So, let us now start on our journey. We begin in 1895 in the San Francisco basement of Charlie, an ingenious machinist, as he tinkers with a mysterious whirring box.

California land baron Elias Jackson "Lucky" Baldwin displays a winning poker hand to his faceless tablemates. In the early 1880s, Baldwin established one of the first casinos at Lake Tahoe, the lavish Baldwin's Tallac House. The casino and resort were on the California side of the lake, and it was only through stealth and guile that Baldwin dodged the fact that gambling was illegal in El Dorado County. "Elias Jackson Baldwin," c. 1895. Image courtesy of the California State Library, Sacramento; California History Section, Digital ID: 2008-0882.

CHAPTER ONE

Black-Legs, California Prayer Books,
and Twisting the Tiger's Tail

GAMES OF CHANCE

J. Linville Hall was a pious Connecticut printer and author of the first published journal of the California Gold Rush. With a company of enthusiastic Hartford gold seekers, Hall arrived in San Francisco in 1849, and among the first phenomena to catch his sharp-eyed notice was the prevalence of gambling. He wrote: "The principal amusement is gambling, which is carried on to an unlimited extent; and the perfect indifference with which thousands are lost and won would astonish you."

While J. Linville Hall's observation certainly reflected the Gold Rush milieu, it would have been nearly as accurate decades earlier and later as well, and in fact it still rings largely true today. Gambling in California has always been an alluring Aladdin's cave and, at the same time, a constantly bothersome, sometimes deadly diversion. Wagers were common before Europeans came to the region and during the time of the Californios, and games of chance were widespread even when they were officially illegal in the Golden State. Today over $12 billion is generated annually for the state's economy through legal gambling in card rooms, at racetracks, and courtesy of the state lottery. For some of that staggering revenue we can thank a tubercular San Francisco machinist named Charlie and his 1899 invention—a hypnotic whirring contraption that enticed the willing with a combination of four elements: a familiar custom, a momentary respite, a distressing stumbling block, and the promise of a better day.

Charlie's original name was Augustinus Josephus Fey, and his invention was the modern slot machine, the omnipresent monarch of today's casinos. Born in Bavaria in 1862, Fey showed sophisticated technical proficiency and natural inventiveness from childhood. He left home at age fifteen, settled in France, and then crossed the channel to England. In London, Fey worked for a nautical instrument company, and his five-year residence in Great Britain supplied him with a first-rate command of English. In 1885, he immigrated to the United States, where he briefly lived with his uncle in Hoboken, New Jersey.

Restless, the twenty-three-year-old Augustinus soon headed west, arriving in San Francisco later that same year. His dreams of a new life in the rollicking City by the Bay quickly dissipated, however, when he was diagnosed with tuberculosis. Told he had but a year to live, Fey vowed to fight the "wasting-away disease" by any means necessary. He decided to undergo creosote treatment. Creosote, a chemical derived from wood, coal, or petroleum, is today most often used as a wood preservative, as an expectorant, and as "liquid smoke" in food preparation, but in the late nineteenth century it had more extensive, if questionable, medical applications, including in therapies for coughs, stomach irritability, ulcers, epilepsy, leprosy, neuralgia, diabetes, and, through the early decades of the twentieth century, tuberculosis.

Creosote cured Fey and, furnished with a clean bill of health, he found employment as an instrument maker and machinist with the California Electric Works. He also legally changed his name from Augustinus Josephus Fey to Charles August Fey, reportedly because he hated being called "Gus." Friends and family started to address him as "Charlie," which Fey enjoyed.

Two of Charlie's fellow employees at the company were the recent German immigrants Theodor Holtz and Gustav Frie-drich Wilhelm Schultze. All three shared a fascination with mechanical gadgets, particularly the coin-operated devices that were gaining popularity in end-of-the-century San Francisco. In the 1880s, gambling contraptions, or "slot lotteries," were becoming the rage in saloons and cigar stores. They were fundamentally vending machines, with winnings dispensed via a human attendant rather than directly from the apparatus. The payout was usually a voucher called a "trade stimulator," which could be redeemed for liquor, cigars, chewing gum, even postage stamps. Mechanized poker games were the most popular type, and in some saloons the prizes could range from one drink for a pair of kings to one hundred drinks for a royal flush. These slot lotteries were often bulky and unreliable, though, and patrons disliked receiving tokens; they craved cash rewards.

In 1893, Gustav Friedrich Wilhelm Schultze received the first United States patent issued for a gambling machine. It was a more compact slot lottery with an automatic payment mechanism, but it still only issued coupons. In 1894, Fey and Theodor Holtz became business partners when they formed Holtz and Fey Electric Works, and in 1895 Fey developed in his basement a modified version of the Schultze design that paid out coins. It was an immediate hit and proved very lucrative to Fey, Holtz, and the establishments that installed the devices, having agreed to a fifty-fifty revenue-sharing agreement.

By 1899, Charlie Fey had created his ultimate "slot machine"— the Liberty Bell. It featured the elements of slots we recognize today: three spinning wheels with staggered stops, a pull lever that activated the wheels, multiple symbols on each wheel, many different winning (and losing) combinations, and varying payouts. After cheaters started inserting metal slugs that let them play for free, Fey also added a "detecting pin," which could distinguish real coins from the phonies. Thus went the creation of the One-Armed Bandit of legend and lore, and it has prospered ever since. In 1937, the seventy-five-year-old Charles August Fey was proclaimed the "Thomas Edison of Slots" at

the convention of the National Association of Coin Operated
Machine Manufacturers.

o   o   o

Of course, gambling in California did not begin with Charlie
Fey and the Liberty Bell. Games of chance had been played in
the region since the dawn of recorded history. Long before the
arrival of Europeans, Native Californians gambled in a variety of ways. Some tribes, such as the Luiseño, Cahuilla, Yuma,
and Kumeyaay, commonly wagered on the game of *churchurki*,
known as *peon* by later Spanish explorers. It starts with two
teams of four people facing each other while singing and drum-
ming. One side covertly passes a small white stick from hand to
hand while their competitors attempt to keep track of the stick's
whereabouts. At a signal from an umpire, the singing and drum-
ming ceases and the players commence betting on which opponent has ended up with the stick. These contests attracted enthusiastic audiences, and they're still played in some California
Native communities today. As attorney Joseph Lancaster Brent
recalled in 1852, the matches "produced enormous excitement
and extravagant betting. The bystanders took sides, including
the women, who were desperate gamblers."

During the time of the Californios—the term used for
Spanish-speaking residents of the Mexican province of Alta
California—gambling was also popular and widespread. As an
example, we can look to the game La Carrera del Gallo, a test of
horsemanship and pluck that was played on ranchos, in town
plazas, and even in the quiet missions of Spanish and Mexican
California. The event started with a well-greased live rooster
buried in the ground up to its neck while about two hundred
yards away the participants waited on horseback. As French
observer Auguste Bernard Duhaut-Cilly noted in the 1820s, the
competition commences when, wagers having been made, the
horsemen, "with one hand on the saddle-bow, dart forth swiftly
as though hurled from a catapult, stooping low, so that in passing they may be able to snatch up the fowl by the neck." Mostly

they failed, and the riders tried again and again, but if even one intrepid contestant succeeded in removing the rooster from its predicament, the game was not over. With the rooster in hand, the lead horseman was then rushed by all the others, who would attempt to wrest the rooster from his control. As the pursuing pack overtakes the rider, "a melee of horses and riders follows. They get sprinkled with feathers and blood; the rooster is torn to pieces; and the horsemen, tumbling over one another, become the butt of the laughter of their companions as well as of the fair spectators of the game." Auguste Bernard Duhaut-Cilly likened the enthusiastic reaction of the female onlookers to that of damsels of the Middle Ages when chivalrous knights jousted for their favor.

This spirit of competition, and the chance for onlookers to gamble on such contests, persisted into the Gold Rush. It should not be surprising that taking chances would be a favorite pastime for the forty-niners, who had already taken the greatest gamble in leaving their homes and families for the mere possibility of striking it rich. Searching for those elusive golden flakes was a cosmic crapshoot, and risk-taking saturated the air and haunted the dreams of the hundreds of thousands of argonauts from around the world who descended on the San Francisco Bay Area, increasing the population by nearly 400 percent within only four years.

The explosion of San Francisco from a tiny harbor town to a city of twenty-five thousand in a little over a year brought the full range of cosmopolitan attitudes and mores—both good and bad. From this hub, tentacles of hedonism would snake throughout Gold Country, and gambling in particular became pervasive. On the subject of local gambling, an 1855 survey of the city titled *The Annals of San Francisco* succinctly concluded, with emphasis, "*Every body did so.*"

In Old California, gambling venues, whether legal or illegal, came in all forms, including grimy shacks, seedy card rooms, barrelheads in dingy backstreets, tree stumps in mining camps, blankets on the ground, and glittering, raucous palaces in budding urban areas. The larger establishments were usually called "gambling saloons" and offered, as Gold Rush witness Samuel Colville observed, "naked . . . and unmasked depravity, daily, nightly, and unblushingly." Dr. Israel Lord noted the supplementary delights of these dens, recalling that nearby the gambling tables, "rather like a dream than reality," was a spread of "oyster and lobster and salad and sauce and fruit and flesh and fish and pies and cakes . . . . Everything is got up, arranged and conducted with a view to add to the mad excitement of gambling."

As California developed, a more conservative, family-oriented population emerged. While some tolerated the gambling halls, it was more common for members of this community to condemn what they saw as the tawdry and appalling realities of these establishments, and to advocate reform. The halls came to be seen less as palaces and more as distasteful, even sleazy dens of abandonment. (Critics routinely referred to the gambling sites as "gambling-hells.") Particularly toward the end of the century in San Francisco's Barbary Coast—the city's red-light district at the time—gambling halls joined with nearby establishments to form a neighborhood conglomeration of card rooms, brothels, saloons, restaurants, opium dens, and dance emporiums. Despite its since-romanticized reputation, it was a grim district, devoid of the frivolity and hearty companionship of legend. In 1871, Albert Evans, a California correspondent for the *New York Tribune* and *Chicago Tribune*, visited the Barbary Coast, and his description would apply for the remainder of that century. He called it a place where

> thieves, murderers, prostitutes, and vagabonds from every clime beneath the sun meet and mingle on a common level, and vice, and crime, and wretchedness, and moral and physical degradation unutterable are stamped on the face of every denizen of the evil neighborhood, marking him or her as an outcast, a leper, a pariah, among the children of men.

Ignoring the warning "This ain't the place for you, stranger; better walk the other way," Evans entered a gambling saloon, which he recalled in detail: "The air is close and hot, and the smell none of the most agreeable. Perhaps two hundred men are in the room, but there is no hum of conversation, and even the smokers hardly place their cigars to their lips often enough to keep them lighted.... The silence is only broken by the chink of coin, and the monotonous voice of the dealer."

o   o   o

Through the years and in diverse locales, wagering was all the rage. In Old California, the most popular games were faro and montebank, with two-card Mexican and four-card Spanish versions. Gamblers could also wager on roulette, keno, poker, and blackjack, which was also called twenty-one or "vingt-et-un." There were also many games that we would not recognize today, including card games such as "thimble rig," very similar to three-card monte; "seven-and-a-half," an Italian predecessor to blackjack; and the French game "rouge-et-noir" (or "trent-et-quarante"). "Hokey-pokey," a name we link today with a silly song and dance, was a popular four-card version of stud poker. Among the curious table games were three-dice "chuck-a-luck"; the British dice game "crown and anchor"; "tub and ball," which featured a four-inch spotted ball tossed into a velvet tub; and "strap and pin," which utilized a leather strap and a needle. The rules were often convoluted and subject to the whims of the game operators. Bets could also be placed on the infamous bear-and-bull fights, dog-versus-badger battles, cockfighting, rat killing, billiard contests called "rondo," ten-pin bowling competitions, footraces, horse races, pugilism, drinking, and even boomerang throwing.

Gambling was so ingrained in the new California culture by this time that it featured its own lexicon, comprising both traditional terms and new formations that often drew on American West slang. "Black-legs" were gamblers; "California prayer books" were decks of cards; "bracing" meant fixing a game;

Gambling has always been an important feature of the California social landscape.
"Alex Colberg's Bar," Mendocino County, c. 1900. From an original negative in
the Georgia-Pacific Corporation Archives, Portland, Oregon. Image courtesy of the
California State Library, Sacramento; California History Section, Digital ID: 2011-1708.

a "four-flusher" was a cheat or bluffer; a "muck snipe" was
some poor unfortunate who had been "cleaned out" at poker; a
"mouth bettor" gave only verbal promises to pay, never a paper
IOU; a "capper" was a gambler's accomplice who made false bets
to sweeten the pot; and a "tinhorn" was a flashy gambler prone
to trickery. Several terms referenced the fact that the backs of
the playing cards frequently featured an image of a Bengal tiger:
"twisting the tiger's tail" and "bucking the tiger" both meant
playing faro or poker, and the names "Tiger Town" and "Tiger
Alley" were used to refer to gambling districts.

The gamblers themselves came in with an eclectic mixture of
skill levels, from novices or "greenhorns" to professionals, plus
the range of players or "punters" (those who had *some* skill) in
between. While a few succeeded, most failed. Many went at it
with optimism but eventually echoed the sentiments expressed

by San Franciscan William Peters in an 1851 letter to his friend Emily Howard, whom he charmingly referred to as Mademoiselle Emilie: "I have to admit that I was not exempt of that contagion but I have lost enough to feel disgusted and I no longer gamble; bah! It is not my destiny to be rich, so I don't expect it and do not envy those who are, for they don't seem happier than those who aren't." New York newspaper correspondent Bayard Taylor also found it astonishing to witness miners wagering, and losing, everything: "Here are lost, in a few turns of a card or rolls of a ball, the product of fortunate ventures by sea or months of racking labor on land." At the other end of the spectrum were the more successful professional gamblers, a curious amalgam of cold-blooded outlaws and slippery tricksters.

The common denominator was that players of all types were addicted to some mixture of the swift, glitzy games of chance, the possibility of a quick fortune, and the boisterous ambience awash in tobacco smoke, whiskey, free food, judgment-free rowdiness, bonhomie, and the everlasting optimism that today might be the day everything changed. That compulsion could manifest itself in as many ways as there were gamblers.

In his 1881 *Reminiscences of a Ranger*, Horace Bell, a Los Angeles lawyer and newspaper publisher, recounted the story of a "distinguished Virginian" named Pete who was devoured by the eternal cravings of the gambling bug. Pete lived in Los Angeles and had heard that San Francisco was overrun with rats, in part because it had few cats to control the vermin. "Consequently," as Bell reported, "[Pete] went to work and gathered up all of the cats he could get, either by hook or crook (rumor had it that most of the feline merchandise was obtained by the former process), caged them up and shipped them to San Francisco." Pete cornered the market and was "supreme dictator" as to price. In San Francisco, he sold his cats, numbering several hundred, for fees as high as $100 (nearly $3,000 today) and made a fortune. But, as Bell wrote,

Alas, poor Pete! His riches soon took wings. Like all great men of the period, Pete was addicted to gambling, and the

product of his magnificent cat speculation went to fill the
coffers of the gambler princes of the Bay City. It was said
that Pete lost every dollar ... [and] the crestfallen forestaller
of the San Francisco cat market returned to the bosom of
his devoted Angel [Los Angeles], a wiser if not a richer man.

o   o   o

While it is perhaps not shocking that gambling would be popular among those who had come to California in the thrall of
gold fever, it is notable how broad a net gambling cast over
Old California. In 1855, authors Frank Soulé, John Gihon, and
James Nisbet wrote in *The Annals of San Francisco*:

> Gambling was ... *the* amusement—*the* grand occupation
> of many classes—apparently the life and soul of the place
> .... Judges and clergymen, physicians and advocates, mer-
> chants and clerks, contractors, shopkeepers, tradesmen,
> mechanics and laborers, miners and farmers, all adventur-
> ers in their kind ... unblushingly threw down his golden
> or silver stake .... Therefore, they staked and lost—staked
> and won—till in the end they were rich indeed, or penni-
> less. But poor or rich, the speculative spirit continued ...
> and either in direct gambling, or in nearly similar opera-
> tions in mercantile, land-jobbing, or general business, the
> inhabitants ... seemed to be one great horde of gamesters.

Gambling in Old California was open to all, regardless of age,
gender, nationality, and ethnicity, and, in fact, it was one of the
few racially integrated social activities in nineteenth-century
California. While people from various classes, races, and nationalities frequently worked together in the gold diggings or agricultural fields, it was uncommon for these groups to socialize
with each other away from the workplace. But gambling was
for everyone, and sources from the time include many stories of
women, children, and men from minority populations wagering
in public with the dominant Anglo-American male populace.

Some gamblers were clearly in over their heads. Hinton Rowan Helper witnessed a violent incident featuring a poker player named Ned, a pistol-packing Massachusetts native who was all of nine years old. John David Borthwick, a Scottish visitor in 1852, wrote: "Seated round the same [gambling] table might be seen well-dressed, respectable-looking men, and, alongside of them . . . little urchins . . . ten or twelve years of age, smoking cigars as big as themselves."

Chinese immigrants were also prominent on the scene, not just as gamblers but as game operators and proprietors of gambling emporia. They had imported the ancient game of fan-tan, and it was very popular, particularly in the Chinatowns that developed in the 1860s and 1870s. In 1889, Jesse B. Cook, future police commissioner of San Francisco, walked a beat in Chinatown, and in 1931 he recorded his memories from that time in the *San Francisco Police and Peace Officers' Journal*. Cook commented on the Chinese gambling he noticed while on patrol, logging sixty-two lottery agents and fifty fan-tan parlors, some with as many as twenty-four tables.

A lottery was also spearheaded by Chinese immigrants, and for decades it reached throughout the state and was serious business. In 1895, George Weeks, a newspaper editor in Bakersfield, reported that a Chinese laborer had given his colleague a quarter to play the lottery for him during the friend's visit to San Francisco. When the traveler returned, he sorrowfully informed the worker that the ticket purchased was a loser, but a few days later it was discovered that, in fact, the ticket had paid $250 (about $7,300 today) and the secretive scoundrel had squandered it all on wine, women, and song. The angry victim confronted the dishonest coworker and demanded his money. When none was produced, a .44 Colt revolver was drawn from a hiding spot and, as Weeks chronicled, "the next instant the thief lay dead on the ground with a bullet through his internal economy."

The newspapers and other opinion leaders of the era stereotypically—and also inaccurately and unfairly—presented the excesses and misconduct of gambling culture as evidence of a universal flaw within the Chinese people as a whole. While there were of course bad actors and criminal elements within the Chinese community, as there are in all communities, this labeling of *all* Chinese gamblers as underhanded and lawless added to the dominant culture's widespread racist perception of Chinese immigrants as not just unacceptably foreign and unassimilable but also deviant.

California's Chinese population was already fighting an uphill battle against the ruling population. Most did not speak English, many were not familiar with Anglo-American customs, and the majority of these young male immigrants viewed themselves as *Gam Saan Haak*, or guests of Gold Mountain—that is, short-term immigrants hoping to quickly prosper and then return to their families in China. For both social and practical reasons they banded together to form self-sufficient communities in what was otherwise an isolated and unwelcoming land. As Geling Yan, a modern Chinese American writer, put it: "They of course clung together in groups, like . . . sardines shipped from China . . . . They sensed that there would be danger, and that they must stick together." While people of other ethnicities and nationalities also used the camaraderie of the gambling halls as respite from the strains and insecurities of life, these parlors were especially important for the Chinese immigrants because they served as vital communal centers offering fellowship and reassurance. It was not the gambling as such that drew them, it was the gathering of kindred spirits navigating an uncertain world.

o   o   o

For all its diversity, California still has a relatively small number of inhabitants of African descent. Today, less than 7 percent of Californians are African American, and although the numbers were even lower in Old California (less than 1 percent of the population), the black community made its mark on the state in many unforgettable ways.

Before California gained statehood, slavery was legal but commonly resented in the region, and in 1850 California entered the union as a free state. For enslaved people who were brought to the area, California offered a quick way to escape slavery, and for both them and the free blacks who came on their own, it offered the promise of economic advancement.

In the gambling world, African Americans established halls that primarily catered to their own community, but they welcomed other races as well. San Francisco had several African American–owned and –operated gambling halls, the two best known being the Cornucopia and the Atheneum. Some black Californians also used white-owned gambling parlors, although not to wager but to change their lives in other ways.

Consider the experience of George Washington Dennis. Dennis was brought to Gold Rush San Francisco by a slave trader who was also his father. He worked for his slaveowner-father as a porter at perhaps the most famous gambling saloon of the era—the El Dorado Hotel. As George performed his duties, he would gather coins accidentally dropped by gamblers at the monte and faro tables, and within three months he had accumulated enough cash to buy his freedom from his father. Soon, he had enough to purchase the freedom of his enslaved mother as well. George Dennis then rented a gambling table at the El Dorado for $40 per day (the equivalent of $1,200 in 2019). George did not gamble, however; instead, his mother used the table to sell homemade hot meals to the always hungry and often cooking-averse argonauts. She averaged $225 in daily revenue (about $6,750 today).

Few accounts of black gamblers during this era exist today, and none by black writers have been discovered, but one story we have is especially lively and evocative. In his 1853 reminiscence *California Illustrated*, John M. Letts recounted the dramatic entrance of an African American adventurer named Jim to a store and occasional gambling hall Letts had established at Mormon Bar, a mining camp on the North Fork of the American River. As Letts recalled:

> About nine in the morning I saw, approaching the store, a
> strange looking being, mounted on a gray horse, a poncho

thrown over his shoulder, over which was slung a huge rifle, skins wrapped around his legs, a pair of Mexican spurs on, and a slouched hat which partially obscured his copper complexion.

Although Letts refers to this caller only as "Jim," his subsequent description clearly identifies the man as James Beckwourth, the renowned scout, explorer, and entrepreneur. The son of a white Revolutionary War officer and his slave, Beckwourth first arrived in California prior to the Gold Rush, but he left after a short stay, returning only after gold was discovered in 1848. During the Gold Rush, Beckwourth established trading posts, founded the settlement of Beckwourth, improved an immigrant trail that became known as Beckwourth Trail, and was credited with discovering a low-elevation pass in the northern Sierra Nevada that was dubbed Beckwourth Pass—all names still in use today. James Beckwourth was also an accomplished professional gambler. As John Letts noted:

> Jim, with his other accomplishments, was considered one of the best "monte" dealers .... On visiting the frontier towns, he would spend his time in gambling. Sometimes he would win several thousand dollars in one night, and the next day he would have every man drunk in town; what he could not spend in drink, he would give to the poor, or to his friends. Money was an incumbrance to which he would not submit.

After three days in Mormon Bar, Jim departed, and Letts figured he would never see the visitor again. However, three weeks later, Jim returned, his pockets stuffed with cash. Upriver, Jim had "fallen in with a Mormon who had some money," and they became partners in a monte game—Jim would gamble and his colleague would be the "banker." Within a few days, they had won $13,000 (the equivalent of $400,000 today). The partners split their winnings and parted company. Jim drifted back to Mormon Bar and told Letts he was on his way to Sacramento

City to spend his bounty. For several hours Jim rested at Letts's store and, to pass the time, Jim joined a card game and won several hundred more dollars. He then mounted his horse, Old Gray, and headed toward Sacramento with "as much money as he could conveniently carry." According to Letts:

> On his arrival, [Jim] looked upon Sacramento City as his guest, and emptied his handkerchief in drinking its health. He had all the inhabitants drunk who were disposed that way, and many of them much against their will. He was quite successful in getting rid of his money, and one week after his advent, he had invested his last dollar.

o   o   o

Another small but significant part of the gambling community in Old California were women, who made up only about 8 percent of the overall state population during these early years, with most clustered along the central coast from Monterey to San Francisco and in Sacramento. Fewer women lived in the interior valleys, foothills, Sierra Nevada, and the still sparsely populated region of Southern California. Consequently, women were a draw everywhere they went, including gambling parlors. Particularly during the Gold Rush, women were often employed as dealers or suppliers of the games. As the French observer Albert Benard de Russailh reported in 1851, "The saloons and gambling-houses that keep women are always crowded and are sure to succeed." Frequently, male gamblers were attracted to a particular establishment less for the gambling than for the opportunity to be in the presence of a "real live woman," and these uncommon meetings were recurrently mentioned in diaries and journals of the era.

In the Tuolumne County mining camp of Sonora, Canadian merchant William Perkins spoke for many when he admitted that "even a staid and sedate man like myself will at times spend a few quarters for the enjoyment of a genial smile from a pretty face, or perhaps the still greater stimulus of a flirtation." Perkins especially recalled the "pretty and handsomely dressed French-woman behind the counter" of his local gambling saloon. He was most likely referring to a young French woman mentioned in a letter written by Elizabeth Gunn, a member of a prominent pioneer family in newborn Sonora: "New houses are going up all the time . . . . [One] was built by a French girl, only seventeen, for her mother and little brother and sister and herself. She earns her money by going to the gaming houses and dealing out the cards to the players, and she makes a good deal."

As the decades wore on and California became more culturally conservative, the numbers of women involved in the gambling business, whether as patrons or employees, diminished as the practice was deemed unladylike, harmful to the social fabric, and in need of stringent regulation. In 1898, a *San Francisco Call* editorial pronounced that "pool-rooms" (parlors for wagering on horse races, akin to present-day off-track betting venues) should immediately prohibit women; the pool-rooms, which were "haunted" by women, wrote the *Call*, were threatening to make women and girls "unfit" for "the honorable occupations of life."

The names of many of Old California's women gamblers have been lost to history, but one that remains comes with a tragic tale not easily forgotten—the story of Madame Moustache.

Accurate, verifiable details are scant, but Eleanore Alphonsine Dumont was most likely born in France in the mid-1830s. She first appears as a gambler in Nevada City, Nevada County, California, in 1854. Many depictions of her life are embellished, and the most extensive and cited account, published in 1879 by the *National Police Gazette*, a sensational tabloid often divorced from historical reliability, is no exception. "She arrived one day on the stagecoach," the *Police Gazette* imagined, "a pretty, fresh-faced, dark-eyed woman, apparently about twenty years of age, and her stylish appearance created much commotion among the rough inhabitants of the town." Then known as Madame Dumont, Eleanore rented a table at a local gambling saloon and commenced a game of vingt-et-un, the French version of twenty-one, or blackjack. In partnership with a violent gambler named Dave Tobin, she prospered and soon opened her own round-the-clock gaming parlor that featured twelve tables of vingt-et-un, faro, and monte.

After being threatened and beaten one too many times by Tobin, Eleanore left Nevada City. She established and ran games—usually with success—in a series of mining camps, including a few in California, such as Columbia in Tuolumne County, and many others in Nevada (Eureka and Virginia City), Utah (Corrine), Idaho (Silver City and Salmon), Montana (Bannack, Helena, and Fort Benton), the Dakota Territory (Deadwood), Arizona (Tombstone), and on Missouri River steamboats. She garnered a small fortune, and it was during this time that Madame Dumont's patrons began to call her "Madame Moustache," due to the growth of facial hair on her upper lip.

In the 1860s, Eleanore made her way to San Francisco, where she spent a year as a brothel madam before returning to gambling in the California goldfields. After winning several thousand dollars at one camp, she purchased a ranch in Carson City, Nevada, spending all her earnings on its improvement. In the early 1870s, most likely in 1872, Eleanore married the charming yet conniving Jack McKnight, who quickly squandered what was left of her money, emptied her bank accounts, transferred all her property to his name, and then sold her ranch without her knowledge. When the scoundrel finally deserted her, he left Eleanore saddled with his personal debts as well. The once great Madame Dumont was now penniless and had little choice but to resume her career in gambling. She also began to drink heavily. A few weeks later, McKnight was found dead of shotgun wounds, and although no charges were brought, Dumont was considered the likely murderer.

By 1878, Madame Moustache had gravitated to Bodie, a raucous boomtown founded in 1876 on the California side of the eastern Sierra Nevada. At the time, Bodie boasted a community of two thousand hastily constructed buildings and almost seven thousand residents. As Bodie's newspaper, the *Standard Pioneer Journal of Mono County*, reported on May 29, 1878:

Madame Moustache, whose real name is Eleanore Dumont, has settled for the time in Bodie, following her old avocation of dealing twenty-one, faro, etc., as force of circumstances seem to demand. Probably no woman on the Coast is better known . . . . She appears as young as ever, and those who knew her ever so many years ago would instantly recognize her now.

Eleanore Dumont opened a game at Bodie's Magnolia Saloon and initially thrived. But by September 1879, Madame Moustache's luck had turned sour. With her vingt-et-un bank dwindling, she borrowed $300 from a friend to keep the game afloat, yet within a few hours the funds were exhausted. Now busted, Eleanore rose from the table without a word and wandered away. The *Bodie Morning News* recounted the rest of the story in its issue of September 9:

Yesterday morning a sheep-herder, while in pursuit of his avocation, discovered the dead body of a woman lying about one hundred yards from the Bridgeport road, a mile from town. Her head rested on a stone, and the appearance of the body indicated that death was the result of natural causes . . . . Deceased was named Eleanor Dumont, and was recognized as the woman who had been engaged in dealing a twenty-one game in the Magnolia saloon. Her death evidently occurred from an overdose of morphine, an empty bottle having the peculiar smell of that drug, being found beside the body.

Following her probable suicide, Bodie's gamblers passed the hat and provided a proper burial on Bodie's boot hill. Mourners attended from as far distant as Carson City, 120 miles to the north. No funds were earmarked for a headstone, and the exact location of Madame Moustache's grave is now unknown.

Gambling was considered part and parcel of the Old California experience, and in later years it was looked back on with fond nostalgia, as in this re-creation of an 1849 gambling house, incorporated as a tourist attraction at the 1894 California Midwinter International Exposition held in San Francisco. "Gambling House," 1894, photograph by I. W. Taber. Image courtesy of the California State Library, Sacramento; California History Section, Digital ID: 2010-6069.

o o o

By 1854, the tides were turning on the world of gambling in California, and gaming for money began growing in disfavor, primarily due to the crime associated with wagering. In 1855, the California State Legislature approved Senate Bill 149, banning a few gambling pursuits. It was the first step in a thirty-year effort to pass effective antigambling legislation that eventually led to prohibitions on virtually all forms of gambling in the state. The 1855 sanction was widely ignored, however, and its failure to curb the spread of gambling led to dozens and dozens of further restrictions, prohibitions, and amendments over the following decades. The craving for respectability and the presumed link between gambling and social and political corruption lent urgency to the call, and people from around the community took up the cause. In the early years of statehood, the main target of gambling restrictions were the proprietors rather than the individual gamblers who patronized them.

The laws were severe in theory but ineffectual in practice, and when a specific game was proscribed, it was relatively easy to get around the law by slightly modifying or renaming the game, thereby allowing the replacement to continue unchecked. Of course, the variant would then be banned and altered again, and then again, in a spiral of action and reaction that persisted for decades. Also, many iterations of the restrictions banned only particular kinds of games, leaving others alone. In 1860, for instance, all "banking" games were outlawed—meaning all games in which a player bets against "the house"—while other games were allowed. Even as late as 1879, draw poker skirted prohibition because it was deemed a game of knowledge and skill, not merely a game of chance.

In 1872, California Penal Code 330 made gaming illegal, but it still focused exclusively on the game owners. It wasn't until 1885 that the code was amended to include players, although the penalties were smaller for patrons than for proprietors until 1891, when the penalties were equalized. With additional modifications over the years, the original 1872 rule remains operative today, and the current Penal Code 330 still lists games that were common in the nineteenth century but haven't been popular for over a century.

Following the institution of the 1872 Penal Code, gambling did not disappear, as its opponents had hoped, but was instead driven underground. Some proprietors moved to Nevada, where gambling was still legal, but among those who stayed in the Golden State, gambling continued to flourish, now confined to illegal clubs in not just gritty urban districts such as San Francisco's Barbary Coast but also hidden in suburban and rural locales.

In 1879, the California government once again responded to continuing demands that the abomination of gambling must be immediately curtailed. In the new state constitution approved that year, Article XI, Section 11, gave law enforcement enhanced means to control gambling. This greater jurisdiction was best defined by a ruling in the 1891 case of George F. Tuttle, a San Francisco gambler arrested for operating an illegal off-track horse betting parlor in violation of a city ordinance. In the decision of *Ex Parte Tuttle*, the Supreme Court of California determined that, as summarized in the supporting case law citations for Article XI, Section 11,

> any practice or business the tendency of which, as shown by experience, is to weaken or corrupt the morals of those who follow it or to encourage idleness, instead of habits of industry, is a legitimate subject of police regulation. Gambling is such a practice.

Nevertheless, the gambling economy thrived, in part because civic officials often looked the other way, whether because they had been bribed or because they were being intimidated by criminal syndicates or good, old-fashioned muscle. Unlawful gambling dens and backroom casinos sprang up all over, many, if not most, of them tied to saloons. In July 1889, the *San Francisco Municipal Report* noted that 2,966 licensed, legitimate saloons were operating in the city, and although no one knows exactly how many of them harbored illicit gambling parlors— not to mention how many gambling venues were housed in *unlicensed* saloons or other similar establishments—we can assume the number was significant.

Other businesses catered to the clandestine gambling market as well. Most were secretive, but a few were slightly more open and transparent, some for decades, including, most notably, the San Francisco company of Will and Finck.

Frederick Will and Julius Finck founded their company in 1864 and sold fine cutlery and knives, sporting goods, and, quietly, unlawful gambling devices. In their early days, Will and

Finck offered rigged faro dealing boxes that allowed the dealer to furtively preview the next card in the deck or to issue two cards at once, meaning he or she could choose the more advantageous card. The company also sold an extensive variety of marked cards—some with rounded corners and others subtly "stripped," or cut to be slightly smaller than standard cards and therefore readily identifiable by touch to the cheat; Will and Finck's surreptitiously published 1896 catalog requested that the purchaser of these cards give custom directions about "just what you want them for, and what cards you want stripped." The company also sold acid fluid to "shade" cards (slightly alter the tint of the decorative backs), nail pricks to punch tiny holes in some cards in the deck, and shiny gold stickpins that concealed a pencil used to place miniscule, virtually invisible marks. Another popular item was the "reflector"—a miniature mirror that could be hidden in a ring, a tobacco pipe, paper money, even a phony stack of seven half-dollars—which allowed the gambler to see the victim's card faces as they were dealt.

Will and Finck also offered several types of altered dice, including one pair rigged to always come up craps and a separate weighted pair guaranteed to come up seven on every roll. The catalog noted, "In ordering dice, please state which side you want to come up." The dice were proudly proclaimed to be "loaded, our own manufacture."

Other popular products included the best-selling "bug"—a small clip that could be quickly attached to the underside of a table or to a pant leg, where a card might be hidden—and a wide range of "holdouts"—devices that could remove cards from play, thereby controlling the action. In 1888, on commission from a notorious black-leg named P. J. Kepplinger, Will and Finck designed an elaborate mechanical holdout that operated within a coat or shirt sleeve and permitted Kepplinger to draw cards up his sleeve and later noiselessly retrieve them at will. The company sold many models and modifications of the Kepplinger Holdout, including a vest version that permitted "cold decking," or replacing an entire deck of cards with a stacked deck, and a "table holdout," which was manipulated by knee power. Some holdouts sold for as much as $100, or $2,900 in today's money.

The Will and Finck Company was a mainstay of San Francisco's Market Street for nearly seventy years. On the surface, it was admired for its sponsorship of public events, such as picnics and baseball games, but those who were aware of its shadowy history also remembered the pockets that it emptied and the illicit fortunes it had made thanks to the firm's remarkable inventory of cheats and deceptions. The company that first opened in 1864 finally closed its doors for good in 1932. It had weathered the deaths of its founders, several partnership changes, and the devastating 1906 San Francisco earthquake and fire, but it could not survive the Great Depression.

o   o   o

The flamboyance, the deception, and the heart-thumping possibility of either striking it rich or losing it all perfectly fit the spirit of Old California. Hazarding everything on the mere promise of a new life was the founding principle of nineteenth-century California, and risk-taking became a defining—even if not always venerated—trait that has marched inexorably through the decades of the state's history. In 1857, former military officer, banker, and future Civil War general William Tecumseh Sherman wrote from San Francisco that, in California, "everything is chance, everything is gambling." One hundred and fifty years later, the celebrated California historian Kevin Starr eloquently added that "such a hope, such a psychology of expectation, fused the California experience irretrievably onto a dream of better days: of a sudden, almost magical, transformation of the ordinary."

BAR-ROOM IN CALIFORNIA.

For nineteenth-century Californians, drinking alcohol was equal parts recreation, therapy, companionship, and commerce. "Bar-Room in California," by Frank Marryat, author and artist of *Mountains and Molehills; or, Recollections of a Burnt Journal* (New York: Harper and Brothers, 1855). Image from a volume in the author's personal collection.

CHAPTER TWO

Anti-Fogmatics, Coffin Varnish,
and Oh-Be-Joyful

THE DEMON DRINK

Many Californians are proud of their flair to produce, and to consume, intoxicating beverages. Next to gambling, drinking was the Golden State's favorite pastime throughout the nineteenth century, and that legacy has stretched into the state's modern economy and character. A 2018 report notes that California is first in the number of producing wineries in the United States and first in the total units of craft beer brewed. For decades, boosters have claimed that California is the national vanguard of alcohol manufacture, consumption, and quality, and today California assumes this mantle with pride and more than a little justification. In the nineteenth century, however, many in the alcohol industry were plagued with a gnawing feeling that California would never quite measure up to Europe.

Case in point: In his 1928 reminiscence titled *California Copy*, newspaper publisher and reporter George F. Weeks wrote about a time in the early 1890s when an arrogant self-anointed oenophile from Europe tried to disparage the state's homegrown wine. According to Weeks, the unnamed man considered himself

> an authority on wines—an expert of the experts . . . . He could distinguish vintages of whatever character, year, or origin. He had all the technique of his profession at the end of his tongue, and allowed it to become known that if there was anything about the wine business which he did not know, he would be glad to be [shamed].

Over the coming months, this supercilious connoisseur spoke before various civic groups and private clubs, and, as Weeks continued,

> he was pleased to speak very patronizingly of the efforts of California wine growers. He was, in fact, disposed to give them credit for their laudable efforts. "But of course, don't you know, you cannot compete in any manner with European wines, and never will." . . . His attitude of kindly forbearance as that of an adult toward a child was not disguised.

The outsider's haughty condescension quickly irritated San Franciscans, and they decided to test this so-called expert's aptitude. At one exclusive gentlemen's club, the members secretly exchanged the contents of six bottles of California vintage and six bottles of French vintage. The critic was then informed that the club members felt that a recently released California wine was excellent and compared favorably to French product. They beseeched the wine snob for his expert opinion, which he was delighted, even eager, to provide.

As George Weeks reported, the first wine served was a French wine from a California bottle.

> The expert sipped it, inhaled its aroma, rolled it on his palate, and went through all the motions of his profession, after which he proceeded to render his well-considered

verdict. It was very good wine indeed—in fact, much better than most of the California product which he had sampled. But of course it was not, it could not in fact, be equal to the same class of the imported variety. All sorts of technical explanations were given in support of its alleged inferiority. He acknowledged that it bore a certain faint resemblance to a high-class French variety, but was radically inferior thereto.

Next, the California wine in the French bottle was presented to the self-important sophisticate:

After sampling this the expert grew enthusiastic. Here, now, was a wine that was a wine. He compared the two vintages, swallow by swallow, almost drop by drop, always to the disparagement of what he supposed was the California product and in praise of the French.

The self-appointed expert, wrote Weeks, was "listened to patiently, and evidently did not detect or understand the covert glances of amusement exchanged by those who were in the secret .... He was not of course told outright how many different kinds of an ass he had made of himself." The Wine Authority soon found his humiliating performance was public knowledge when the deception was happily leaked to the press.

o   o   o

While Californians might have been self-conscious about the quality of their product at times, there was never any doubt that intoxicants—wine, beer, and spirits of all kinds—have always been an integral social feature of life in the state. Native Californians had been using mood-altering alcoholic beverages for centuries, often as a part of rituals or as a means to induce dreams or trances, as in the case of the *Datura* plant (often known as *toloache* in Mexican Spanish, *jimsonweed* by Anglo-Americans, and by several different names among Native Californians, including *naktamush* by the Luiseño and *tanai* by the Yokuts). A member of the nightshade family, the plant was used—with great caution due to its poisonous properties—by Natives from Southern California to as far north as the Lower Sacramento Valley; they made it into an alcoholic (and sometimes hallucinogenic) brew by soaking and fermenting the crushed roots and seeds. This mixture was not consumed in social settings but was used primarily as an element in elaborate supervised rituals.

When Europeans arrived in the area that would become California, the role of alcohol in Native communities changed rapidly. The production of wine and spirits by Spanish and California missions was an integral part of the barter and trade economy of Old California, and the quantities and types of alcoholic beverages, not to mention the increased access to them, often led to irresponsible overindulgence among both Native Californians and Europeans.

What differed, however, was the way in which drinking to excess was interpreted, and tolerated, by the then dominant culture, now made up of Spanish, Mexican, and Anglo-American settlers. The general attitude was that the drunkenness of a Californio or a white imbiber was considered an individual and often comical fault, whereas the drunkenness of a Native person was judged as wicked and threatening, and a demonstration of racial inferiority. This racist double-standard fueled the spread of long-standing but inaccurate "firewater myths," which claim that Native people have a natural, genetic craving for alcohol, are particularly susceptible to alcohol addiction, become uncontrollably violent when inebriated, are incapable of self-discipline, and must have restrictions and prohibitions imposed by outside, non-Indian authorities for their own welfare. Modern studies have repeatedly poked holes in these theories, but in Old California these fallacious concepts were commonly accepted.

On June 30, 1834, the United States Congress incorporated these myths into federal law in the form of "An Act to Regulate Trade and Intercourse with the Indian Tribes, and to Preserve Peace on the Frontiers." The act applied to white and Native people only in the so-called Indian Country, which the law defined as

> all that part of the United States west of the Mississippi, and not within the states of Missouri, Louisiana, or the territory of Arkansas, and, also, that part of the United States east of the Mississippi river, and not within any state to which the Indian title has not been extinguished.

This geographic boundary was very fluid during the era as lands were usurped by white settlement and the borders that defined states and territories shifted, but it generally applied to California as a whole.

The new law served to consolidate and strengthen previous regulations. For example, the trading posts had to be licensed and the traders were limited to trading only fur and hides and were no longer allowed to "barter, trade, or pledge" for any Native personal belongings, such as cooking utensils and clothing. The act imposed a penalty of $500 ($14,250 today) on any individual who "shall sell, exchange, or give, barter, or dispose of, any spiritous liquor or wine to an Indian (in the Indian country)." A fine of $300 ($8,600 today) would be levied against anyone introducing or attempting to introduce alcohol for personal noncommercial use in Indian Country, and it made lawful the government confiscation of any liquor and the seizure and forfeiture of all personal property of any person—white, Native, or otherwise—possessing liquor in Indian Country.

When California attained statehood in 1850, this 1834 federal law influenced legislation that was then enacted by the first California State Legislature. Called "An Act for the Government and Protection of Indians," the bill addressed many issues related to the Native population and essentially stripped Native Californians of their rights. Two provisions specifically related to alcohol: Article XV ordered fines and prison terms for "any person in this State [who] shall sell, give, or furnish to any Indian, male or female, any intoxicating liquors (except when administered for sickness)," and Article XX noted that Native

Californians could be declared "vagrants" simply by being in proximity to alcohol. Once identified as a vagrant, a Native American person could be auctioned into bondage immediately: "Any Indian . . . who shall be found loitering and strolling about, or frequenting public places where liquors are sold . . . shall be liable to be arrested . . . . [If appropriate government authority] shall be satisfied that he is a vagrant . . . [that authority could] hire out such vagrant within twenty-four hours to the highest bidder . . . for any term not exceeding four months." Article XX, the "involuntary servitude" section of the act, was repealed following the ratification of the Thirteenth Amendment to the United States Constitution in 1865, but other conditions, including those related to the distribution of alcohol to Native Californians, remained intact until the act was fully repealed in 1937.

As distribution penalties were relaxed, however, the overall restrictions on alcohol purchases by Native Californians, initiated in the 1850s, stayed on the books for many decades. While national Prohibition ended in 1933 with the passage of the Twenty-first Amendment, proscriptions on sales of alcohol to Native Americans continued for another twenty years. In the wake of a widely publicized 1952 incident in which twenty-two World War II and Korean War veterans from the Modoc tribe of northeastern California were not allowed to purchase aftershave lotion because it contained alcohol, the California State Legislature passed Senate Bill 344 in April 1953, which allowed alcohol sales to Native Californians. This bill was followed in August 1953 by H.R. 1055, a congressional action that lifted longstanding restrictions on alcohol sales to Native Americans nationwide.

o   o   o

While Native Californians were being persecuted with alcohol sanctions, the production and consumption of wine, beer, and spirits exploded throughout the rest of Old California. During the mission era and California's time as a Mexican province, wine was commonly produced for both personal and religious purposes, made possible by not only an abundance of wild grapes but also the missionaries' introduction of the Spanish variety *Vitis vinifera* (nicknamed the Mission grape), which made wine of a higher quality. The region's first sustainable vineyard was planted at Mission San Diego del Alcalá in 1779 under the supervision of Father Junípero Serra—founder of the California Franciscan mission system and credited as the "Father of California Wine"—and the Mission grape dominated California viticulture from this period until the 1880s. Carlos N. Híjar, who had arrived in California from Mexico in 1834 as a member of the Híjar-Padrés colonization expedition (led by his uncle José María Híjar), recalled the early days of California winemaking:

> The wine of pastoral days was made in this manner: Suitable ground was selected, and a *desvan* or platform placed thereon. This was covered with clean hides, and the grapes piled upon it . . . . Indians . . . were put to treading out the grape juice, which was caught in *coras*, or in leathern bags. These were emptied into a large wooden tub, where the liquid was kept two or three months, under cover of grape skins to ferment.

Secular, mercantile winemaking grew out of the mission system, originating in Southern California at the turn of the century, with commercial production happening primarily in Los Angeles. In 1805, the village had a population numbering less than five hundred, but it soon became the epicenter for California vineyards and wine. As Thomas Pinney notes in his excellent 2017 book on the history of wine in Los Angeles, the hamlet was becoming known as the "City of Vines."

In 1833, Jean-Louis Vignes, a wine barrel maker recently arrived from the French vineyards of Bordeaux, planted the first documented European vines in Los Angeles. Vignes would ultimately plant tens of thousands of vines, yielding ten thousand gallons annually. Residents and visitors alike, wrote his friend

William Heath Davis, an American maritime trader headquartered in Alta California, were "delighted with his California wines, of different vintages, some as much as eight or ten years old, of fine quality."

Vignes's neighbor and competitor was William Wolfskill, who had come to viticulture without the pedigree or knowledge of Jean-Louis. Wolfskill was a trapper, trader, and carpenter who had arrived in Los Angeles in 1831. He knew nothing about winemaking. In 1836, Wolfskill purchased a small plot of land with a few grape vines and quickly expanded his wine-making business. With the profits from his efforts, he secured more acreage, planted more vines, and, within ten years, was cultivating nearly forty thousand vines. By 1856, William Wolfskill boasted sixty thousand bearing vines and operated four wine cellars that together stored one hundred thousand gallons. Twice he would win the "Best Vineyard" prize at the California State Fair. Vignes and Wolfskill were the dominant figures in California wine through the Gold Rush and into the first years of statehood.

The Gold Rush unsurprisingly brought increased demand for wine, especially from the rapidly growing population of the San Francisco Bay Area, and vines were planted throughout that region during this time. As journalist Benjamin Parke Avery recalled in 1878, the coastal valleys near the bay were ideal for grape growing: "They are commonly oblong, nearly level, or rolling like the Western prairies, extremely fertile, and have a climate more sheltered from the sea-wind and fog . . . . Their gently rolling surfaces rise into mound-like hills on either side—the best soil for the wine-grape." With this development of its own vineyards, Northern California was no longer dependent on what the English sailor, artist, author, and argonaut Frank Marryat called "the Wine of the South."

Starting in the 1860s, the wine districts near San Francisco were aggressively promoted by Hungarian immigrant and wine huckster Agoston Haraszthy. While some (including Haraszthy himself) have elevated Haraszthy to the exalted position of "Father of California Viticulture," that claim ignores the fact that others as far back as the eighteenth century might have a more solid claim to the distinction. Haraszthy maintained that he was the first to advertise California wine to a wide national market, but he was not. Haraszthy declared that he had introduced the popular Zinfandel wine grapes to California, but he did not. What Haraszthy *did* accomplish, however, was being the best, most enthusiastic advocate of California wine, optimistically touting its future and raising public awareness of the region's burgeoning industry through numerous newspaper and journal articles and the publication of his book *Grape Culture, Wines, and Wine-Making* in 1862.

Old California wine production, consumption, and commercial success was doing well on its own but was further aided by a botanical catastrophe that struck European vineyards in the last half of the nineteenth century. Beginning in the 1850s, American grape vine specimens were displayed by collectors at botanical gardens throughout England, but unbeknownst to anyone until it was too late, the cuttings were infected with a louse called *phylloxera* that feeds on the roots and leaves of grape vines. The American vines were resistant to the pest, but most European vines were not, and over the next thirty years, the infestation spread and an estimated 70 to 90 percent of all European vineyards were laid waste by *phylloxera*. As it took many years to restore the European vineyards to health, California winemakers filled the breach. By 1900, the California wine industry was a leader throughout the world, making regular exports to Canada, Mexico, South America, Europe, and Asia.

o o o

As with the history of wine in California (and perhaps all things in the state's history), there is no consensus as to who first produced beer commercially in the region. It is generally, but not universally, acknowledged that William McGlone rightfully earned that distinction. The intriguing McGlone was a sailor from Massachusetts who had arrived in California in November 1837 aboard a whaling ship named the *Commander Rogers*.

McGlone found himself stranded in Monterey when the *Commander Rogers* suffered a series of unfortunate accidents, including, first, a powerful storm damaging the vessel while at anchor, and then, after repairs were made and the whaler set sail again, another squall that snapped the masts and shredded the sails. The captain beached the ship to save its precious cargo of whale oil, but the *Commander Rogers* was beyond redemption.

To make ends meet, forlorn William McGlone held many temporary jobs before finally obtaining employment in Isaac Graham's whiskey distillery near Salinas, where he learned the fundamentals of fermentation. Some sources suggest that, sometime in the early 1840s, McGlone briefly sold his beer to the public, and as preeminent California historian Hubert Howe Bancroft noted, McGlone was thereafter referred to as "Billy the Brewer." McGlone may have been the first to bring beer to the people of California, but he was certainly not the last. The cultural explosion of the California Gold Rush saw to that.

Starting in 1848, more than three hundred thousand eager argonauts and merchants inundated the Land of Gold. There were immigrants from virtually every corner of the world, including notable contingents from England, Ireland, Germany, France, Switzerland, Italy, Austria, Denmark, Mexico, Chile, Australia, China, and of course thousands from the United States itself. They were thirsty and in demand of alcoholic refreshments, particularly beverages that reminded them of their various homelands. In 1849, Adam Schuppert opened his San Francisco brewery, which many scholars consider the first dedicated beer-making facility in California. In Southern California, Harris Newmark, who had arrived in 1853 and spent the next sixty years in the southland, recalled that John Murat founded one of the first breweries in Los Angeles, called the Gambrinus Brewery, yet, as Newmark wrote, "the quality of the product dispensed to the public left much to be desired; but it was beer." And that was enough to satisfy consumer cravings.

To meet skyrocketing demand, many other breweries followed, as did increased wine production and the importation of a wide variety of liquors of outrageously varying quality. A tidal wave of saloons swept through California, and by 1852, in San Francisco alone, there were 350 such establishments serving a population of 36,000, or one saloon for every 103 residents. By 1860, the number was 800 public houses supplied by 24 breweries, dozens of local vintners, and many import enterprises. By 1889, there were 2,966 licensed saloons in the city, plus many unlicensed establishments. While San Francisco was the hub of alcohol trade in the state, smaller markets—including Sacramento, the southern coastal cities, inland Gold Country, and other districts—experienced comparable growth. In 1850, Bayard Taylor, the twenty-four-year-old Gold Rush correspondent of the *New York Tribune*, observed, "The most common excesses into which the Californians run, are drinking and gambling." This notion was corroborated in 1855 by English observer Frank Marryat: "Drinking is carried on to an incredible extent here; . . . a vast quantity of liquor is daily consumed."

Available alcoholic beverages ranged from high-quality liqueurs imported from back East, to foreign and domestic wines, to locally brewed beers, to tainted consumables, to the rankest homemade swill. Nineteenth-century Californians commonly drank ale, varietal wines, brandy, cider, rye, blackberry liquor, bourbon, and various varieties of "whiskey," which included the best Irish and Scotch products but also adulterated "red-eye," which might be supplemented with turpentine, ammonia, gun powder, cayenne pepper, or strychnine to provide an additional "bite." There were also many mixed drinks to tempt those so inclined, some of which are still familiar today (the old fashioned and mint julep) and others less recognizable, such as the "blackstrap" (a mixture of rum and molasses), the "mule skinner" (whiskey and blackberry liqueur), the "stone fence" (whiskey and cider), and the "peach and honey" (peach brandy with a dollop of honey), the last of which was particularly popular in Los Angeles. *How to Mix Drinks, or The Bon-Vivant's Companion*, an 1862 recipe book for mixed drinks and cocktails, listed over six hundred possibilities.

With alcohol consumption so prevalent, California developed an extensive lexicon to describe both intoxicating beverages and degrees of drunkenness. Some of the terms were Golden State originals, but many came in with the swift influx of people from around the country and the rest of the world. While there were numerous appellations for specific cocktails and of course brand names for beer and wine, the all-purpose terms used for alcoholic beverages in general during the nineteenth century were equally clever and enlightening, among them "deadshot," "coffin varnish," "bug juice," "family disturbance," "aguardiente" (literally "firewater" in Spanish), "tonsil varnish," "oh-be-joyful," "John Barleycorn," "pair of overalls," "grog," "gutwarmer," "lotion," "brave-maker," "anti-fogmatics," "tarantula juice," "bottle courage," and "pop skull." The lingo for getting or being drunk was just as idiosyncratic: "shot in the neck," "brick in one's hat," "squiffled," "corned," "boosy," "mauled," "soaked," "fuddled," "been in the sun," "bent an elbow," "jingled," "loaded for bear," "on a tear," "roostered," "primed," and "batted." Without question, the most commonly used term for drinking was to say someone had "gone on a spree."

The foremost practitioner of inventing labels and classifications for levels of drunkenness was Alfred Doten, a pleasure-chasing gold seeker and journalist who lived and worked mostly in California from 1849 until his death, in 1903. Doten drank prodigiously but still managed to keep a daily journal that chronicled his liquor-fueled life for over fifty years. His frequent references to imbibing compelled him to invent new expressions for cataloging and categorizing his various degrees of intoxication. In his journal he classified nights of drinking as a "tall spree" or "small bit of a spree," or a "soiree" or "bender" or "jollification," or a "corrective for a stomach," or a "jubilee." Doten was never "drunk" but "tight" or "less tight" or "a little tight" or "very tight," and sometimes "obscure" or "very obscure indeed" or "somewhat obscure" or "a little obscure."

During this era, the saloon was the revered temple of tippling. In its ideal configuration, it was part music hall, part gambling den, and part bar, and its purpose was to dazzle the eye, excite the senses, and gently escort the customer away from good judgment toward muddled abandon. Acerbic Scottish observer John

Californians had a wide variety of alcoholic beverages from which to choose, ranging from cheap and possibly deadly homebrews to fancier top-shelf brands. Here the owners and employees of the Sebastopol Brewery proudly display their wares, c. 1890. Image courtesy of the California State Library, Sacramento; California History Section, Digital ID: 2008-1175.

David Borthwick described the typical "gambling saloon" in 1853:

> Another very attractive feature is the bar, a long polished mahogany or marble counter, at which two or three smart young men officiated, having behind them long rows of ornamental bottles, containing all the numerous ingredients necessary for concocting the hundred and one different "drinks" which were called for. This was also the most elaborately-decorated part of the room, the wall being completely covered with mirrors and gilding, and further ornamented with china vases, bouquets of flowers, and gold clocks.

Some bartenders became celebrities in this atmosphere. Duncan Nichol was in charge at San Francisco's Bank Exchange Saloon in the 1870s. He is credited with inventing "pisco punch," considered the most popular beverage of the Barbary Coast. Nichol kept the formula a closely guarded secret, only allowing that it used pisco brandy, a Peruvian potion. As Thomas Knox revealed in his 1872 book *Underground, or Life Below the Surface*, pisco punch had quite a kick:

> It is perfectly colourless, quite fragrant, very seductive, terribly strong, and has a flavour somewhat resembling that of Scotch whiskey, but more delicate, with a marked fruity taste . . . . The first glass satisfied me that San Francisco was, and is, a nice place to visit . . . . The second glass was sufficient, and I felt that I could face small-pox, all the fevers known to the faculty, and the Asiatic cholera, combined, if need be.

The king of the nineteenth-century bartenders was Jerry Thomas, who plied his trade throughout the country but was best known for his tenure in San Francisco. It was Thomas who cowrote *How to Mix Drinks, or The Bon-Vivant's Companion* in 1862, the first mixology book published in the United States. The preface of the book, by coauthor Christian Schultz, a winemaker and professor of chemistry, calls Thomas "the Jupiter Olympus of the bar." The cognoscenti nicknamed Thomas "The Professor," and Edward Peron Hingston, an English visitor to San Francisco in 1870, breathlessly exclaimed that Thomas was "an accomplished artist," gushing that he was a "star" who also dressed the part: "He is a gentleman who is all ablaze with diamonds. There is a very large pin, formed of a cluster of diamonds, in the front of his magnificent shirt, he has diamond studs at his wrists, and gorgeous diamond rings on his fingers."

Thomas took credit for inventing the popular eggnog-based "Tom and Jerry" Christmas cocktail, although others disputed his claim. It was generally acknowledged, however, that Thomas was responsible for the dramatic "blue blazer," a flaming Scotch whiskey concoction. As Thomas described it in *How to Mix Drinks*, the technique is to combine "in one mug" whiskey and boiling water and then "ignite the liquid on fire, and while blazing mix both ingredients by pouring them four or five times from one mug to the other . . . . If well done this will have the appearance of a continued stream of fire." Thomas also added this valuable, albeit obvious, advice: "To become proficient in throwing the [flaming] liquid from one mug to the other, it will be necessary to practise for some time with cold water."

o o o

Even among those who believed nineteenth-century Californians guilty of overindulging in alcohol, many contended that, overall, it was a convivial, hail-fellow-well-met, communal experience, with few episodes of excessive drunkenness or obnoxious behavior. The historical record, however, shows otherwise. Although it was common practice to sweep instances of offensive alcohol-fueled behavior under the rug or to dismiss it as harmless frivolity, chronicles of the era comprehensively demonstrate that it frequently led to violence, murder, larceny, assault, and other nefarious components of Old California culture . Daily newspapers are rife with reports of crimes, property damage, physical injuries, and other consequences of these "sprees." In 1857, John David Borthwick considered the root cause of this phenomenon:

> Drinking was the great consolation for those who had not moral strength to bear up under their disappointments . . . . This is a very common disease in California: there is something in the climate which superinduces it with less provocation than in other countries . . . [These individuals] make the voyage through life under a full head of steam all the time; they live more in a given time than other people, and naturally have recourse to constant stimulants to make up for the want of intervals of *abandon* and repose.

Among initial efforts to address alcohol abuse were facilities known as "inebriate homes," which were constructed in California's urban areas. Among the first was the San Francisco Home for the Cure of the Inebriate, founded in 1859 by volunteer firemen who were members of the Dashaway Association, an organization that encouraged its followers to "dash away the intoxicating bowl." The association emphasized total alcohol abstinence, which it tied to personal responsibility. Their facility was originally designed as a boardinghouse for drunken men and women delivered there by local police, but it ultimately transformed into a more comprehensive treatment center of the type routinely called "asylums" during the nineteenth century. The San Francisco Home for the Cure of the Inebriate operated from 1859 to 1898.

Temperance, teetotaling, prohibition, and prayer were touted as other solutions for battling the evils of alcohol. In 1870, the American Association for the Study and Cure of Inebriety pronounced that alcohol abuse was a treatable malady, and the organization's statement of principles declared: "Intemperance is a disease . . . . It is curable in the same sense that other diseases are." The problem was that no one knew what "cure" would work, and methods advertised as "foolproof" were rarely effective. Among the most regularly undertaken regimens were hydrotherapy and "electric light baths." Hydrotherapy, which largely consisted of wrapping the patient in cold, wet sheets for hours, was used to tackle a wide spectrum of conditions and was a leading treatment for alcoholism.

"Electric light baths" sought to harness the potential healing powers of electricity, drawing upon public fascination with the newly invented lightbulb. For a treatment, the patient was placed inside a seven-foot-long, four-foot-wide steel box called a "horizonal cabinet," the interior of which featured sixty-two incandescent bulbs arranged in rows. Between the rows of lights were mirrors that intensified the illumination. In an 1897 *Los Angeles Herald* article entitled "A Novel Bath," practitioners claimed that prolonged exposure to the light would penetrate the "delicate nerve fibers" and aid the "nutritive process." In fact, the longer the exposure, the greater the benefits. The *Herald* article grandly concluded that "the electric bath can be made to keep the tissues in repair, and thus prolong life indefinitely."

If these therapies proved ineffective (and they often did), there were a variety of patented medicinal remedies readily available. Among the cures for alcohol addiction that were marketed throughout the United States were Knight's Tonic for Inebriates, the White Star Secret Liquor Cure, the Boston Drug Cure for Drunkenness, and Morphia-Cure. Not only did these "balms" not work, they were often generously dosed with opium, morphine, cocaine, and, ironically, alcohol.

Meanwhile, some temperance warriors simply resorted to a more direct response: isolating or restraining individual offenders until they dried out. As Bayard Taylor recalled in his 1850 book *Eldorado: Adventures in the Path of Empire*, one inebriated man's friends "took away his money and deposited it in the hands of the Alcalde [mayor], then tied him to a tree where they left him till he became sober."

While many of the consequences of immoderate use of alcohol are quite predictable, if not timeless, there were also some unexpected outcomes, especially within the roiling cultural upheaval of the California Gold Rush. William Perkins, a Canadian gold seeker and Sonora merchant, recollected that, during the Gold Rush, "the most common and fatal result . . . of drunkenness is falling into some of the thousands of deep pits, dug during the summer by the miners, and now full of water. Scarcely a week passes that two or three bodies be not fished out of these holes."

James Ayers, a forty-niner from Missouri who became a newspaper publisher in the rollicking Gold Country village of Mokelumne Hill, in Calaveras County, remembered an 1852 incident concerning a man named Clarke. Clarke, Ayers noted, had the Midas touch—he was renowned in the foothills for his ability to find gold claims—but he was equally celebrated for his knack of losing his newfound wealth by gambling and drinking.

One day Clarke entered Mokelumne Hill after finding yet another rich diggings. Within minutes after arriving in the hamlet, however, he went on a "protracted spree" and quickly spent all his recently acquired funds, meaning he could no longer purchase any liquor. "No problem," said Clarke. Immediately, he left Mokelumne Hill to "make a rich find," fortified with a gift flask of whiskey. Before too long, Clarke was "overcome with fatigue and inebriation" and lay down to take a nap. According to Ayers:

> During his restless sleep he rolled down the side of the hill and landed in a gulch. When he came to his senses he turned over, drew his case knife and commenced to dig up the earth. After a while he uncovered a lump of gold. Then, as he went deeper into the ground with his case-knife, he brought out more nuggets, some of them very large. To make our story short, he had discovered a ravine that was afterwards known as Rich Gulch, and from which many millions were taken.

The key to Clarke's success, Ayers asserted, was that he had "no theory [of discovery]." His method was to drink whiskey until he got drunk and then wander. He would prospect in spots where success was inconceivable—"untrammeled by the laws of science or even by the likelihood of auriferous distribution"—his only secret weapon, according to Clarke himself, being his excess consumption of whiskey. As Ayers concluded, "He was very assiduous in demonstrating the truth of his proposition."

Tales of drunken men abound, but perhaps the most unusual alcohol-induced escapade did not revolve around a human but a horse—a spirited colt named Whitey.

In 1871, Albert Evans, a New Hampshire–born journalist working as a California correspondent for the *New York Tribune* and *Chicago Tribune*, went on a daylong horseback excursion to the top of Mount Tamalpais, in Marin County, with two friends. Before returning to San Rafael, a few miles distant, the three decided to add an exciting finale to the day by engaging in a horse race to end all horse races. And as Evans recalled, "Here the trouble began." The oldest member of the group, known as "The Doctor," was aboard the energetic Whitey; Lloyd was astride the gentle Mousey; and Evans was riding the seemingly docile Juanita. Evans recounted that the Doctor, "by reason of his greater age and presumably riper judgment and greater discretion, was entrusted with the transportation of the saddle-bags, in which were packed a chicken-luncheon, a lot of ammunition, and a few [liquor] bottles."

With a shout, the intrepid racers were off. They jockeyed for position, swooping down the hillside at a furious pace, until they came to a fork in the road. Mousey, Lloyd's horse, with a full head of steam, turned toward the left fork, even though the entrance to San Rafael required taking the right fork. Seeing Lloyd and Mousey's predicament, the Doctor yelled out, "No! No!" to redirect the pair. Unfortunately, the Doctor's estimable steed, Whitey, heard his rider's cry as "Whoa! Whoa!" and therefore stiffened his legs, skidded to a stop, and began to buck. The Doctor was thrown clear, and

something rose gracefully from the rear of the saddle, described a gentle curve in the air, and landed with a loud thud and a sharp jingle on the hard road, a few feet ahead of him. It was the saddle-bags, and the jingle sounded suspiciously like that of broken glass—which we found no difficulty in ascertaining that it was.

At this point, Juanita jumped backward at the commotion, and Evans was dislodged; "the ground in that particular locality is very solid, as I ascertained beyond a doubt." Juanita, now riderless, sniffed at the saddlebags "with distended nostrils and eyes opened wide with horror. Well might she do so! The escaping fluid made the leather curl up like a burned boot, and as I held them up the liquor ran from them much as you may see it run from a clam fresh dug from the sand."

Luckily, the riders and horses were unhurt. Evans dusted himself off, and the Doctor retied the saddlebags to Whitey. With the Doctor back in the saddle, Evans noted that the liquor from the bags was flooding over Whitey's back and "appeared to infuse new spirit into him." Before long it seemed that Whitey had somehow instantaneously absorbed the alcohol and was drunk. The colt reared and kicked and "switched his tail and snorted viciously, then bolted for San Rafael as if life or death depended on his reaching there inside of ten minutes." Whitey rocketed toward San Rafael "like a woodchuck hunting a new hole," and the Doctor held on as best he could. The increasingly tipsy Whitey was having trouble coordinating his back legs with his forelegs, and the result was an ungainly, uncoordinated gallop that caused the Doctor to "roll and pitch like a ship in a cross sea with a head wind." Swaths of daylight frequently flashed between the Doctor's trousers and his saddle.

Mousey and Juanita, saddled with their incredulous riders, now instantly rushed to join their comrade Whitey. "Mousey," Evans wrote, "seemed to rather enjoy the situation, and kept close upon Whitey's heels, while Juanita, thinking it was a race for grand cash, went in to win or die." When Mousey bumped Juanita, Albert Evans's feet slipped from the stirrups, and then he lost control of the reins. He was "at sea rudderless and drifting helpless before the storm."

With their horses dashing hell bent for leather, Lloyd, Albert, and the Doctor had seemingly lost all command as they barreled toward San Rafael. They passed Chinese laborers who waved their broad-brimmed hats in delight at the spectacle, even as the Doctor loudly saturated the countryside with epithets and expletives. Evans, who normally frowned on such coarse language, said he did not express unhappiness with the profanity as he was "very busy at the moment."

In what seemed like seconds, the three racers approached San Rafael: "The hospitable citizens . . . saw us coming, with a cloud of dust spinning out in our wake like the tail of a comet, and with one accord turned out to greet us." Fearing that the riders might dangerously charge through without slowing or stopping, the townspeople spread out and blocked the street, boisterously hollering, "WHOA!" Whitey staggered to a stop and bucked, Mousey braked suddenly, and the Doctor and Lloyd were deposited head over heels before the citizenry. Albert and Juanita continued undeterred, with Evans holding on for dear life, feet flying and arms flapping. Juanita skirted the barricade and "went through a picket-fence, caromed on a market-vegetable cart which stood in the field, and went down with a crash which sounded in my sensitive ears like that which will in due time announce the final dissolution of the universe." When Albert Evans regained his senses, he found himself sprawled in a potato patch. "Thus we made our triumphal entry into San Rafael," he concluded.

And thus ended the wild rides of Mousey, Juanita, and Whitey the inebriated stallion.

DINNER AT STRAWBERRY.

Nineteenth-century dining was frequently haphazard, spirited, and quick. "Dinner at Strawberry," illustration by J. Ross Browne, from Browne's "A Peep at Washoe," *Harper's New Monthly Magazine*, vol. 22, no. 127 (December 1860): 1–17, illustration on p. 15. Image courtesy of the California State Library, Sacramento; California History Section.

CHAPTER THREE

Grizzly Bear Steak, Sourdough
Slapjacks, and Whole Jackass Rabbit

GRACIOUS DINING
AND GLUTTONY

In the twenty-first century, California has become renowned as the epicenter of the "locavore movement," which encourages residents to eat only foods that are grown or harvested within a hundred-mile radius of the location in which they are served. The state is also a pioneer—under the leadership of Alice Waters, the visionary owner of trailblazing Berkeley restaurant Chez Panisse—in the "farm-to-table" or "farm-to-fork" effort to serve only local foodstuffs in restaurants and school cafeterias, preferably either through direct acquisition of goods from producers (dairies, wineries, breweries, truck farms, and fisheries) or as cultivated through community-based agriculture. The objective is the use of local, organic, and sustainable food to, as the Chez Panisse website states, help the diner "partake of the immediacy and excitement of vegetables just out of the garden, fruit right off the branch, and fish straight from the sea."

In nineteenth-century California, eating local wasn't akin to today's "foodie" culture but simply a way of life. While many residents valued and sought out the finest locally produced food, usually they had to make do with whatever they could get, whether domestic or foreign. A case in point concerns the scarcity of chicken eggs in San Francisco during the Gold Rush. In the skyrocketing population composed mostly of young men who did not want or did not know how to cook, the city's cafés, restaurants, and saloons, ranging from the greasiest of greasy spoons to the most elegant of eateries, did big business offering meals varying from the quick and barely edible to the leisurely

During the latter half of the nineteenth century, millions of eggs of the murre, a seabird, were gathered on the Farallon Islands near San Francisco to feed the hungry denizens of the city. "The Egg Pickers, Farralone Island, Pacific Ocean, #250," photograph by E. Nesemann, c. 1885. Image courtesy of the California State Library, Sacramento; California History Section, Digital ID: Farallon Islands, Stereo-3216.

and gourmet. Chicken eggs were in high demand to help satisfy this yawning gastronomic need, but there simply were not enough. A solution arose when someone thought to look toward the Farallones, a group of rocky islands and craggy pillars in the Pacific Ocean thirty miles west of San Francisco.

The islands were the nesting ground of thousands upon thousands of seabirds, and of particular interest to residents of the City by the Bay were the seabird eggs, especially those of the murre. This member of the auk family is about half the size of a duck, but its eggs compare in size to goose eggs, which are two or three times bigger than chicken eggs. Speckled greenish brown and pointy at the end, the eggs, when fresh, have no distinctive odor, but when they get to be several days old, they develop a noticeably fishy smell and taste. The yolk is deep red, and the white remains clear and gelatinous, even when fried. This unappetizing meal looks like a bloody eyeball surrounded by a slimy halo . . . but a fresh egg is a fresh egg. And customers craved them.

While Native people almost certainly harvested murre eggs, the best post-contact documented evidence of "egging" on the Farallones traces back as early as 1827. An estimated few hundred eggs were harvested that year, but the practice became much more popular during the Gold Rush. During the 1850s, "eggers" collected murre eggs by the hundreds of thousands and sold them in San Francisco and environs. Murre eggs were gathered on the Farallones for forty years, with estimates ranging from 900,000 eggs collected annually at the height of activity to 150,000 eggs per season in a slow year. During the Gold Rush era, murre eggs sold for an average twenty-six cents per dozen (about $8 per dozen today).

The Pacific Egg Company, also known as the Farallon Egg Company, sought to monopolize the murre egg trade in the 1850s, but their biggest challenge came when egging grounds were threatened by the construction of a government lighthouse on the islands. Skirmishes, sometimes armed, occurred between the eggers and the lighthouse construction crews, and independent egg companies also established beachheads on the

Farallones to get what they could. The Pacific Egg Company engaged in heated confrontations with its competitors, including one group led by David Batchhelder. The tension grew until, in 1863, there was bloodshed. In an incident known as "The Egg War," Pacific Egg Company personnel clashed with Batchhelder's gang on the islands and, when the dust and feathers cleared, two were dead and four lay wounded. David Batchhelder was convicted of murder, but the verdict was later overturned on a technicality. The Pacific Egg Company emerged victorious and retained a stranglehold on the egg trade for the next eighteen years.

Equally as fascinating as the battles over egg rights was the actual gathering of the murre eggs. For an 1874 article for *Harper's New Monthly Magazine*, Charles Nordhoff visited the islands during the collection season. He memorably described the process:

> From fifteen to twenty men are employed during the egging season in collecting and shipping the eggs . . . . The work is not amusing, for the birds seek out the least accessible places, and the men must follow, climbing often where a goat would almost hesitate. But this is not the worst . . . . The murre remains until her enemy is close upon her; then she rises with a scream which often startles a thousand or two of birds, who whirl up into the air in a dense mass, scattering filth and guano over the eggers.

Nordhoff marveled at the agility and daring of the eggers:

> So difficult is the ground that it is impossible to carry baskets. The egger therefore stuffs the eggs into his shirt bosom until he has as many as he can safely carry, then clambers over rocks and down precipices until he comes to a place of deposit, where he puts them into baskets, to be carried down to the shore, where there are houses for receiving them. But so skillful and careful are the gatherers that but few eggs are broken.

In this manner, millions of eggs were collected from the Far-allones, stretching over several decades until the northern Bay Area community of Petaluma emerged as a production hub for chicken eggs in the late 1890s and early 1900s and murre eggs fell out of fashion. The impact of so much egg gathering was already devastating for the murre population, however, and the Farallon rookery has still not fully recovered. Studies conducted by the United States Fish and Wildlife Service calculate the pre–Gold Rush count of murres as between 1 to 3 million birds; the removal of their eggs and the resulting plunge in reproduction reduced the figure to less than 20,000 murres at the turn of the twentieth century. Due to conservation efforts and reduced pressure on the murre population, the current tally is estimated to be around 250,000, with a guarded prognosis of continuing improvement in the numbers.

o   o   o

Old California culture accommodated a wide variety of cooking methods, dishes served, and dining choices. The consumers might be grizzled gold seekers in a mining camp, loggers in a mountain outpost, salty mariners, struggling townsfolk, urban denizens, or cosmopolitan gentry, but no matter the demographics, they all had to eat. And everyone seemed to fantasize about fine food. As Mariposa County gold rusher Horace Snow recalled in 1854: "Morning begins at dawn and . . . you are awake [but not fully] . . . . You fall into a dreamy mood and think of sirloin steak, plum puddings, mince pies, potted pigeons . . . . And never once imagine that you will awake to disappointment."

Dining was a free-for-all, physical trial throughout the era, and in some cases it was akin to a contact sport, no matter if the food was revolting or refined. In his 1871 *History of San José and Surroundings*, historian Frederic Hall described a meal following the first meeting of the California State Legislature, in 1849. When the dinner bell rang, there was a frantic stampede: "It was

a hazardous undertaking . . . ; the rush was so great, that crowd-
ing through the dining-room door, put one in mind of trying to
drive a four-horse team through a single door of a stable."

In 1851, Englishman William Shaw described a typical Gold
Rush "eating-house" and feeding frenzy:

> At certain hours in the day, the beating of gongs and
> ringing of bells from all quarters, announce feeding time at
> the various refectories; at this signal a rush is made to the
> tables. It is not uncommon to see your neighbour coolly
> abstract a quid [a plug of tobacco] from his jaw, placing
> it for the time being in his waistcoat pocket, or hat, or
> sometimes beside his plate, even; then commences, on all
> sides, a fierce attack on the eatables, and the contents of
> the dishes rapidly disappear. Lucky is the man who has
> a quick eye and a long arm; for every one helps himself
> indiscriminately, and attention is seldom paid to any
> request.

Even as the Gold Rush began to subside, the daily rush on
the region's various eateries did not diminish. In his 1860s
Harper's Monthly series entitled "A Peep at Washoe," journalist
and author J. Ross Browne recounted the dinnertime blitzkrieg
at the stagecoach stop of Strawberry, about thirty-five miles east
of Placerville on the road to Nevada:

> At the first tinkle of the [dinner] bell the door was burst
> open with a tremendous crash . . . The whole house actually
> tottered and trembled at the concussion, as if shaken by an
> earthquake. Long before the main body had assaulted the
> table the din of arms was heard above the general uproar;
> the deafening clatter of plates, knives, and forks, and the
> dreadful battlecry of "Waiter! waiter! Pork and beans! Cof-
> fee, waiter! Beefsteak! Sausages! Potatoes! Ham and eggs—
> quick, waiter, for God's sake!" It was a scene of destruction
> and carnage long to be remembered . . . . When the table
> was vacated it presented a shocking scene of desolation.

Perhaps the most entertaining postscript for rambunctious California eating practices was supplied by British journalist and travel writer Phil Robinson in 1892, when he succinctly described the "savage" approach of the diner in seven memorable words: "Dab, dab, peck, peck, grunt, growl, snort!"

∘ ∘ ∘

Food was always expensive, usually the result of simple supply and demand, but prices were also often predicated on what the market could bear, and this was particularly evident during the cultural upheaval of the Gold Rush. As Joseph Conlin chronicles in *Bacon, Beans and Galantines*, his excellent 1986 examination of nineteenth-century western mining frontier "food and foodways," Gold Rush food costs were astronomical, and price volatility was routine. Charges for commodities could vary wildly from community to community, and prices were generally much higher in remote locations due to limited supplies. In Placerville, some forty miles east of Sacramento, a single slice of bread cost $1 ($30 today); if buttered, you'd pay twice that. During the Gold Rush, a can of fruit in San Francisco cost two thousand times more than in New York City, and in 1850 a boatload of ice shipped to San Francisco from Boston quickly sold out at eighty cents a pound (about $25 per pound today).

Dining out reflected similar cost disparities. In December 1849, Catherine Haun, a recent arrival by wagon train from Iowa, found herself one of the few women in boomtown Sacramento, then a world of rickety shelters and leaky tents. For Christmas Day dinner at an improvised "restaurant," Haun paid $2.50 (about $75 today) for a grizzly bear steak, and $1 ($30) for a side order of cabbage. In New York City, a similar steak dinner with all the trimmings cost between twelve and fifty cents ($3 to $5). Basic foodstuffs were "market-priced," meaning the highest possible sales price. The following chart underscores the remarkable difference in California prices compared to those elsewhere in the United States in 1849–50; in the rightmost columns, you can see the change in prices after the Gold Rush:

	Typical 1849–50 prices in the United States, outside of California	Typical 1849–50 prices in California (2019 equivalents in parentheses)	Typical 1900 prices in California (2019 equivalents in parentheses)
Beans, per pound	9¢	20¢ ($6.20)	4¢ ($1.20)
Beef, per pound	6¢	40¢–75¢ ($12–$23)	15¢ ($4.50)
Butter, per pound	15¢	$1–$20 ($30–$610)	4¢ ($1.10)
Cheese, per pound	31¢	$1–$25 ($30–$762)	17¢ ($5)
Coffee, per pound	5¢	16¢–33¢ ($5–$10)	30¢ ($9)
Eggs, each	1¢	$1–$3 ($30–$91)	2.5¢ (63¢)
Flour, per pound	11¢	25¢–30¢ ($8–$9)	2¢ (60¢)
Ham, per pound	10¢	$1 ($30)	13¢ ($3.90)
Molasses, per gallon	26¢	$2–$4 ($62–$124)	51¢ ($15.30)
Pork, per pound	8.75¢	40¢–75¢ ($12–$23)	15¢ ($4.50)
Potatoes, per pound	1¢	14¢ ($4)	2¢ (60¢)
Rice, per pound	2.25¢	10¢–30¢ ($3–$9)	8¢ ($2.40)
Sugar, per pound	4¢	20¢–50¢ ($6–$16)	6¢ ($1.80)
Tea, per pound	24¢	60¢–$1 ($19–$30)	55¢ ($16.50)

Prices moderated following the Gold Rush, although the most sought-after consumables (such as lobster, French champagne, and Peruvian port) often continued to fetch higher prices in California than elsewhere. By 1900, California food costs were roughly the same as the national averages, in part due to increased availability and improved supply chains, including, most notably, the completion of the Transcontinental Railroad in 1869, which linked California to sprawling national markets that had been inaccessible at midcentury.

Throughout the nineteenth century, California received foodstuffs from seemingly everywhere: Chilean beans, Chinese rice, Australian flour, Argentinian jerky, hogs from Hawaii, and fruits and vegetables from Oregon. A Gold Rush–era cargo ship from Tahiti delivered sweet potatoes, squashes, limes, coconuts, bananas, and oranges. From the state's interior came salmon, while foothill and Sierra Nevada hunters provided deer, elk, and thousands of quail. Grizzly bear was commonly available at midcentury, and grizzly steaks and roast were regularly featured on local menus. In the latter half of the century, California farms, both small and large, offered radishes, lettuce, carrots, beets, melons, peas, and many other truck crops. Merchants organized networks of stores that offered a dazzling array of products. As an example, the Excelsior Tent at Mormon Island, about twenty-five miles east of Sacramento on the American River, displayed a broadside advertisement that promised

> Pork, Flour, Bread, Beef, Hams, Mackerel, Sugar, Molasses, Coffee, Teas, Butter & Cheese, Pickles, Beans, Peas, Rice, Chocolate, Spices, Salt, Soap, Vinegar & c . . . . Every variety of Preserved Meats and Vegetables and Fruits; Tongues and Sounds; Smoked Halibut; Dry Cod Fish; Eggs fresh and fine; Figs; Raisins; Almonds and Nuts; China Preserves; China Bread and Cakes; Butter Crackers, Boston Crackers, and many other desirable and choice bits.

For nearly twenty years, supplying provisions was a major enterprise and a strain on the infrastructure, both existent and improvised. Freight charges from San Francisco to Sacramento, about 100 miles, were higher than freight costs from New York to San Francisco, a span of 3,000 miles. Wagon cargo levies often exceeded $1 a pound ($30 today). When competition increased rapidly, freight rates dropped markedly, but then transport could become problematic. Delivery caravans of wagons pulled by teams of forty or fifty mules jammed the roads. From Marysville in the Sacramento Valley, multiple companies made up of an estimated total of three thousand teamsters and twenty-five hundred mules and horses were employed to deliver food and other supplies to the foothills. In the northern part of the state, near Mount Shasta, communities imported on a weekly basis more than one hundred tons of provisions using nineteen hundred mules.

But the fundamental concern was not the amount of food obtainable or the frequency of delivery—it was the quality of preparation. A major problem throughout the earliest years of the Gold Rush era was that home cooking was often performed by people, usually men, who did not have any experience or apparent culinary aptitude. Gold Rush accounts note hapless miners igniting cook fires with gunpowder, and several descriptions tell of clueless cooks scooping handfuls of rice into pots without first adding water, then placing the pot on the fire and being astonished that the finished product was a solid block of scorched grains and a ruined pot destined for the scrap heap. As Prentice Mulford recalled of his Gold Rush days in a June 1869 *Overland Monthly* article entitled "California Culinary Experiences":

> The human avalanche precipitated on these shores in the rush of '49' and '50' was a mass of culinary ignorance. Cooking had always by us been deemed a part of woman's kingdom. We knew that bread was made of flour, and for the most part so made by woman . . . . Of the knowledge, skill, patience and experience required to conduct this and other culinary operations, we realized nothing.

Cleanliness was usually an afterthought, especially in more secluded areas. The reliably acerbic Hinton Rowan Helper described a typical gold seeker's cooking practices:

> His cooking utensils consist of a frying-pan and a pot, neither of which, except in rare instances, is ever washed. The pot is mostly used for boiling pork and beans, and the old scum and scales that accumulate on the inside from one ebullition serve as seasoning to the next . . . . [The miner] will probably keep a bottle of molasses, which may be seen by the side of the frying-pan, unstopped, and containing an

amount of flies and ants nearly equal to that of the saccha-
rine juice.

Helper's understandable conclusion? "He is not very squeamish
about his diet."

Often the rough mining camp meals were hurried and unappetizing exercises in eating whatever was available. As gold
rusher J. D. Stevenson explained in an April 1849 letter:

> This labor would be more endurable, if at the close of day,
> [the miner] could enjoy the comforts of good food and rest,
> but this is out of the question. He must cook his own food,
> or go without it . . . . The food is rarely such as will satisfy
> the appetite of a fatigued and hungry man . . . . I have seen
> men living for days without any other food than flour
> mixed with water formed into a kind of dough and baked
> in the ashes.

As Stevenson observed, miners would combine flour (preferably
with a sourdough starter) and some form of liquid—whether
water, milk, or alcohol—to form a batter and cook pancakes, or
"slapjacks." Often, the ingredients were a bit mysterious, and
invariably the dubious results were referred to as "some kind of
slapjacks" in letters, diaries, and journals.

Mining camp restaurants and makeshift cafés were not
much better. Frank Marryat, English author of the 1855 Gold
Rush chronicle *Mountains and Molehills*, remarked that at
every hotel eatery one was likely to find "a stereotyped bill
of fare, consisting, with little variation, of a tough beefsteak,
boiled potatoes, stewed beans, a nasty compound of dried
apples, and a *jug of molasses*." Peripatetic Scottish observer John
David Borthwick recalled an 1851 meal near Nevada City that
was "a villainous bad dinner" of "bad salt pork, bad pickled
onions, and bad bread." Unusual meals appeared frequently
on the bill of fare. A case in point was the El Dorado Hotel in
Hangtown (today's Placerville), which offered "whole jackass
rabbit" for $1 ($30) in 1850.

Not surprisingly, bad nutrition led to serious physical complaints and illnesses. As J. D. Stevenson noted during the Gold Rush, "The result is, that living in this way produces sickness and disease, and many who come into the town with heavy purses of the precious metal are broken in health and constitution." A wide panoply of diseases emerged, caused by both poor food preparation and inadequate nutritional knowledge. One of the most common was scurvy, the result of a serious vitamin C deficiency. Edward Gould Buffum, a Rhode Island journalist who had migrated to California during the Gold Rush and, after an abortive attempt as a miner, became editor of San Francisco's *Daily Alta California* newspaper, contracted scurvy in the goldfields and described its symptoms in chilling detail: "I noticed its first attack upon myself by swelling and bleeding of the gums, which was followed by a swelling of both legs below the knee, which rendered me unable to walk; and for three weeks I was laid up in my tent, obliged to feed upon the very articles that had caused the disease, and growing daily weaker, without any reasonable prospect of relief." Buffum survived by altering his diet.

Scurvy could be prevented or reversed by consuming foods high in vitamin C, such as chili peppers, broccoli, parsley, lemons, limes, oranges, strawberries, cabbage, spinach, or potatoes, but these things were not always part of. Gold Rush–era diets, especially in the rough-and-tumble universe of the mining camps. Sonora, in Tuolumne County, suffered a scourge of scurvy and temporarily organized a city government primarily to establish a municipal hospital to address the challenge. To combat the threat, residents also purchased hundreds of bottles of lime juice at $5 per bottle (the equivalent of $150 per bottle today), and canned fruit sold at twenty times the going rate in other Gold Country districts. Depending on a community's circumstances, oranges were sold during the Gold Rush as both food and medicine.

And scurvy was not the only ailment caused primarily by bad nutrition. There was "bilious fever," a catch-all diagnosis for any fever that caused nausea, vomiting, abnormal diarrhea, and a high fever; and other maladies included constipation, cramps, food poisoning, irritable bowels, gastritis, hemorrhoids, kidney disease, ulcers, liver complaints, dyspepsia (or upper abdominal pain), heartburn, and cramps.

But for too many, particularly those in the hinterlands where food delivery could be difficult, the biggest worry was how to fill an empty, growling stomach. W. S. Walker, in his reminiscence of mining life entitled *Glimpses of Hungryland* (1880), recalled a winter morning circa 1865: "Christmas morning found us frying the string our bacon had been suspended with. This we washed down with a tin cup full of pepper-wood tea, and then we sat down to reflect on the peculiarity of the situation." But that was soon forgotten when his ravenous campmate Reed spied a mountain hare and commenced a madcap chase, rifle in hand. A half hour passed, then another, and yet another as Reed zigzagged through the woods, shadowing the frantic rabbit. Walker recalled, "Such wild leaps as that animal made, I have never saw equaled; and Reed made some of the most inhuman jumps and plunges that a mortal ever was guilty of, as . . . he dashed wildly in pursuit." The terrified hare eventually leapt from a cliff into an icy river to escape, and the famished Reed, following close behind, skidded to the cliff's edge and made several attempts to summon the courage to follow the rabbit into the river before Walker finally pulled him to safety. The lucky rabbit escaped.

o   o   o

Even during those days when population outpaced food supplies, it was a matter of pride for villages to offer the finest grub possible to demonstrate that a modicum of civilization could exist in even the humblest of circumstances. For instance, John David Borthwick, who had gagged down a "villainous bad dinner" the night before, dined at the Hotel de Paris in Nevada City in 1851 and relished the meal, which he described as "the best-got-up thing of the kind I had sat down to for some months." The feast of roast beef, soup, cabbage, carrots, turnips, and onions—washed down with copious amounts of coffee and cognac—left Borthwick "powerfully refreshed."

In times and places when and where the food supply chain was fully functional, many Californians preferred "eating out," both for convenience and because restaurants and cafés were often the closest approximation of "home" in a transitory society. The number of customers was prodigious. In 1852, the What Cheer House, a combination rooming house and restaurant in San Francisco, served four thousand meals per day. The nearby Branch Restaurant, which had two locations, fed three thousand a day. By the mid-1850s, the Branch's monthly bill for meat was $8,000 (about a quarter of a million dollars today); for flour, $4,000 ($120,000); for milk, $2,000 ($60,000); and for butter, $200 ($6,000). Daily sales for the Branch restaurants exceeded $2,000 daily, or $60,000 in 2019.

In 1983, Mary Lee Spence, former president of the Western History Association, penned for the *Western Historical Quarterly* an article titled "They Also Serve Who Wait" that provided an intriguing perspective on the ongoing importance of cafés and restaurants during this period. Using employment figures for waiters from the United States Census records of 1900 and 1910, Spence noted that, in 1910, there was one waiter for every 101 residents of San Francisco, a much higher rate than in New York City or Boston. California had one waiter for every 320 citizens in 1900, and one for every 203 in 1910. By comparison, South Dakota had one waiter for every 1,793 inhabitants in 1900.

While everything was understandably rougher in the camps, the dining experience in the larger cities could be very elegant. A prime example can be found in the history of a restaurant that existed under various guises in San Francisco from the Gold Rush to the mid-1980s. Founded in 1849, the establishment was originally known as Poule d'Or, meaning either "The Golden Hen" or, if the French colloquial definition of *poule* is used, "The Golden Prostitute." In 1868, the name was formally changed to the Poodle Dog, and aside from some periodic name enhancements (e.g., Ritz Old Poodle Dog), it was known by that name until it closed in 1983. One of the most expensive eateries in town and an exemplar of French haute cuisine in a port city known for being simultaneously scrappy and sophisticated, the Poodle Dog offered tastebud-tempting delights including "Frog Legs à la Poulette," "Oysters à la Poulette," and "Soufflé Rothschild." Other restaurants followed the lead of the Poodle Dog, offering opulent dining on French or French-sounding cuisine, considered the epitome of chic gastronomy from midcentury onward; the *spécialité de la maison* was habitually known by this grand Gallic term, even if the dish featured simple ingredients and minimal preparation.

While some stylish eating emporia were in midsized settlements such as Sacramento, Monterey, and Los Angeles, most were centered in San Francisco, the hub of fashionable epicureanism. Among the city's finest locales were Jack's, Marchand's, Maison Riche, Maison Dorée, Delmonico's, the Palace of Art, and Monkey Warner's Cobweb Palace. Luxurious dishes of the time included "Angels on Horseback" (oysters), persimmon salad, smothered quail, terrapin stew, artichoke scrambled eggs, mulled buttermilk, "Carmel Chow Chow" (a gourmet vegetable preparation), deviled pork chops, candied rose petals, "Drunken Pigeons" (squab in a rich sauce), "Chicken à la Beautiful Mulatta," "Tripes à la mode de Caen," "San Francisco Tipsy Cake" (pound cake with blanched raisins, fine sherry, and raspberry jelly topped with custard), a very, very spicy pasta topping called Sauce Mount Etna, and many more.

Some creations were named for celebrities, including several in honor of opera divas, who frequented San Francisco. There was Patti Consommé (a soup of chicken dumplings, artichoke hearts, and spaghetti) and Veal Patti—both after the Italian-French prima donna Adelina Patti—and then there was the popular Chicken Tetrazzini, named for coloratura soprano Luisa Tetrazzini. Peach Melba was not invented in San Francisco, but the city helped popularize the dish worldwide due to its fascination with Australian soprano Nellie Melba and its own growing reputation as a global tastemaker and trendsetter. And perhaps the longest lasting contribution was "Louis dressing," named for its originator, chef Louis Coutard; generations of visitors to San Francisco's Fisherman's Wharf and elsewhere in the city have enjoyed Shrimp and Crab Louis thanks to Coutard, and in return, the chef gained lasting culinary fame thanks to the dish. Louis Coutard made the Louis dressing, and the dressing made Louis Coutard.

o   o   o

While French cuisine was especially revered—due not only to its historical association with European and East Coast refinement but because roughly 10 percent of (or thirty thousand) Gold Rush immigrants were from France—other national gastronomies were also evident in the ethnically diverse and cosmopolitan California cosmos. Most notable were Mexican/Spanish/ Californio and Chinese foodstuffs and techniques, and although these are some of the most beloved cuisines in modern-day California, that wasn't always the case.

From the 1820s until the dawn of the Gold Rush era, the hybrid cuisine of Spain and Mexico was dominant in the region. Perhaps a more precise term for this style of cooking would be "Californio," for its captivating fusion of Spanish traditions, Mexican embellishments, and Native Californian elements. Early settlers who came directly from Spain often found the landscape similar in climate and soil to their Mediterranean homeland, and they readily developed agriculture and ranching systems that echoed those of their Spanish roots. There were extensive orchards and vineyards, sprawling cattle ranches, and mission gardens featuring oranges, figs, and other reminders of home. The cuisine had a distinctive Spanish flavor and style.

The first published compendium of Californio recipes, *El Cocinero Español*, or "The Spanish Kitchen," was compiled by Encarnación Pinedo in 1898. The book includes fare that is common in California today (tamales and enchiladas) but it also features rarer time-honored Spanish dishes

and ingredients, such as *membrillo* (quince jam) and empana-
das filled with raisins, saffron, olives, almonds, walnuts, and
sherry. Other entries are evidence of the increasing influence of
Mexican culture during the decades when the region was under
Mexico's control; some of the more than eight hundred recipes in Pinedo's collection are tagged "à la Mexicana," and the
names of the foods reflect some Mexican influence, including
mole and *guajolote* (turkey).

Despite many white Californians enjoying the taste and convenience of Californio fare, widespread approval of the cuisine
nearly disappeared during the Gold Rush, and historians have
for decades speculated as to why it fell out of favor. One theory
is that gold rushers simply stuck to food they were familiar with
and were unwilling to experiment, a notion belied by the rising
popularity of French cookery, which was foreign to most American palates. A more likely explanation is that structural racism
deliberately exiled the food, as Mexican and Californio culture
was considered, at the very least, insignificant or, at the most,
contemptible. As a result, the literature of the period offers very
few allusions to Mexican and Californio food.

At the time, there were many different rationalizations for
not eating Mexican and Californio food, including such false
justifications as the popular rumor that coyotes would not even
eat the flesh of dead Mexicans because their bodies were tainted
with the foul-tasting residue of chili peppers. Another common
excuse was that it wasn't right to consume the cuisine of a hated
enemy from the Mexican War of 1846–48. A few sources placed
some blame on the pervasive guidebooks of the era, which sometimes counseled travelers to avoid Mexican fare. Even as these
assertions were specifically about food, however, underlying
each attack was loathing of the Mexican and Californio cultures themselves. Our notion that Mexican cuisine has *always*
been a beloved California institution is a twentieth-century
conception.

o   o   o

Another major group that brought its cuisine to California were the Chinese immigrants, who were often employed as cooks in eateries of all stripes—in some cases because they liked the work and in other cases because, due to hundreds of restrictive local ordinances and state and national legislation throughout the era, they had few other options. During the Gold Rush era and for decades beyond, Chinese immigrants were mostly relegated to a few professions: farming, gardening, laundry service, manual labor (especially on the railroad), mining, domestic work, and cooking for both private and public clientele.

California saw a huge influx of Chinese immigrants during the Gold Rush, with the most reliable records indicating that from 1850 to 1855 the number topped 27,000—an exponential leap from the approximately 400 who came to California between 1840 and 1850. During the construction of the Transcontinental Railroad in the 1860s, Chinese immigration increased dramatically again (90 percent of the construction workers on the Central Pacific Railroad were Chinese), and most of them gravitated to Gold Country, where the census of 1860 reveals that 35 percent of foreign-born residents in the Sierra Nevada counties were Chinese, who also accounted for 18 percent of the overall population in that area.

Numbers made little difference when it came to acceptance, however, and in fact over time the record is evidence of how strong anti-Chinese sentiment was in Old California. The discriminatory Foreign Miners Tax imposed unfair levies on Chinese and other immigrants from 1854 to 1870, and when the Transcontinental Railroad was completed in 1869 and Chinese railroad workers went looking for new jobs, violent attacks on individuals and communities escalated as anti-Chinese societies blossomed. It all culminated with the Chinese Exclusion Act of 1882, which prohibited Chinese laborers from entering the United States for ten years. (California's Chinese population at the time was 300,000, including 39,579 immigrants who had come to California that year alone.) The law was renewed twice—in 1892 and 1902—and extended indefinitely in 1904, until it was finally repealed in 1943.

Chinese immigrants were regarded warily by the dominant white culture and were considered especially unassimilable and "alien" in personal habits, dress, and other ethnic customs, including their style of food. Many Chinese immigrants worked in restaurants, but it wasn't uncommon for establishments to try to conceal their Chinese workforces, advertising themselves as serving only "American food" or proclaiming to be "English kitchens" (even though such dodging was often to no avail, since the cooking quarters were usually in full view of the customers).

The reaction to Chinese cooks versus their Chinese cooking, however, was sometimes flat-out contradictory: on one hand, the cuisine (usually of the Cantonese variety, since that's were most of the immigrants were from) was praised for its tastiness and attractiveness, while, on the other hand, patrons distrusted the cooks and expressed disgust at the individual ingredients and techniques they used. Descriptions of the supposedly "filthy" conditions of Chinese cookery were common throughout the era, and they were accompanied by revoltingly stereotypical depictions of the Chinese employees themselves. For example, the Reverend Otis Gibson observed in 1877 that most of San Francisco's Chinese restaurants were "exceedingly filthy places" where "many dishes taste of rancid oil." In his 1902 book *By the Golden Gate*, Joseph Carey opined that "[the Chinese] eat things too, which would be most repulsive to the epicurean taste of an Anglo-Saxon. Even lizards and rats and young dogs they will not refuse."

Despite the rampant anti-Chinese fervor of the times, however, Chinese food and restaurants were quite popular in nineteenth-century California. Although never ascending to the positions held by French and so-called American cooking, Chinese food was attractive because it was cheap, quick, and tasty. Usually the Chinese restaurants charged one fixed price for access to an all-you-can-eat selection of various dishes.

Some patrons bucked the negative commentary and naturally found much to celebrate in Chinese cooking and the skills and work ethic of the "Celestials" who made it. In 1852, English-man William Kelly gushed, "The Celestials carry off the palm for superior excellence in every particular. They serve every-thing promptly, cleanly, hot, and well-cooked." William Shaw, who regularly found fault in much of California's fare, com-mented in 1851 that "the best eating houses in San Francisco are those kept by the Celestials and conducted Chinese fashion."

It was, however, a double-edged sword for Chinese restaurant proprietors, chefs, and food workers. On the one hand, Chinese cooking provided a livelihood and a means to preserve their Chinese culture abroad. On the other hand, due to pervasive legal and commonly practiced unwritten restrictions on Chinese employment, the food service industry remained a potent exam-ple of the lack of economic opportunity and social mobility for some immigrant groups.

o   o   o

In many respects, the dining preferences and habits of Old Cali-fornia perfectly reflected the dynamic of the era: it was adven-turous, eclectic, and persnickety, and the feasting of the period encapsulated the dreams and desires, and also the harsh realities, of nineteenth-century California. In January 1885, an event in New York City exemplified this kaleidoscope of gracious dining, gluttony, and everything in between. It was the annual dinner of the Associated Pioneers of the Territorial Days of California, an organization of veterans of the California Gold Rush. The reunion exhibited the yearning of the members to revisit their youth and smother the past in nostalgia. It was a moment that saw the emotional confluence of authenticity and wistfulness. As the *New York Times* reported, the gathering of aging forty-niners featured a menu that reflected their recollections of the Days of Gold, a banquet commemorating the meals and fellowship once shared. It was a dazzling, ethnically diverse array including "grizzly bear steaks with frijoles, ribs of antelope with tortillas, carne seco with Chili Colorados, fried salt pork with slapjacks, stewed jackass rabbit with moscal [mescal], mule (rump) steak with hardtack, and mysterious stew à la Chinese." Of course, the menu did not represent what was actually consumed nearly forty years earlier but was instead a fantasy representation of their fading memories. It was a synthesis of the ideal and the everyday, a meal served with stardust and grit.

The leading choice for tobacco consumption in nineteenth-century California was a cigar, and the industry was very prolific and profitable. The number of cigars produced was staggering, with one report noting that, from 1867 to 1881, the average *monthly* output of cigars was nearly six million. "Portrait of Soldier," photograph by Jacob Shew, c. 1865. Image courtesy of the California State Library, Sacramento; California History Section, Digital ID: 2008-0327.

CHAPTER FOUR

Spittoons, Quids, and Cigarillos

TOBACCO CULTURE

I n 1604, the world's most powerful enemy of tobacco
    unfurled his banner and charged into battle against nico-
    tine. King James I of England issued "A Counterblaste to
Tobacco," in which he decried the "manifolde abuses of this
vile custome of *Tobacco* taking." Tobacco chewing and smoking
was a popular and flourishing activity throughout the British
Empire and was to be a major source of revenue in the soon-to-
be-established North American colonies, but James I foresaw
only "perpetual stinking torment" from the continued consumption and propagation of tobacco. His "Counterblaste" concluded that tobacco use was "a custom loathsome to the eye,
hateful to the nose, harmful to the brain, dangerous to the lungs,
and in the black, stinking fume thereof nearest resembling the
horrible Stygian smoke of the pit that is bottomless."

Despite the king's best efforts to ban or temper tobacco usage
(with efforts including boosting the import tax on tobacco
products by 4,000 percent), the good and true subjects of the
realm ignored the edict. The same snub would have occurred
if a nineteenth-century California civic leader, statewide official, or reformer had dared to suggest a similar widespread

prohibition, as fondness for tobacco was ubiquitous. The men, women, and children of Old California happily and frequently smoked, chewed, and snorted their cigarettes, cigaritos, cigarillos, cigars (commonly spelled "segars" through most of the century), plugs, and snuff. Tobacco was touted for its curative powers and for being an enjoyable respite, a genteel creature comfort, a contemplative tool, and an emblem of status; tobacco products were produced by the millions and sold everywhere, used in every setting, and featured in a parallel economy as barter currency.

But while tobacco was considered an omnipresent and pleasurable diversion, that doesn't mean it was free from criticism in California. Many considered it an unwholesome and disgusting habit, and they didn't keep such opinions to themselves. Consider this commentary from the January 6, 1851, edition of San Francisco's *Daily Alta California*. In its editorial "Things Theatrical Which Should Be Amended," the newspaper railed against the offenses common among the theatergoing public—such as crying babies, patrons in shirtsleeves, and catcalling and laughing during dramatic scenes—but it saved its most vicious invective for those who chewed tobacco. The editorial board ranted against

> the odious, nauseous, abominable habit of creating . . . seas
> of . . . that villainous spittal crushed from the foul weed
> by masticating grinders as constant in their milling as an
> over-shot water wheel, and squirted from discolored lips,
> which seem made only to act as a spouting horn for the
> emission of a nasty semi-liquid which would disgust the
> very herd of swine that swallowed the devils.

Furthermore, the editorial seethed,

> this filthy outrage upon decency is still in practice to such
> an extent that one is not safe in taking a seat at a theatre
> . . . . The floors are flooded, the seats are bespattered, huge
> quids [remnants of chewed tobacco] lie unburied like

corpses of foul toads thrown from some snake's overloaded stomach, and the effluvia arising from these combinations [are] of a most odious weed and bad breath, tinctured, too, perhaps, with the fumes of exceedingly bad rum. . . . This habit should be remedied. . . . Let them bolt the quid. . . . Let this nuisance be abated.

"Tobacco taking," as King James I phrased it, had been an aspect of California culture for centuries—well before California became California—and use of *Nicotiana*, the scientific designation for what the Europeans called "Indian tobacco," has been traced back at least as early as the ninth century. It was a staple crop throughout Mesoamerica and the Western Hemisphere, far antedating the appearance of Europeans in the region, and in fact tobacco was one of the primary products introduced into Europe through the "Columbian Exchange" (named after Christopher Columbus), the extensive system by which flora and fauna, technology, diseases, and humans themselves were transferred between Europe, Africa, and the New World during the fifteenth and sixteenth centuries. The indigenous population of North America used tobacco for trade, ritual and ceremonial purposes, and medicine, but they seldom smoked it as an individual indulgence, or at least not until the arrival of the Europeans. In many Native communities, tobacco was smoked almost exclusively by men, although women shamans were allowed to partake under certain circumstances.

Smoking, rarely chewing, was a social ritual that usually occurred after evening meals, during ceremonies in sweathouses, and at other communal events, and tobacco was also widely given as a medicine. Whether used alone or in mixtures with other plants, tobacco was used for poultices to treat ailments including rheumatism, swelling, rattlesnake bites, and eczema, and it was smoked to help relieve earaches, toothaches, asthma, tuberculosis, sore throats, colds, and many other afflictions.

With the dawn of Spanish California in the eighteenth century, tobacco usage exploded as it grew beyond ceremony into custom. Mostly, it was smoked in cigars, cigaritos, cigarillos, or pipes, and it was indulged in by all classes, all genders, and all ages, a practice that continued well into and beyond the Mexican era of California history. In the 1820s, hide merchant William Heath Davis recounted that

> the Mexican ladies when smoking were in the habit of holding the cigarito between the thumb and finger; the rich using a gold or silver holder, to prevent staining the fingers with the tobacco, and the poorer classes a holder made of *gamuza*, or fine deer skin—with two little pockets, into which they slipped the thumb and finger. Holding up the cigarito, as they placed it in the mouth or removed it, they displayed their pretty little hands to advantage, the fingers extended with an air of coquetry, all very graceful and becoming, and quite captivating to the observer.

Davis also noted that convention dictated that

> no boy or man, though the latter might be sixty years of age, ever smoked in the presence of his parents. . . . If a young man was smoking in the street, and met an old man coming along, so great was the feeling of respect and deference for the latter, that the former would cease smoking and throw his cigar away, and politely raise his hat in salutation, whether they were acquainted or total strangers.

That said, tobacco addiction was so prevalent that at times it could eclipse even religious piety. *New York Tribune* correspondent Bayard Taylor noted in his 1850 book *Eldorado: Adventures in the Path of Empire* that he once attended a Catholic mass in Monterey and noticed that, "during the sermon, several of the [Californios] disappeared through a small door at the end of the gallery. Following them, out of curiosity, I found them all seated in the belfry and along the coping of the front, composedly smoking their cigars."

o o o

In Mexican California, the assorted forms of cigarettes were usually wrapped in cornhusks, with cigarette papers and commercially pre-wrapped cigarettes becoming readily available in the 1840s; Euro-Americans usually favored paper while Californios generally preferred cornhusks, and many descriptions of the period remark on the constant preparation of these nicotine delivery devices across the social spectrum. Forty-niner Prentice Mulford recalled meeting a Californio he dubbed "Don Somebody" who "seemed always in a chronic state of corn-husk cigarette. When not smoking he was rolling them; when not rolling or smoking he was lighting them."

The California Gold Rush transformed the region into the most culturally diverse population in the world, and likewise it featured a myriad of tobacco traditions. So universal was tobacco taking that it even played a role in the publication of the first regional newspaper during the American era. On August 13, 1846, the *Californian* released its first issue, but since newsprint was unobtainable, the publishers used what they had readily available: paper that wrapped tobacco destined for cigars.

Tobacco for chewing—another habit that expanded with the coming of Euro-Americans—was often sold in sheets, like slabs of ribs from a butcher shop, and one could obtain plugs cut from these tobacco blocks of "chaw," occasionally flavored to make the taste less acrid. Chewing tobacco was an acquired taste and beware to those who did not understand how it was consumed. By way of example, consider Charles Peters, a Portuguese sailor who arrived in California in 1846. In 1915, Peters recollected his first encounter with chewing tobacco aboard a ship en route to California:

> One afternoon the captain and the first mate left a large plug of chewing tobacco, from which each had cut a piece and put in their mouths, on the cabin table. I thought that it would make me more of a sailor if I followed their example, so I took a good sized chunk in my mouth and

began to chew. I swallowed the saliva it produced, not knowing it was necessary to expectorate it. The result was I became the sickest boy that ever fell into a bunk on a ship. The captain thought I was going to die but never knew what disease I had, because I was afraid to tell him the cause. I have never tried to chew tobacco since.

Unsurprisingly, the Gold Rush upheaval exponentially increased tobacco consumption in the area. Scottish writer John David Borthwick described the scene in San Francisco soon after his arrival in 1850. It seemed that everywhere he looked there were "Mexicans wrapped up in their blankets smoking cigaritas . . . ; Frenchmen in their blouses smoking black pipes; and little urchins, or little old scamps rather, ten or twelve years of age, smoking cigars as big as themselves."

Smoking by children was especially noteworthy to the argonauts; it was not a particularly unusual occurrence in Old California, but it was surprising, even shocking, to the recently disembarked. Author and social reformer Eliza Farnham recalled that, in the topsy-turvy Gold Rush universe, "the children participate in all the vices of their elders. I saw boys, from six upward, swaggering through the streets, begirt with scarlet sash, in exuberant collar and bosom, segar in mouth, uttering huge oaths, and occasionally treating [buying drinks for] men and boys at the bars." In 1852, Sir Henry Vere Huntley, a British naval officer and representative of an English gold mining company, visited California and remarked that children "not more than six or seven years of age" were "already very conversant with the cigar."

It was impossible to escape the noxious weed. Since restrictions on public tobacco usage were unenforceable, if not virtually nonexistent, the smell and residue of widespread consumption was everywhere. Carl Meyer, a Swiss forty-niner, remarked that "the American's vice and passion for chewing tobacco has been often related by travelers and the fact is probably well known that during a meal the American either lays the half-chewed tobacco quid down on the table or holds it in his hand so that

Tobacco, in its various forms and usages, was ubiquitous in early California, and tobacco shops were a common sight in cities large and small. Moses A. Gunst (in the top hat), owner of the M. A. Gunst Cigar and Tobacco Store in San Francisco, established a chain of cigar stores throughout California and along the Pacific Coast and became a millionaire by age forty-five."M. A. Gunst Cigar and Tobacco Store, San Francisco," photograph by I. W. Taber, c. 1880. Image courtesy of the California State Library, Sacramento; California History Section, W. H. Davis Collection, Digital ID: 1998-0706.

he can resume chewing it as soon as possible." Meyer also mentioned that he had seen miners cradle foul, dripping quids in their palms while receiving the Eucharist in church.

In 1851, William Shaw, an Englishman who had arrived in California via Australia, memorably described his tobacco-infused lodgings: "When coiled up in your blanket, the smoking, chewing, and (as a necessary consequence) random expectoration, often prevented repose. Towards morning the heat and effluvia became intolerable; on some occasions . . . I have been oppressed with a vomiting sensation." The spittoon became the omnipresent brass quintessence of the tobacco culture, and as Sir Henry Huntley bemoaned, there was "smoking and spitting everywhere—one cannot walk in the saloon without kicking over 'spittoons,' as the receiver is called, the very sight of which invites a discharge from an American mouth."

For the Gold Rush generation, smoking was also part of the communal culture, a way to pass the time and to interact with others. Writing about the spectacle of twice-monthly mail distribution in San Francisco, in which thousands would wait for hours outside the main post office until it was their turn to approach one of the six small service windows—John David Borthwick pointedly noted that "smoking and chewing tobacco were great aids in passing the time . . . in perfect tranquility."

In the mining camps, smoking could also be an avenue to welcome companionship or a distraction from annoyance or irritation. John Swan, an English sailor who made California his permanent home in 1843, remembered this of his days in the goldfields:

> We thought we should pass a pleasant night but were disappointed . . . [as] the whole party [attempted] . . . to keep clear of the mosquitoes who were bleeding them so freely and making them pay toll to them . . . . After tossing about and trying to sleep for some hours, it was given up for a bad job by the whole party for that night, and the campfires were started afresh and were soon surrounded by men determined to make the best of a bad job; and smoking, singing, and spinning yarns was indulged in by the whole party more or less till daylight.

Tobacco chewing was widespread among the gold seekers, and in fact it was more unusual to spy a miner *without* a bulging cheek of chaw. In one particular instance, this habit led to unforeseen and potentially deadly consequences. In his memoir *The Autobiography of Charles Peters* (1915), Peters recounted a conversation with William Parks, who owned a rich claim on the Yuba River that employed dozen of miners. One of Parks's workers was a young man named Bill, who, Parks said, "always seemed to have a large quid of tobacco in his mouth and was an inveterate spitter." While shooting the breeze with the local storekeeper, Parks commented that Bill must be one of the biggest tobacco chewers in the area, at which point the shopkeeper laughed and told Parks that Bill never chewed tobacco and had never bought a plug of tobacco in his store. Suspicious, Parks confronted Bill.

Noticing his cheek puffed out apparently by a larger quid than usual, [I] stopped and remarked: "Bill, that's a mighty big quid you have in your mouth. Let's see it?" There was a stare of thunderstruck astonishment for a moment, then a gulp, followed by a gurgle and the man fell prostrate, strangling to death. He had a large [gold] nugget concealed in his mouth and had tried to swallow it. It was too large for his gullet and it had stuck in his throat, shutting off his breath at his windpipe. It took several minutes to get the nugget out of his throat and he came very near strangling to death.

o o o

The development of a more settled society over time did not diminish tobacco consumption in California. On the contrary, the production and sale of tobacco products became big business and the market grew. In particular, the demand for cigars was enormous. In San Francisco, cigar-making factories were one of the largest employers in the last half of the nineteenth century. The majority of cigar rollers were Chinese and nonunion, and that didn't sit well with some people. In 1876, one San Francisco cigar manufacturer angrily testified before Congress that Chinese cigar makers outnumbered white workers by forty to one and that Chinese cigar rollers were paid half of what whites were earning. The manufacturer interpreted this difference not as a disadvantage to the Chinese workers but to the white ones who could not compete with the lower wages. This disparity and competition contributed to decades of open racial hostility and labor strife. In 1875, a local union of white cigar makers known as the Cigar Makers' Association of the Pacific Coast required that any cigars made by their members carry a stamp bearing the trademark of the association and the following legend:

CIGAR MAKERS' ASSOC'N.
The cigars contained in this box are made by WHITE MEN.
This label is issued by the authority of the
Cigar Makers' Association of the Pacific Coast and
adopted by law.

The stakes were high, as cigar making was a very profitable enterprise. The workforce was large, and the quantity of cigars produced was staggering; by one account, each roller was expected to make at least fifteen hundred cigars per shift. *San Francisco Municipal Reports*—annual public official papers providing academic data—documented the enormous output, which numbered in the millions monthly:

Fiscal Year	Number of Firms	Number of Workers	Expected Monthly Production	Actual Number of Cigars Produced
1867–68	60	1,132	3,000,000	35,672,000
1868–69	n/a	n/a	3,500,000	38,692,000
1869–70	63	1,597	4,152,000	38,414,000
1870–71	151	2,500	n/a	60,000,000
1871–72	n/a	n/a	n/a	50,000,000
1872–73	n/a	n/a	n/a	55,400,000
1873–74	115	Data incomplete	n/a	n/a
1874–75	120	4,000	n/a	95,000,000
1875–76	251	3,000	7,000,000	113,000,000
1876–77	200	4,000	7,000,000	107,000,000
1877–78	200	4,000	7,000,000	107,000,000
1878–79	200	4,000	7,000,000	107,000,000
1879–80	200	3,200	9,000,000	82,000,000
1880–81	200	3,500	9,000,000	91,000,000

For the reform-minded, the mountains of cigars, the putrid rivers of tobacco juice, the clouds of pipe and cigarette smoke, and the troubling specter of smoking children prompted national anti-tobacco movements that gained adherents in Old California. The American Anti-Tobacco Society, formed in 1849, warned the mostly unaware public that the addictive demon of tobacco caused a plethora of illnesses, from insanity to cancer. From 1857 to 1872, a Massachusetts publisher produced the *Anti-Tobacco Journal*, which colorfully decried the filth, cost, and health dangers of tobacco, and in 1883, the WCTU (Women's Christian Temperance Union) established its Department for the Overthrow of Tobacco Habit, linking an anti-tobacco platform to its efforts to mitigate the perils of alcohol. In the 1890s, other national organizations arose that focused on prohibiting the sale of tobacco to minors.

These organizations had little impact in Old California. Most residents viewed the "tobacco habit" as a personal, adult affair not subject to legislation or the reform impulse. Many found the anti-tobacco crusaders to be self-righteous and annoying, echoing the attitude of Mark Twain, who, when inundated with facts and figures from an anti-smoking activist he dubbed "the Moral Statistician," responded: "I don't want any of your statistics; I took your whole batch and lit my pipe with it."

In California, there was the occasional notice of the establishment of a local chapter of the Anti-Tobacco League or an isolated call for prohibition, and only infrequent editorial comment condemning "tobacco taking," with most of that targeted at smoking by children. The California legislature took note of the concerns over tobacco sales to and use by minors under the age of sixteen and, in 1872, amended the California Penal Code accordingly. But even this prohibition was poorly enforced, and critics railed against what they perceived as the ongoing and unimpeded assault on the health and morals of young people. In 1874, the *Russian River Flag* published an observation entitled "Going Off in Smoke" that condemned cigarettes as the gateway to tobacco addiction for adolescents:

As sure as a boy is led into smoking cigarettes, he will become a confirmed smoker, and will take to his pipe and plug tobacco, or to his two-bit cigar whenever he can raise the money. At present it may be set down for a fact that the California boy is going off in smoke. Every hoodlum smokes. Every truant from school smokes. Every precocious boy who knows more at ten years than he ought to know at twenty, smokes. Every gamin smokes . . . . There is a law against selling liquor to minors. But there is no law forbidding the sale of tobacco, in its most seductive form, to every boy who is old enough to ask for it. The schoolboy carries the cigarette in his pocket . . . . School-girls try the cigarette for the "fun of the thing" . . . . The cigarette has become the curse of juvenile California.

Reformers called for raising the minimum age of tobacco purchase to eighteen or twenty. In 1891, to emphasize growing public concern, the prohibition on providing tobacco was given a separate designation in the California Penal Code, but the law itself did not change, and the minimum age for tobacco sales remained at sixteen.

Not finding legislation to be effective to their cause, reformers tried a different approach in the 1890s. Adopting a tactic from the temperance movement, anti-smoking pledges were circulated to children and teenagers, and at least 250,000 "took the pledge" nationwide. In California, the most energetic application of this concept was employed by the *San Francisco Call* in 1894. Launching what it characterized as a "crusade," the *Call* established the Boy's Anti-Cigarette League, inviting each boy of San Francisco to join the "army of health" and "abstain from cigarette smoking until he is 21 years of age, and to use his influence to suppress cigarette smoking among minors." Starting in mid-January 1894, with the official approval of the school boards, the newspaper distributed anti-cigarette, anti-smoking pledges to schoolboys throughout the city.

Accompanying the pledges were a series of passionate *San Francisco Call* articles specifying the arguments for their "crusade." In many respects, the lines of reasoning were familiar, having been repurposed from well-publicized anti-liquor campaigns. The *Call* appealed:

> Look around you. You will find the streets full of puffers of the cheap brands of cigarettes. The messenger-boys, the waifs and odds and ends of boydom are puffing away. The sallow-faced young men lounging at grocery corners and saloon doors are puffing away. The gamins and "wood rats" pick up the halfburned butts and rapturously ignite them.... Like a cancer the cigarette habit is spreading over the land.
>
> Money is procured by any means to gratify the cigarette propensity.... The first steps in duplicity, underhand dealing, evasiveness and absolute lying are learned and practiced. The boy is developing into a thief or worse.

And from another article:

> Cigarettes are called "coffin nails".... Ninety-nine out of a hundred murderers use tobacco, and the most common form used is that of cigarettes. The principal item of expense in penitentiaries and insane asylums is tobacco.

Ten days after launching the Boy's Anti-Cigarette League, the *Call* published a "Healthy Roll" of 1,068 boys who had signed the promise. Three weeks later, in a February 16 article entitled "Make It Lasting," the *San Francisco Call* claimed to have nearly 10,000 signed pledges for the league.

While dramatic, the Boy's Anti-Cigarette League did little to influence public policy. The minimum age for tobacco sales did not change, and enforcement of the rule continued to be deficient. As the *Los Angeles Times* reported in 1900: "There is scarcely a tobacconist in Los Angeles who does not violate [the minimum age limit] at least a dozen times a day, as it is notorious that youths of tender years form a large proportion of the great army of cigarette smokers." It was not until 1911 that the

California State Legislature increased the minimum age for tobacco sales to eighteen. In 2016, the state raised it again, to twenty-one years old.

o   o   o

Throughout the era, anti-tobacco sentiment was common fodder for the prominent humorists of the era, who used it more often as a punch line than as an alarm. George Horatio Derby, a satirist better known as the Veritable Squibob, invented a dialogue between fictional characters Old Man Bowers and the youthful Mr. Jones, in which Jones congratulates Bowers for quitting smoking:

> "And why, Mr. Bowers," said Jones, "have you given up smoking?"
> "Because I chews," replied the old fellow, with a quiet chuckle.

Even more typical were asides tossed into newspapers as filler, such as this riposte from the *Red Bluff Independent* of July 25, 1862: "An anti-tobacco lecturer spoke so powerfully against the use of tobacco, that several of his audience went home and burned their cigars—holding one end in their mouths by way of punishment."

In this vein, newspapers also frequently goaded the anti-tobacco reformers by reviving the well-loved tale of a centenarian who happily smoked until meeting his untimely demise. A version of this probably apocryphal story was published dozens of times over the decades, and while the structure of the account remained consistent, there were endless variations as to the details, including age, gender, location, and the method of smoking. But the ending was always the same. Consider this example from the *Sonoma Democrat* of December 10, 1881, as it reports on the death of James Reilly:

[Reilly] had been a consumer of the fatal weed for more
than three-quarters of a century. During all that long
period he brazenly disregarded the appeals of the anti-tobacco propaganda and defiantly diffused the baleful nicotine through his system, until death cut him off in his
career of folly and self-defilement at the age of 101 years.
While lighting a pipe his clothes caught fire from some
falling sparks, and assistance came too late to save his life.

o   o   o

Tobacco played no favorites. Its impact was felt across the span of
nineteenth-century California, and it inarguably influenced—
directly or indirectly, negatively or positively—California's society, culture, economy, and health. Everyone who lived in Old
California was touched by the taste, smell, smoke, and discarded
relics of tobacco, even the animals.

In perhaps the most bizarre case of tobacco addiction ever
recorded, a dog in Sonora became a victim in the late 1890s. The
pooch in question was an American Water Spaniel named Sport.
He was owned by George McGowan, who, ironically, was a cigar
merchant in Sonora, Tuolumne County. Sport was a remarkable dog by all accounts. He was an excellent hunter, could walk
a tightrope, and when asked to "smile" could relax his jaw into
an amusing approximation of a grin. As the *San Francisco Call*
profiled, "The dog is the acme of sociability and a great favorite
among children, though, it cannot be said that he is as fond of
them as he is of tobacco."

Sport acquired his taste for tobacco on a hunting trip with
McGowan in the Sierra Nevada. McGowan and Sport visited a
nearby shepherd on their journey, and this shepherd happened
to possess a large quantity of tobacco to help him pass the long,
lonely days and nights in the high meadows. One day, he discovered that a portion of his tobacco had disappeared mysteriously.
The shepherd noticed more missing the next day, and the next
and the next. He confronted George McGowan, but the hunter
knew nothing about the loss. The shepherd hiked to neighboring

valleys, watercourses, and forests looking for the culprit. He found no one. And yet still the tobacco continued to vanish.

After another day searching for the thief, the shepherd returned to his cabin and, as the *San Francisco Call* reported, he was "surprised upon entering . . . to find Sport lying on the floor upon his back in what appeared to be a beastly state of intoxication with tobacco juice in large quantities oozing from his mouth." Mortified, McGowan paid for the lost tobacco and returned with Sport to Sonora. But that wasn't the end of the story. The cigar shop proprietor soon learned that his dog had become a "tobacco fiend," and Sport required one half-pound of tobacco daily to satisfy his habit. The *Call* noted that Sport

> displays a wonderful appetite for the noxious herb. He not only masticates it, but eats it as voraciously as he would devour a succulent chop. When Sport evinces his desire for tobacco he acts in all respects like a human opium fiend, who insists on the gratification of his abnormal taste at any cost . . . . He trembles violently and emits piteous whines which one finds it impossible to ignore. Only after he has been provided with the weed will he desist in his pleadings and finally succumb to its effects.

George McGowan shortly heard from others in Sonora that even a half pound wasn't enough for his canine addict. Sport was doing tricks all over town to beg tobacco, and even stealing chaw from the pockets of residents napping on their porches.

After several years of unsuccessfully attempting to wean Sport from his addiction, McGowan sought treatment for his dog through the services of one Dr. McClelland. Sport visited the veterinarian's office several times a day and, as the *Call* recounted, "invariably carries some trifling article in his mouth with which he hopes to bribe [McClelland] into giving him some tobacco in return." The doctor slowly reduced Sport's daily dose of tobacco to one quarter-pound and administered "hypodermic injections of nitro-glycerin and sulphate of strychnia in order to cure a habit which has held possession of [Sport] for almost four years." The treatment largely worked, although Sport would occasionally fall off the wagon and stealthily liberate a tobacco plug from an unsuspecting target. Sport's tobacco habit became so renowned that a New York City show-biz impresario offered George McGowan $300 in gold (about $8,300 today) for Sport. McGowan declined.

When James I warned of the "manifolde abuses of this vile custome of *Tobacco* taking" in 1604, it is a safe bet that His Royal Highness, or anyone else for that matter, never thought it would be applied to an American Water Spaniel from Tuolumne County.

In this 1897 publicity photograph, boxer Jimmy McVey (left) squares off against
James J. "Gentleman Jim" Corbett. Corbett, a San Francisco native, was a local
hero and became the World Heavyweight Champion in 1892. "A Hook Punch to
the Point of the Jaw," 1897. Library of Congress Prints and Photographs Division,
Digital ID: cph3b45787u.

CHAPTER FIVE

Demanding Satisfaction, Frogstickers,
and the Slogging Fraternity

DUELING, KNIFE FIGHTS, FISTICUFFS, AND ANIMAL BAITING

They were both named Johnny and they were looking for a bit of fun, although their definition of amusement was, I hope, very different from yours and mine. In 1868, Johnny Nyland and Johnny Devine were denizens of the wild San Francisco district known as the Barbary Coast, which was, as chronicler Herbert Asbury noted, "a hell-roaring swirl of crime and debauchery" teeming with "murderers, thieves, burglars, gamblers, prostitutes, and swindlers of every degree."

And Nyland and Devine didn't just live there—they were considered among the most sadistic residents of one of the most violent neighborhoods in the country. The two Johnnys were like peas in a pod: both were burglars, enforcers, brawlers, thieves, pickpockets, and pimps. They were toughs for hire and were especially adept with guns, brass knuckles, and knives.

They were also runners for a crimp, which was the term used for someone who would, through physical assault or drugging, render unsuspecting men, usually sailors, unconscious and then kidnap them into service on maritime vessels. The men would awaken and find themselves out to sea, serving on a ship against their will. This practice came to be known as "being shanghaied" (presumably based on the destination of many of the ships), and it was common in port cities where filling out a crew could be challenging. The crimps would provide the kidnapped sailors for a fee, often under contract, and the enterprise could be lucrative. Crimps relied on "runners" to steer or strong-arm the sailors to the boardinghouses, and Johnny Nyland and Johnny Devine were runners for San Francisco's premier crimp, James "Shanghai" Kelly.

Of the two Johnnys, Devine was more notorious and was once described by the *San Francisco Call* as "one of the most dangerous of the habitués of the Barbary Coast." Devine's heinous activities were so well known throughout the city that terrified residents gave him the nickname "the Shanghai Chicken"—"chicken" being nineteenth-century slang for an unpredictable or overly excitable person. The Chicken, as the newspapers branded him, was a force to be reckoned with, but he was perhaps just as famous for being fearsome as he was for getting caught. Over one nine-month period, Devine was arrested twenty-nine times.

It might be an understatement to say that the Chicken sometimes had trouble controlling himself. He was once hired for $50 to rough up a man who was holding a grudge against another, and although the job was to simply intimidate the grudge holder, instead the Chicken mugged the victim, who remained in the hospital for months. During his criminal career, Johnny Devine was detained numerous times for burglary, battery, and pimping, and he was once paid $20 for killing a man with a rock. Everyone was a potential victim, no matter how high-ranking. In November 1866, for example, Nyland and Devine were jointly arrested for viciously beating the captain of the British ship *Mary Ann Wilson*.

On June 13, 1868, these ne'er-do-wells indulged in a spree. They resolved to get drunk, roam around the Barbary Coast, stir up trouble, and assault anyone they could. Both carried guns, and Johnny Nyland brandished a massive knife that he claimed he had lifted from a dead policeman. The *Daily Alta California* described the weapon as "an immense butcher knife, almost as heavy as a butcher's cleaver." The Johnnys started at Billy Lewis's saloon and managed to shoot and knife several patrons before being rudely ejected. They then lurched into William Maitland's bar, where, for no apparent reason, Nyland immediately cut a chunk out of a sailor's head with his enormous knife. A melee ensued and Nyland rushed the proprietor. During the scuffle, Maitland yanked the knife from Nyland's hand, at which point the Shanghai Chicken came to the assistance of his friend and lunged at Maitland, who swung the huge knife at Devine. As the *Alta California* reported, "It struck the 'Chicken' exactly at the wrist joint, and cut clean through, merely leaving a small strip of skin, which was not enough to hold up the weight of the hand."

Bloodied and battered, the two Johnnys were tossed from the saloon, with Devine grasping his nearly severed hand. They walked two blocks to Doc Simpson's drugstore and asked the pharmacist if he could sew the hand back onto the bloody stump. When the Shanghai Chicken presented his injury for examination, the thin shred of skin that was still connected to the hand gave way and the hand flopped onto the counter. Johnny Devine collapsed and was taken to the hospital. His hand could not be reattached, but even that did not slow down the Chicken for long. He soon had his arm fashioned with a large iron hook, which he honed to razor sharpness and used to inflict horrible wounds in the further execution of his nefarious duties.

This blood-spattered event was chronicled in the newspapers, but only as one among the many unexceptional incidents in the usual daily litany of crime and punishment. The violent maiming of the Shanghai Chicken was viewed as nothing special, just another colorful vignette of life in Old California.

o   o   o

Using violence to resolve personal or institutional grudges was not, of course, unique to the Barbary Coast, or to California, or even to this particular era, and yet in looking at how fighting functioned in Gold Rush society, we can learn much about the time, the place, and the people involved. In the nineteenth century, there were certainly those who viewed California as a pastoral Eden, a terrestrial paradise, a golden land, but the historical record is rife with accounts of aggression and depravity, and it wouldn't be inaccurate to say that, from 1820 to 1900, California was especially barbarous. During the Gold Rush generation, the unprecedented population boom coupled with the constant churning of multiple cultures and nationalities made Old California particularly prone to interpersonal hostilities.

In his groundbreaking research on homicide in Los Angeles from the 1820s to the twenty-first century, historian Erik Monkkonen concluded that the years between 1830 and 1870—covering both the Mexican and American eras—saw the highest per capita percentage of murders in the region's history. During that four-decade span, the homicide rate in Los Angeles averaged 120 murders per 100,000 residents, peaking in 1853 with nearly 375 murders per 100,000 residents—far exceeding the rates of other major cities, including San Francisco, Chicago, and St. Louis. By comparison, the homicide rate for the same forty-year period in New York City averaged 6.3 per 100,000, and today's rate for both metropolitan areas is about 10 per 100,000.

While many of these deaths were the result of individual moments of anger and passion, many were also due to communal violence. Between 1851 and 1874, according to records of the Los Angeles County Sheriff's Department, the city witnessed forty legal hangings and an additional seventy lynchings, including thirty-two by vigilance committees. On October 24, 1871, nineteen Chinese immigrants were murdered in the city's ghastliest single incident of mob violence.

Such depravity was underpinned by a wide variety of physical, psychological, and legal assaults perpetrated and perpetuated by the dominant Anglo-American segment of society. Members of minority communities—especially Mexicans, Californios, people of African descent, and Chilean and Chinese immigrants—suffered dangerous, even deadly, onslaughts, and in many cases the legal system was no help. Racist laws on both the local and federal level (e.g., the Chinese Exclusion Act of 1882) upheld inequitable ordinances, prohibitions on legal testimony, unfair evictions, immigration restrictions, and criminal profiling, with the result that individuals suffered the full range of bodily harm, workplace harassment, public demonstrations of racism such as mob rallies, and other large and small offenses, usually without hope that the wrongdoers would be held accountable.

The unparalleled scope and diversity of California's societal development in the nineteenth century led to the expected culture clashes, and in this uncertain world, clannishness became a byword and a survival technique. A multiplicity of rings, bands, posses, and gangs emerged as individuals sought the support and safety of others with whom they shared a race, nationality, or life experience, and tensions between groups often boiled over.

Some criminal organizations received special public notice and scorn, such as the Gold Rush–era "Sydney Ducks" or "Sydney Coves," a squad of Australian immigrants and former convicts who had clustered in a San Francisco enclave called Sydney Town. After the immigrants' attempts at mining had proved unprofitable, many resumed their prior disreputable occupations, and Sydney Town soon became rampant with protection schemes, extortion, robberies, arson, muggings, murders for hire, and prostitution. City authorities and law enforcement had a curious response: they turned away, mostly from fear. Ultimately, the police would not enter Sydney Town. When the Sydney Ducks set massive fires as distractions from their other criminal activities, the residents of San Francisco responded, in part, with the infamous vigilance committees of the 1850s.

The original San Francisco Committee of Vigilance was formed in 1851, having sprung up when a group of citizens decided they could no longer tolerate what they viewed as the inability of the city administration and law enforcement to address rampant criminality. The committee was essentially an extralegal militia, and its motivation was best expressed by an editorial in the *San Francisco Evening Picayune* of June 14, 1850, that said: "Our people have endured the state of things . . . until patience has ceased to be a virtue. Under the force of imperative necessity . . . , they have entered upon the discharge of their self-imposed and solemn duty and will not desist until . . . the city is freed from the scoundrels who infest it."

The 1851 Committee of Vigilance functioned for only three months, but it was revived in 1856. This later iteration also lasted three months, but in both cases the committees were known for their aggressiveness, often acting as violent as the criminals they sought to eradicate. Overall, the committees hanged eight people and forced the resignations of several government officials.

While the vigilance committees had some immediate impact on slowing down crime, San Francisco was overwhelmed by massive population growth, and crime continued largely unabated. In the ensuing years, the population of Sydney Town swelled to create the notorious Barbary Coast district, which operated largely unchecked into the twentieth century.

Another bunch of hooligans was homegrown. Grandly calling themselves the San Francisco Society of Regulators, the gang was known far and wide as "The Hounds." Comprising American veterans of the Mexican War and members of the Nativist movement (which touted the superiority of white, native-born Americans), the Hounds primarily attacked Spanish-speaking immigrants, Californios, and Chinese people throughout Old California, and with special emphasis on Gold Country. The Hounds harassed their enemies, destroyed property, and took delight in torturing innocent victims.

In larger cities, such as San Francisco, the Hounds were sometimes arrested and formally tried, with the result that many received large fines and were sentenced to hard labor in prison. By contrast, in Gold Country, where law enforcement was virtually nonexistent, local residents often took such matters into their own hands, and several Hounds were captured and unceremoniously hanged.

o o o

California was, as advertised, a land of earthly and psychic rewards, but it was also extremely perilous. Obstacles loomed and threats lurked around every corner; it took great resilience and resourcefulness not just to prosper there but to merely survive. A combative spirit was in some ways not an advantage but a necessity.

In Old California, the most discussed and scrutinized modes of fighting were gun duels, knife fights, prizefighting, and animal baiting. In each case, these examinations reflected the most persistent theme of the era: contradiction. The paradox was that each of these activities was simultaneously officially condemned and openly practiced, an accepted flaunting of legal prohibitions.

Dueling with guns, either pistols or rifles, was a time-honored method of settling disputes in the nineteenth century, as we know from such memorable duels in American history as those between Aaron Burr and Alexander Hamilton (1804), Andrew Jackson and Charles Dickinson (1806), and Wild Bill Hickok and Davis Tutt (1865), the last of these a famous public "quick draw" duel. Other prominent figures barely avoided duels through apology or negotiation, most notably Abraham Lincoln and Mark Twain (although not against each other). Dueling was considered a reasonable means of bypassing a capricious judicial system and was viewed as a test of manliness and character. "Demanding satisfaction" was the code for these "affairs of honor," and dueling was seldom about killing an opponent and more about proving that one was brave enough to face the consequences should someone actually die. Unilaterally retreating from a duel was considered a demonstration of cowardice.

Prior to the Gold Rush, gunfights were part of California life, but they were not as prevalent as dueling with swords or knives. Richard Henry Dana, Jr., in his 1840 memoir *Two Years Before the Mast*, noted that, in 1830s California, duels were usually fought over marital infidelity:

> A few inches of cold steel has been the punishment of many an unwary man, who has been guilty, perhaps, of nothing more than indiscretion of manner . . . . The ready weapons of a father or brother, are a protection which the characters of most of them—men and women—render by no means useless; for the very men who would lay down their lives to avenge the dishonor of their own family, would risk the same lives to complete the dishonor of another.

With the advent of the California Gold Rush, gun dueling became more frequent. In 1855, *The Annals of San Francisco* stated that, from its earliest days, the Gold Rush saw "numerous duels," and for that year it specifically mentioned twenty duelists by name and referenced many other unnamed participants.

The duels often drew large crowds, as confirmed by English observer Frank Marryat in this description of an 1853 duel in San Francisco:

> Dueling in particular became quite the rage . . . . When I reached the Plaza, I found a large concourse of people already assembled to see the sport; and it was such a novel and delicious excitement to stand in a circle and see two men inside of you exchange six shots apiece, that had the matter been more generally known, I do not think there would have been room for them to fight!

Just as numerous as the duels themselves were denunciations of the practice. In 1851, a witness to a duel that occurred near Nevada City wrote to the *Sacramento Union* that "the man killed was named Dibble, and Lundy the person who wound him up, making only the *fifth* man he has killed in duels. I suppose he considers it a real honor to murder a man. I call it nothing but murder." In 1859, Eliza Farnham, a California author and social activist, dismissed dueling as simply "polite murder," sarcastically adding, "I have no quarrel with the duel. It is the cheapest, most expeditious and decent method for dispatching worthless and troublesome men."

The prevalence of dueling led to a lively debate at the 1849 California Constitutional Convention. With many of the convention delegates themselves recent arrivals from states in which dueling was either practiced or prohibited, the two sides debated a middle-ground provision to penalize those who fought in duels. The proviso stated that any citizen who should "fight a duel with deadly weapons, or send, or accept a challenge to fight a duel, . . . or knowingly assist in any manner those [who do]" should "not be allowed to hold any office of profit, or to enjoy the right of suffrage."

The spirited proceedings following the introduction of the proposed article reflected the diverse backgrounds and attitudes of the delegates.

> Lewis Dent, delegate from Monterey, originally from Missouri:
>> No clause that you can introduce in the Constitution will prevent a man from fighting a duel, if it be in defence of his honor. There are few men who will not risk their lives when their honor is at stake . . . . It may be said that it is a false sense of honor, but there may be circumstances in every man's life to induce him, if he possess one particle of manliness or one principle of liberty, to defend his honor at the risk of his life.

> Winfield Scott Sherwood, delegate from Sacramento, originally from New York:
>> It is no mark of courage for one man to shoot another in a duel. I have known great cowards to fight duels. Nor does it sustain a man's honor. The experience of all the

northern States of the Union, proves that the honor of
men can be sustained without fighting duels.

Morton M. McCarver, delegate from Sacramento, originally from Kentucky:
Suppose an individual calls out his friend and shoots
him down, and suppose another murders a citizen for
his money, what difference is there in effect between
the two cases. They have both committed murder; the
object was different, but the result is the same. In either
case, a citizen of the State is slain. The one murderer is
hung; the other is merely deprived of a political right.

In the end, the California Constitutional Convention of 1849
adopted a dueling provision as Article XI, Section 2, but it was
a curious provision. It did not penalize all forms of dueling but
instead only those involving political officeholders, as well as
clashes over disenfranchisement. The law was generally ignored,
however, and political gun duels continued, often with dire
results.

o   o   o

Perhaps California's most infamous duel was the one that
occurred on August 2, 1852, and under circumstances that
could be considered timely today, for it was a confrontation
between a newspaper editor and a politician. Edward Gilbert
was the dynamic, fire-eating editor of California's leading newspaper, the *Daily Alta California*, based in San Francisco. In a
series of scathing editorials, Gilbert accused Governor John
Bigler of political chicanery and showboating in his handling of
relief and rescue efforts for California-bound travelers brought
to a halt in Nevada's snowbound Carson Valley. Editor Gilbert
included in his condemnations Bigler's appointed relief party
agent, the imposing James Denver. Denver did not brush off
the criticism but responded that Gilbert was motivated by "an

envious and malicious heart." Gilbert counterattacked, calling Denver a toady of Governor Bigler and a "political hanger-on," to which Denver snapped back, calling upon Gilbert to seek Denver out and "when so found he may rest assured that he can have any 'issue upon the matter' he may desire." Incensed, Gilbert called for an apology, and if he received none, he wrote, "it only remains to me to demand the satisfaction known to the code of honor." Denver accepted the challenge. Edward Gilbert, who had suffered the humiliation both of withdrawing from a duel a year earlier and of the subsequent accusations of his spinelessness, felt this duel could restore his reputation.

As the aggrieved party, James Denver had the choice of weapons and chose Wesson rifles at forty paces. Denver was a veteran of the Mexican War and, from all accounts, an expert rifleman. Gilbert, on the other hand, was proficient with pistols but clumsy with rifles.

The dueling ground was a few miles northeast of Sacramento. After forty paces, the combatants wheeled and fired. Both missed. Many believed Denver deliberately shot wide. Thinking the affair over, Denver laid down his rifle and began to leave the field of honor, but Gilbert, as the challenger, demanded satisfaction and insisted the duel continue. This time Denver did not miss. A bullet ripped through Gilbert's left side, just above his hipbone. Mortally wounded, the editor never spoke a word again and expired within minutes. Following this denouement, James Denver stopped at a nearby inn and had breakfast. He was not arrested, and most observers reported that Denver had tried to end the duel peacefully but to no avail.

Gilbert's corpse was transported to San Francisco, where a throng attended his funeral. The Reverend Osgood Church Wheeler conducted the service, and as the *Sacramento Union* reported on August 3, 1852, the reverend "inveighed, though gently yet most powerfully against the cruel and bloody code by which [Gilbert] had been cut down in the flower of his youthful manhood and usefulness." Edward Gilbert was thirty-three years old.

On August 2, 1852, California state senator James Denver (left) killed former congressman and founder/editor of the *Daily Alta California* newspaper Edward Gilbert in a duel to settle a dispute over an editorial. Denver image courtesy of the California State Library, Sacramento; California History Section, Digital ID: 2007-0026. The Gilbert image was originally published in Frank Soulé, John H. Gihon, and James Nisbet, *The Annals of San Francisco* (1855), and is from that volume in the author's personal collection.

Five months after the duel, Governor John Bigler appointed James Denver as California's Secretary of State. In 1855, Denver was elected to Congress, and in 1857, President James Buchanan named James Denver as governor of Kansas Territory, which included the area that later became Colorado. The state's capital city is named in honor of James Denver. In 1884, Denver was considered a viable presidential candidate, but his chances were ruined when his opponents successfully (albeit inaccurately) accused Denver of initiating the duel with Edward Gilbert some thirty years earlier.

Dueling in California was revisited several times by the state government. Commentators constantly decried that the constitutional prohibitions were not enforced and called for stricter penalties and fines to be recorded in the criminal code. In 1860, in a written message issued on his last day in office, Governor John B. Weller noted his exasperation with the inefficacy of California's remedies: "In regard to dueling; many valuable lives have been sacrificed in this State under what (I think) has been mis-called the 'code of honor' . . . . If gentlemen who adjust their differences without a resort to arms are taunted with cowardice, it cannot be expected that duels will not be fought." In 1872, stern penalties for dueling were placed in the penal code in Title 8, Chapter 7, Sections 225–32, effectively banning dueling, and these restrictions remained in place for the next 122 years, until they were repealed as outmoded in 1994.

o   o   o

Through the 1870s, when firearms became more reliable and easier to obtain, knives were often the dueling weapon of choice. Virtually everyone had a knife, ranging from utilitarian pocketknives to some variation of what was broadly called a "Bowie knife," named after its most famous user, the frontiersman Jim Bowie. In general, a Bowie knife is twelve to fifteen inches long and has a five- to twelve-inch clip-point blade, meaning the forward portion looks partially clipped off, but there were many adaptations, including knives with interchangeable blades, push daggers or dirks, folding knives, knives featuring other accessories such as a corkscrew, and even a combination pistol and knife called a "cutlass pistol." The so-called California knife was a Bowie option featuring local adornments such as abalone or gold inlaid in the handle.

The historical literature of Old California is brimming with descriptions of vaqueros, Californios, soldiers, outlaws, settlers, and miners carrying knives, usually as part of their identifying "uniform." In the case of the gold seekers, knives were also an indispensable mining tool. In addition to the term Bowie knife, which was often used generically, the weapons were also called "frogstickers," "pigstickers," "long knives," "rifleman's knives," "scalping knives," "belt knives," "sheath knives," and "Arkansas toothpicks." Some manufacturers assigned more fanciful names to their knives, such as "Self Defender," "I'm a Real Ripper," "Hunter's Companion," "I Can Dig Gold from Quartz," "Texas Ranger," "Alabama Hunting Knife," and "Gold Seeker's Protection." Edwin Bryant, in his popular 1848 guidebook and memoir *What I Saw in California,* stated that every Californian should possess "a hand-saw, auger, gimlet, chisel, shaving-knife, etc., an axe, hammer, and hatchet . . . . [And] every man should have in his belt . . . a hunter's or a bowie-knife."

Prior to the Gold Rush, early Southern California settler Horace Bell recalled, "Knives and revolvers settled all differences, either real or imaginary. The slightest misunderstandings were settled on the spot with knife or bullet, the Mexican preferring the former at close quarters and the American the latter." As the Gold Rush unfolded, knives were so abundant that some observers, such as the nomadic Scotsman John David Borthwick, considered them an effective constraint on crime: "It seemed to me, that as every one wore his bowie-knife, the prospect of getting his opponent's knife between his ribs deterred each man from drawing his own, or offering any violence whatever." Borthwick also observed that at events that prohibited weapons, such as dances or the theater, "several doorkeepers were in attendance, to whom each man as he entered delivered up his knife or his pistol, receiving a check for it, just as one does for his cane or umbrella at the door of a picture-gallery."

But even as they were seen as a deterrent to criminal activity, knives were also of course under the control of their unpredictable users and were often lethal. Upon his arrival in California in 1841, pioneer John Bidwell asked a prominent physician what disease "prevailed most in California," and the physician's answer was "the knife."

Knife fighting was never specifically banned in California, even though it was a common feature of assaults, murders, and other crimes. In 1872, when the penalties for dueling were redefined, knives were listed as a prohibited "deadly weapon" that might be used in a duel, but as with similar laws, enforcement was lax.

Knife fighting reached its zenith between the 1840s and the 1860s, when the Gold Rush brought together a perilous brew of people from all over the world. Conflicts often came to quick, fatal resolutions at the ends of knives, although occasionally in weird ways.

For an example, we can turn to the epicenter of the Gold Rush: the mining town of Coloma. In October 1848, as Jacob Wright Harlan recounted in his memoir *California '46 to '88*, a young merchant named Von Pfister had just arrived in town and was setting up shop. For safety's sake, Von Pfister slept with a pistol and a Bowie knife tucked under his pillow. One night, a drunken miner named Pete Raimond broke into Von Pfister's tent, accosted him, and demanded liquor. The merchant told Raimond that he had no liquor, as his not-yet-opened store was still awaiting shipments of goods. Raimond staggered off and attempted to break into other buildings looking for alcohol, but, finding none, he angrily circled back to Von Pfister and confronted him once more. Words were exchanged and a heated fracas ensued. During the scuffle, Raimond discovered the Bowie knife and plunged it deep into Von Pfister's heart. The fatally injured shopkeeper crawled to a neighbor's cabin and fell dead at the door, the knife sticking out of his chest.

Pete Raimond was instantly captured and, lacking all remorse, proudly proclaimed he had killed Von Pfister with the merchant's own knife, a fit punishment for not having any liquor. The townsfolk deliberated whether to shoot or hang Raimond immediately or deliver him to the authorities at Sutter's Fort. Deciding on the latter, they sent Raimond to a secured jail cell, although he wasn't there for long, as on the night of his arrival Raimond and two other jailbirds overpowered the guard and escaped.

They headed to Southern California and when they arrived near Santa Barbara, the three fugitives heard of an old man who had made a rich gold strike and therefore was a prime robbery target. Raimond and his rough companions found the man, stole the gold, and murdered the whole family, including the miner, his wife, his two daughters, and a nursemaid. An eyewitness who had escaped the detection of the criminals sped to inform others of the murderous rampage, and warnings were soon distributed from Santa Barbara to points south to be on the lookout for the three desperadoes. Traveling farther south, the fugitives made it close to San Juan Capistrano before they were surrounded by a posse of Californios. Pete Raimond and one other outlaw were mown down in a hail of bullets, while the third darted into the ocean and drowned.

o   o   o

In addition to the ineffectual laws that attempted to curb fighting with knives and guns, there were also ineffectual laws that attempted to curb fighting without weapons of any kind, and particularly if that fighting was done for money. Prizefighting—defined in an 1850 statute as a clash in which "any persons shall, without deadly weapons, . . . upon any wager, or for money or any other reward, fight one with another"—was classified as a felony, and participants could be sentenced to prison terms of up to two years. If a death occurred during a bout, the sentence could be from three to ten years. The law also stated that anyone "aiding and abetting" a prizefight could be punished as well, as happened to John Warrington, who was in January 1850 dismissed from his position as a doorkeeper for the California State Assembly for being "absent without leave during business hours" to "witness a brutal prize fight."

The standard technique of prizefights in the mid-nineteenth century was bare-knuckle boxing, and fatalities were not uncommon. There were rules of a sort—many followed the "London Prize Ring Rules," written by the British Pugilists' Protective Association in 1838—but in most respects these contests were untamed, bloody, fight-to-the-finish slugfests. The rulebook called for a ring twenty-four feet square bounded by two ropes suspended from wooden stakes. A line or "mark" bisecting the ring was scratched or laid out, and each round began with the boxers placing their toes on the line as a sign that they were able to continue. There was no standard length of time per round, and no limit on number of rounds. A round ended with a knockdown, and the next round started thirty seconds later if both boxers could "toe the mark" unaided. The bouts could last for dozens of rounds before one fighter became unable to continue or conceded defeat. In 1889, the heavy-weight championship between victor John L. Sullivan and Jake Kilrain lasted seventy-five rounds.

Kicking, gouging, head butts, low blows, and biting were fouls. In 1867, Scottish nobleman John Douglas, the 9th Marquess of Queensberry, endorsed what became known as the Queensberry Rules, a code that eventually superseded the London Prize Ring Rules and, most notably, called for fighters to wear gloves. In California, however, professional bare-knuckle matches continued to be popular, although illegal, for the remainder of the nineteenth century.

Terms popularized by bare-knuckle brawling are still part of our vocabulary today. "Start from scratch" is a reference to the mark scratched across the middle of the ring, and the terms "high-stakes gambling" and "stake money" originated from the practice of tying the bag of prize money to one of the wooden stakes lining the fighting ring.

In 1872, when California wrote its first penal code, efforts were made to clearly delineate the parameters of illegal prize-fighting. Title 11, Section 412, "Crimes Against the Public Peace," was entirely composed of an extraordinary 269-word sentence that spelled out in detail the activities that defined a prizefight, "with or without gloves," and the penalties that could arise. The code did allow "sparring exhibitions . . . in domestic incorporated clubs," which were licensed. Professional promoters skirted the law by staging their prizefights in private clubs and advertising them as mere demonstrations, but everyone, including local law enforcement, knew the truth and turned a blind eye.

The bare-knuckle fights of the Gold Rush era were not exercises in the "sweet science" or "manly art" touted by boxers today. They were brawls or, to use the vernacular of the period, "slogs." As the *Sacramento Union* described one 1864 fight featuring Johnny "Shanghai Chicken" Devine (before he lost his hand), the "pummeling" had "no science but plenty of pluck." The "Slogging Fraternity," as the *Daily Alta California* dubbed the fighters themselves in 1885, tended to be hulking figures, with little athleticism beyond a powerful punch; the battlers generally stood toe-to-toe and commenced to swinging freely. The face was not a primary target, as it is today, in part because bare-knuckle boxers preferred the softer body targets that would not injure their hands.

Pugilists tended to be from the toughest and most intimidating elements in the social order, and many of them had come from hardscrabble upbringings and turned to boxing as a way to make money after having abandoned work in farming or a trade, or having failed in the goldfields. By day, boxers were frequently employed as strong-arm criminals, enforcers, political thugs, or saloon bouncers, and they were often good fits for government jobs that required strength and an aggressive nature, such as firemen and election precinct officers. Within the community of prizefighting, some "sloggers" were able to make a name for themselves and become quasi-celebrities.

Throughout the century, fighters were usually of Irish, Australian, or British heritage, and although the majority were white, there were also pugilists of color, most notably Peter Jackson, the renowned black Australian champion. Dozens of professional boxers were transplants to California from the fisticuff hotbeds of the eastern United States, eager to ply their trade on new and fertile ground.

Crowds numbering from the hundreds to the thousands jammed exclusive clubs, such as San Francisco's Olympic Club, to watch and bet on boxing contests. Prominent figures attended the matches, and a few even tried their hand at the game. Mark Twain was a boxing aficionado and fancied himself a skillful amateur . . . until he had his one and only fight. As chronicled by his friend William Wright (better known by his pen name Dan DeQuille), Twain's adversary "let one fly straight out from the shoulder and 'busted' Mr. Twain in the 'snoot,' sending him reeling . . . with two bountiful streams of 'claret' spouting from his nostrils" and "a vast, inflamed and pulpy old snoot."

The first great American boxing luminary was the Irish American bare-knuckle brawler John L. Sullivan, celebrated as the "Boston Strong Boy," who epitomized the image of the brutish boxer. For nearly a decade in the late nineteenth century, Sullivan could honestly proclaim, "I can whip any son-of-a-bitch in the house." But a new kind of pugilist was emerging to threaten Sullivan's reign—a "scientific boxer" who relied more on strategy than strength to vanquish his opponents.

His name was James J. Corbett, and Californians loved him, especially since he was one of their own, a Golden State superstar. When he began training at the Olympic Club in 1885, Corbett was a San Francisco bank clerk who was considering becoming a priest, but he was instead hired as a boxing instructor at the club after impressing the staff with his skill, not only as a boxer but as a baseball second baseman. He soon began to fight regularly and gained devotees for his technique, grace, and gallant manners. Corbett was beloved by fans, but other fighters, including John L. Sullivan, denigrated him with the nicknames "Pompadour Jim" and, most famously, "Gentleman Jim," a way of making fun of his habit of always being impeccably dressed. The sobriquets were not meant as compliments, but Corbett appropriated them as part of his personal brand, much to the dismay of his rivals.

On May 21, 1891, "Gentleman Jim" Corbett fought Peter Jackson, the World Colored Heavyweight Champion (the only title available to black boxers in the nineteenth century), at the California Athletic Club in San Francisco. Tickets to this illegal bare-knuckle prizefight were $20, the equivalent of $600 today. About eight hundred spectators stuffed the small venue. The bout began with energy and panache, and both men were in top form. As the *Daily Alta California* reported, "In the fifth and sixth rounds there was some very hot work, the fighting being fast and clever," and in the fourteenth round, "Corbett got in a good one on Jackson's nose . . . . [and then] repeated the visitation on several occasions, which caused Jackson to show considerable solicitude for his face." Out in the streets, thousands of people had gathered to hear the latest developments from the seemingly endless battle.

By the thirtieth round, both fighters were exhausted, but they gamely soldiered on and on and on . . . for thirty-one more rounds. In the sixty-first round, the contest had deteriorated into "fruitless sparring," and the referee, after consultation with the club's directors, declared the match a draw, infuriating the patrons, who cried: "What did we pay twenty dollars for? Keep them there all night!"

Both Gentleman Jim and Peter Jackson believed that public dissatisfaction with their bout would end their careers, but they were wrong. Both continued to work as prizefighters, and to great acclaim. Jackson would retain his World Colored Heavyweight Championship title until 1896, and, on September 7, 1892, Gentleman Jim Corbett won the World Heavyweight Title by knocking out John L. Sullivan in the twenty-first round.

James Corbett continued to defy expectations, using his boxing career as a platform from which to jump into other forms of entertainment. He appeared in one of the first movies designed for public viewing—an 1894 short entitled *[James J.] Corbett and [Peter] Courtney Before the Kinetograph*—and in a dozen other films (often playing himself) over the next thirty years. Corbett acted in theatrical productions—receiving excellent reviews for his lead performance in the potboiler melodrama *A Naval Cadet*—and he toured extensively on both the lecture circuit and the vaudeville circuit. He also wrote a best-selling autobiography that was eventually fictionalized as the 1942 motion picture *Gentleman Jim*, starring Errol Flynn.

James J. Corbett was a paradox—a gentle soul in a brutal profession. Perhaps the best coda for the bundle of contradictions that constituted the "Gentleman Pugilist" is found in an 1892 interview of Corbett conducted by a young female correspondent for the *Sacramento Union* known as "Beselena." Never having met a fighter before, but aware of the loutish legacy of fighters such as John L. Sullivan, Beselena was anxious before her meeting with Corbett. Upon talking with him, however, she soon discovered that he had "nothing of the 'animal' about him; in fact, he impressed me as being distinctly human."

o   o   o

While observers might debate whether members of the slogging fraternity were "animals," there were several options for those wishing to indulge their preference for *actual* animal fighting.

Animal baiting—contests pitting one animal against another—is extensively documented in Old California, and the most prevalent incidents in midcentury were the death matches between bulls and bears, usually now-extinct California grizzlies. Wagering on the outcome of a fight was customary, and the bloody affairs were well attended, with some Gold Country mining camps constructing arenas to accommodate the spectators. Gold Rush diaries, journals, and letters are crammed with gory accounts of the battles, and the clashes not only captivated the eyewitnesses but also piqued the curiosity of those far away from the goldfields. One example was an article printed on August 15, 1854, in the *Pittsburgh [Pennsylvania] Daily Post*, based thousands of miles away from the event itself. Perhaps more unusual than that, however, was the detail that the bull emerged victorious in the fray; usually the more powerful grizzlies won easily.

A great bull and bear fight occurred . . . in California. A fearful scene occurred. The bull was wild, and the bear, a grizzly of large size, was caught a few weeks previously. The instant the animals beheld each other they made a spring, the bear raising himself to strike, and the bull lowering his head for a plunge. The contest was tremendous, and in about twenty minutes the bull with one ear bitten off, his nose torn and neck severely mangled, laid his ferocious adversary completely dead in the centre of the arena. The owner of the bull offers to let him fight any bear not exceeding him in weight that can be produced, for a wager

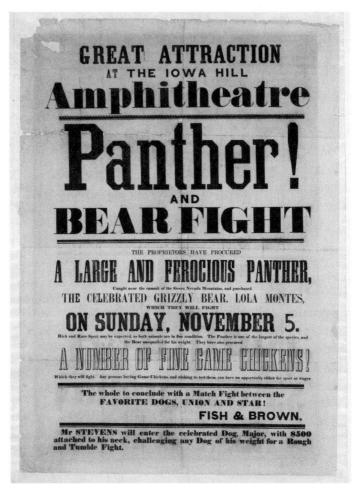

Animal baiting in Old California was a popular entertainment, as evidenced by this
poster from Iowa Hill, Placer County, c. 1855. "Great Attraction at the Iowa Hill
Amphitheatre," Collections of the University of California, Berkeley, Bancroft Library,
Robert B. Honeyman, Jr., Collection of Early Californian and Western American Pictorial
Material; BANC PIC 1963.002:1801–E.

of any sum between $1000 and $5000 [the equivalent of $31,000 to $155,000 today].

Often, the observers were less interested in the gruesome contest itself than they were in the betting, the colorful pageantry, and the cheap liquor. On one occasion in Iowa Hill, in Placer County, a surprising turn by a grizzly provided this lasting memory:

> In process of time, the Bear and Bull, both in excellent train, were placed in proper position before the anxious multitude, but disgusted at what seemed to him a farcical degeneracy, his bruinic majesty, Samson-like, burst the thongs which confined him, and darting through the crowd, he scattered them headlong and in terrible haste from before his path. Throwing people and benches out of his way, he made tracks for his native woods, trusted with no muzzle, and bothered with no clog. Beyond the severe fright, we believe no one received any injury.

While bull-and-bear skirmishes received the bulk of the commentary, they were far from the only cases of animal baiting during the nineteenth century. There were cockfights, dogfights, and raccoon baiting, and Iowa Hill was once the site of a highly publicized battle between a grizzly bear and a mountain lion (the latter identified as a "panther" on the event poster). Owners of fighting animals frequently had a "stable" of combatants, and the most vicious creatures quickly gained reputations and followings. Two types of animal clashes drew special notice: badger baiting and rat catching.

Badger baiting, or badger drawing, had for many years been a venerable tradition in England, and in Old California the rowdy activity was quickly adopted during the rough-and-tumble Gold Rush years. Badgers would square off against one or several dogs in a fight to submission or until the badger was successfully wrenched from its enclosure, usually a small box or barrel. Dogs were specially bred for the task, and dachshunds were considered the ideal badger opponent—"dachshund" literally translates as "badger dog."

Badger baiting was not clandestine but openly practiced, and even though the fights were ultimately declared illegal in the late 1850s, published accounts of badger baiting in California continue into the early twentieth century. The *Sacramento Union* reported on a typical badger-and-dog fight on December 12, 1858:

> A badger baiting affair came off yesterday afternoon . . . between an unusually large badger and John Legget's celebrated dog "Leo." After a contest of about ten minutes, the dog was taken off, severely bitten in the breast and side, the badger being apparently uninjured. Within ten minutes thereafter, another wager was made, and another dog entered. The latter contest lasted between ten and fifteen minutes, when the owner of the dog was willing to take him off and call it a drawn game, the badger, in aiming at [the dog's] throat, having caught him by the collar and there held him. Persons who pretend to be posted in this kind of "sport" (!) say that there is no dog in California that can whip that badger.

Rat catching, or rat worrying, was another well-established animal baiting activity in nineteenth-century America, common on the East Coast before it first appeared in California in the 1840s. Ostensibly designed as a public health benefit, these contests were primarily offered as animal bloodsport. The premise was simple: live rats were captured and then set upon by one or several dogs, usually of the rat terrier breed. Spectators would place bets on the number of rats slain in a round or on how quickly they were dispatched. These contests were especially popular in port cities, such as San Francisco and Monterey, but the historical record indicates that rat worrying was also common in inland cities and mining camps. On November 11, 1853, the *Sacramento Union* recounted a rat-catching exhibition at a riverside saloon:

Saturday last, the house of J. W. Foard &. Co. amused
themselves by clearing out the rats. Commencing at the
front part of their store room, bags, barrels, and every kind
of package was removed for the purpose of coraling this
particular kind of vermin. When they had been driven
into a corner, an excellent terrier dog was let in among
them, which in a few moments time destroyed fifty-seven!

Twenty-six years later, the *Los Angeles Herald* of July 1, 1879,
chronicled another rat-catching episode, proving little had
changed from the preceding generation.

At a rat catching match at East Los Angeles yesterday, Dan
Welsh's bull dog killed 30 rats in one minute and thirty
seconds, a remarkable feat for a dog of his age. The dog,
which is eight years old, is quite a hero in his way, having
won a number of severely contested battles in the upper
counties and enjoys the reputation of being a regular cat
exterminator.

As California matured following the Gold Rush and became
more family oriented and socially conservative, animal baiting
became increasingly problematic for civic authorities. The savage nature of these occasions was not in keeping with the public
advancements California wished to exhibit to the nation and the
world, and concerted efforts were made to outlaw or at least cur-
tail the matches. The City and County of Sacramento pioneered
restrictions as it passed an ordinance to regulate animal fighting
on August 11, 1859. It read:

It shall not be lawful for any person to aid or encour-
age any dog fight in any of the streets or alleys within the
city, or in view of any such street or alley; or to assist at
or exhibit any prize fighting, or sparring match; or any
bull, bear, dog or cock fight; or any badger baiting, or rat

catching match; or any fight of a bull or bear against each other or against any other animal or animals, etc.

The ordinance was renewed in subsequent years, and other cities and communities followed suit. In 1905, prohibitions against animal baiting were incorporated into the California Penal Code as Part 1, Title 14, Code 597b, which stated, in part:

This statute forbids anyone from causing a fight between any animal or creature for amusement or gain, or allowing an animal fight to take place on [his or her] premises. It also makes it a misdemeanor for anyone to be present at an animal fight . . . . Any human being . . . who, for amusement or gain, worries or injures any bull, bear, dog, or other animal, or causes any bull, bear, or other animal . . . to worry or injure each other, or any person who permits the same to be done on any premises under his or her charge or control, or any person who aids or abets the fighting or worrying of an animal or creature, is guilty of a misdemeanor.

This statute has been amended and supplemented seven times since 1905, and as recently as 2012. It has also been ignored and violated countless times by those who pursue the practices covertly.

o   o   o

In its various forms, the fighting culture of nineteenth-century California is characteristic of the period known for pitting legality against illegality within an atmosphere that found barbarity both abhorrent and fascinating. And more than a century and a half later, contemporary California is not far removed from those Old California attitudes. Even though the Golden State declared cockfighting illegal in 1939, arrests for the bloody practice are still common, and in 2017, the single largest cockfighting bust in United States history seized seven thousand fighting roosters in rural Los Angeles County. In 2006, the California legislature authorized professional mixed-martial-arts matches, and the initial MMA event, held in Anaheim, sold more than thirteen hundred tickets. In 2018, the first legal bare-knuckle prizefight in the United States in over 130 years was held in Wyoming. There are presently efforts underway to legalize bare-knuckle brawling in California.

Courtship and marriage in Old California were often complicated, but they were also a source of enjoyment and celebration. Here, famous Yosemite Valley photographer George Fiske and his second wife, Caroline Paull, admire their wedding cake in 1897. Image courtesy of the California State Library, Sacramento; California History Section, Digital ID: 2012-1301.

CHAPTER SIX

Sparking, Philanthropic Importation,
and the Hospital

COURTSHIP, DIVORCE, AND PROSTITUTION

I n Old California, romantic relationships, including the
often complicated aspects of sexual desire, courtship, and
divorce, were further complicated by a society characterized by impulsiveness and impermanence. Life was transitory,
thoughts of the future were suppressed, and traditional expectations yielded to relentless cascades of urgency. As John David
Borthwick wrote, "The every-day jog-trot of ordinary human
existence was not a fast enough pace for Californians . . . . The
longest period of time ever thought of was a month." Old California was also somewhat removed from the reality that governed mainstream society; always partly fact and partly fable,
California has for centuries symbolized the venerable fairy
tale wish to live "happily ever after" according to one's own
desires. In the new El Dorado, the old rules—the time-honored

standards many immigrants had grown up with—did not strictly apply.

The April 1854 edition of *The Pioneer, or California Monthly Magazine* proudly reinforced the idea that California was a vanguard of "social fermentation." As author Casper T. Hopkins pronounced,

> We live faster than any other people. We think more promptly; a thousand times more freely than our fathers of the east and of Europe. Our passions are stronger; our intellects keener; our prejudices weaker . . . . We enjoy to the full our present opinions; glorying in the isolation of our social position and our comparative freedom from social formalities, each cares to conform his actions solely to his own will and pleasure.

The major factor in defining the distinctive nature of nineteenth-century sexual relationships in California was the disproportionate ratio of men to women. The numbers were roughly equal in pre–Gold Rush California, but the population explosion of the 1850s greatly altered the demographics, and for the rest of the century the tidal wave of male argonauts engulfed large cities, small mining camps, and almost everything in between.

An exact count of women during this time period is difficult to establish, as the rapid influx of new Californians, their tendency to move frequently, and the inefficient and often inaccurate data collection methods of the times make the results of the state's early censuses suspect. However, the best available figures indicate that women made up about 8 percent of California's population in 1852. In the gold camps, the percentage of women was less than that, and among certain ethnic groups the disparity was even more stark and startling. For example, among Chinese immigrants in California in 1855, women represented only 2 percent of the total population; fifteen years later, Chinese men still outnumbered Chinese women by thirteen to one.

Women during the Gold Rush era may have been scarce, but they did not go unnoticed. In 1856, Eliza Farnham, who had come to California from New York in 1849, recalled that

> at that period in the history of San Francisco, it was so rare to see a female, that those whose misfortune it was to be obliged to be abroad felt themselves uncomfortably stared at. Doorways filled instantly, and little islands in the streets were thronged with men who seemed to gather in a moment, and who remained immovable till the spectacle passed from their incredulous gaze.

Also in 1856, authors Theodore Barry and Benjamin Patten memorably observed, "We remember the day, when a woman walking along the streets of San Francisco was more of a sight than an elephant or giraffe would be today."

As the years passed and the Gold Rush faded, more and more women came to California, and while the chasm narrowed, the gender gap remained. By 1860, women constituted 28 percent of the population, and although the percentage jumped to 42 percent by 1870, it remained in the range of 42 to 45 percent for the rest of the century. It was not until the mid-twentieth century that the male and female populations approached 50 percent.

The population discrepancy was further complicated by Old California's unique amalgamation of social and sexual mores, which represented dozens of different cultures, not to mention the personal proclivities of individuals from within those communities. By the mid-nineteenth century, Northern California was the most ethnically and socially diverse spot on Earth, and that was reflected in the multiplicity of sexual behaviors and attitudes on display there.

In Old California, courtship—or "sparking" or "spooning" or "wooing"—mirrored what was happening in other communities dominated by Victorian-era rules and customs, with the major difference being that everything happened faster on the

West Coast. In general, and even across lines of race, ethnicity, and nationality, men of the era expected their potential soul mates to be exemplars of virtue, piety, and respectability, which often included serving as a shield to the baser instincts of husbands tempted to consort with "bad" women. Steeped in such romanticism and Victorian sentimentality, men in California were fixated on these ideals of marriage even as their opportunities to fulfill that dream were limited by the availability of "acceptable" partners.

Books published during this era offered varied advice on courting and marriage, and among the most popular were the racy novel *Harry Coverdale's Courtship and All That Came of It* (1854), by Frank Smedley, and the self-help tomes *My Courtship and Its Consequences* (1855), by Henry Wikoff, and Mrs. Madeline Leslie's *First or Second Marriages, or, The Courtesies of Wedded Life* (1856). Some residents might have turned to local newspapers, which were filled with advertisements for lectures aimed at helping the lovelorn, such as Frederick Coombs's "Courtship and Matrimony, Phrenologically Analysed."

Spiritualist mediums also stepped up to proffer otherworldly guidance. The mysterious Madame Bryon, advertised as "The Greatest Wonder in the World," could be "consulted with entire confidence on all affairs of life, embracing Love, Courtship, Marriage, Sickness, & c." She also "restores drunken and unfaithful husbands[;] has a secret to make you beloved to your heart's ideal; and brings together those long separated." Magazines and newspapers added to the dialogue by serving up mawkish poems such as this syrupy verse entitled "Courtship or Marriage?," published in the *Daily Alta California* on February 22, 1891:

> Marriage is an ordered garden,
>   Courtship, a sweet tangled wood;
> Marriage is the sober summer,
>   Courtship, spring, in wayward mood;
> Marriage is a deep, still river,
>   Courtship, a bright laughing stream;

Marriage is a dear possession,
 Courtship, a perplexing dream;
Marriage is the blue day's beauty,
 Courtship, the capricious morn;
Marriage is the sweet rose gathered,
 Courtship, bud still fenced with thorn;
Marriage is the pearl in setting,
 Courtship is the dangerous dive;
Marriage, the dull comb of honey,
 Courtship, the new-buzzing hive.

o   o   o

While men were used to having the power when it came to both courtship and marriage, the single women in Old California—whether never married, newly divorced, or widowed—found they often had their pick of suitors and were not as inclined to settle as they might have been in their hometowns. That said, the men were also more curious and assertive in this bold new land, and the women often faced relentless pressure to marry posthaste. As with everything in that time and place, relationships moved fast, and whereas it might take months or even years to develop a romantic connection back home, in Old California a bond could be forged in a matter of hours.

In June 1875, the *Sacramento Union* reported on a verified incident in Alameda County in which a Livermore rancher, aged sixty, made the acquaintance of a well-known and "upright" woman, aged fifty-five. The two struck up a conversation and, instantly smitten, the rancher asked, "How would you like me for a husband?" The woman responded with another question: "How would you like me for a wife?" On the spot, they agreed to marry. The rancher rode into Oakland that afternoon to obtain a marriage license, and the couple was joined in matrimony the next day.

While such super-speedy marriages were unusual, short courtships were not. Even as California became more conservative and conventional following the Gold Rush, sparking was attended by a sense of intensity and urgency not exhibited elsewhere. A prime example of this hurried nature can be seen in the case of Isaac Tibbetts Coffin, who kept a remarkable nearly-daily diary of his life in Dutch Flat, Placer County, from 1863 until a few weeks before his death, in 1903. In 1856, at age twenty-four, Coffin arrived in California from Salem, Massachusetts, where he had held a number of jobs, including shoemaker, farmhand, racehorse groomer, and cook and skipper on cod and mackerel fishing schooners in the Atlantic. Driven by Gold Rush dreams of instant wealth, Coffin settled in the mining camp of Dutch Flat and subsequently pursued careers as a miner, mine owner, photographer, and owner of the Dutch Flat Water Works. Unmarried and unattached when he put down roots in California, he sought to change those circumstances, and then did, rather quickly. Coffin would ultimately have four marriages, two ugly divorces, and seven children and stepchildren.

With his first wife, Anna, whom he married in 1868, the spooning was traditional and lasted many months. His description of their courtship included charming passages of their long romantic walks, whispered encounters, and even a lyrical account of the two lovebirds counting tadpoles in a pond. The marriage ended with a dreadful, mean-spirited divorce in 1879, and from that point onward, Coffin's diary entries about courtship lacked such amorous interludes and dreamy musings and were instead practical and brief—sometimes very brief, in accordance with the courtships themselves, each one of which was progressively shorter.

Coffin met his second wife, Cynthia, in June of 1881, and they were married in October. This marriage also ended in divorce, in 1883. The sparking of Coffin's third wife, Ruth Ella, was similarly short, lasting from February 1886 until their marriage in April of the same year. Sadly, Ruth Ella died after a long illness in 1892, but Coffin soon moved on to Dora, who would become his fourth and final wife. Their intense wooing (almost entirely through the exchange of letters) began in mid-August of 1894, and they married about a month later.

Often, hurried courtships and impulsive marriages led to divorce, and California happened to have the most liberal divorce law in the United States at the time. On March 25, 1851, the state legislature passed "An Act Concerning Divorce," under which the California District Courts were given exclusive jurisdiction to grant divorces. The grounds on which a divorce might be granted included "natural impotence," adultery, "habitual intemperance," desertion, willful neglect, consent obtained by force or fraud, felony conviction, or extreme cruelty, the last of which was the most frequently cited cause for a divorce action.

Critics were shocked and scandalized by the ease with which a divorce could be achieved. In their eyes, California was becoming infamous for the number of divorce decrees it racked up, as well as the readiness of, and even enthusiasm with which, married couples sought to end the bonds of holy matrimony. As the law was being debated in the state legislature, the *Daily Alta California* editorialized on January 26, 1851, that lax divorce laws invariably led to "evil, much evil, and only evil."

> It is against the whole principle of all laws of divorce that we enter our protest. They are all reprehensible, all opposed to good morals, . . . all tending to encourage immorality, dissatisfaction and alienation of feeling, . . . all an insult to the Bible and the principles of Christianity . . . . Divorce has become of so easy attainment nowadays that men take wives with as much *sang froid* as they purchase a horse, knowing that if they become dissatisfied their bargain can as easily be unmade again. And women with similar impressions fish for partners with as much unconcern.

And yet, despite these objections, divorces continued to be issued at a swift pace and in significant numbers. William Morris Stewart, who was California's attorney general in 1854 and became the first United States senator from Nevada about a decade later, recalled serving on a divorce jury in California's Nevada County in 1851. In his memoir, Stewart wrote that the jury had been informed by the judge that "there were ten divorce cases on hand and he wanted to dispose of them that day." Promised that they would be able to return to their mining camps by evening, the panel members prepared the jury room by stocking it with "a demijohn of whiskey, a bucket of water, and twelve tin dippers [cups]." As they considered the cases before them, Stewart observed that the "charge in each case was extreme cruelty, and the principal witness for each plaintiff—in all cases the wife—was her new friend who was engaged to marry her as soon as she could get the old love off." All ten cases were decided in rapid order, ten divorces were granted, and, as Stewart noted, "there were ten weddings that afternoon and evening."

o   o   o

The divorce laws were continuously liberalized by subsequent state legislatures and court decisions throughout the nineteenth century, and the statistics show that women sued for divorce more than men, approaching a ratio of three to one. Throughout the century, studies indicate that female plaintiffs were granted divorces more than 70 percent of the time. Old Californians had twice as many divorces per capita than residents of any other state in the Union.

These unusual circumstances made California a laboratory for a variety of sexual relationships, and among them was a practice both old and yet, in some ways, new: prostitution. The difference in California following the advent of the Gold Rush was that the overwhelmingly male population afforded prostitutes a sense of deference, if not outright respect, that was not common elsewhere in the United States. At least in the early years of the rush, men were more likely to treat a sex worker with appreciation—at least if she conformed to a certain standard, which usually meant she conducted herself with propriety, appeared demure, and spoke English. For a brief time, some prostitutes and madams even became social luminaries and reveled in the mixture of notoriety and prominence. As California native and renowned philosopher Josiah Royce commented about the prostitutes of San Francisco, "There were some women in the city . . . but they were not exactly respectable persons, yet they were the sole leaders of society."

Most sex workers were women, but there were also male and gender-nonconforming people in the business in Old California. Prostitution was a job, and often it was the only job available for people stuck in poverty, individuals who had been abandoned by their families, people of color, those facing language barriers, victims of rape, impoverished mothers with young children, and any other people desperate to survive. In contrast to the high-class madams and courtesans, these "unglamorous" sex workers were mostly invisible or scorned, and although they found customers, they were not as readily accepted into the public social fabric of Gold Rush California.

It was in this atmosphere that Hinton Rowan Helper offered his snide compliment listing "prettier courtezans" as a prominent example of California having the "best bad things." Romanticizing prostitution was a familiar facet of Old California, and the record includes countless takes on the subject; the famed Gold Rush humorist Alonzo Delano flippantly referred to prostitution as "philanthropic importation." For most, ignoring the underlying brutality of the sex trade was routine, and in its place grew the mythology that idealized the prostitutes as "Soiled Doves," "Daughters of Joy," "Fair but Frail," and "Ladies in Full Bloom." These women of western legend and lore were generally stunning, charming, and alluring ornaments on the arms of infatuated gentlemen, and their glamorized bordellos were glittering refuges for the world-weary seeking an oasis of loveliness in a desert of disillusionment and defeat. In reality, of course, prostitution was, at its core, far from glamorous, and even deadly.

The history of prostitution in Old California is long and tortuous. Selling sex was exceedingly rare in Native California, but with the arrival of Europeans, the practice soon became widespread, and the first victims were the Native Californians themselves. During the Gold Rush, Native girls were frequently kidnapped and forced into sexual slavery, even as the tribes attempted to protect themselves. One Nisenan mother stated that, because kidnappers tended to prize physical beauty, she would deliberately dirty her children's faces to keep them from being stolen and sold into the sex trade.

Adult Native women were also captured and driven into prostitution by newcomers. In El Dorado County in 1853, two Native men unsuccessfully attempting to free their captive wives were shot, one fatally, and the women remained under the control of their white abductors. In 1856, the *San Francisco Daily Evening Bulletin* reported that in one mountain reservation "some of the [government] agents, and nearly all of the [government] employees [were] daily and nightly . . . kidnapping the younger portion of the females, for the vilest purposes . . . . [These] wives and daughters [were] prostituted before the very eyes of their husbands and fathers, by these civilized monsters."

The Native population fought back against sexual assault as they were able. In 1855, a Nisenan woman was abducted by a miner named Big Tom, and when he refused to return her to her people, a Nisenan male relative attacked Big Tom's camp in retaliation, killed all the white people present, and dismembered Big Tom himself. In 1859, near Hoopa, in Humboldt County, four white soldiers sexually assaulted a Native woman who then fatally stabbed one in retribution.

In some cases, the violence may have stopped after the Natives fought back, but other times it led to a cycle of retaliation. In 1858, along the Klamath River, a handful of white settlers described by the *Sacramento Union* as "a parcel of abandoned characters" were "in the constant habit of committing the grossest outrages upon the [Native women]." The Native people in the region avenged this maltreatment by "shooting the aggressors and killing their stock," but the white community not unsurprisingly came down on the side of the settlers and, dismissing the severity of their attacks on the local tribes, considered the Natives' acts of revenge as the initial catalyst. In a surprisingly sympathetic interpretation of the matter, however, the *Union* concluded that their reciprocal violence against the settlers unfortunately "made the pretext for fresh outrages upon the poor redskins."

o   o   o

It's hard to say how many women were involved in sex work during the Gold Rush era—prostitution was generally not considered an occupation by census takers—but we do know that although most women who were in California during the Gold Rush were *not* prostitutes, there were some communities in which the percentage of women associated with the sex trade is considered significant.

Either way, the prevalence of the sex trade led to a widely held, but erroneous, belief that virtually all women in California during the Gold Rush were involved in the sex trade. In 1852, Henry Sheldon, an itinerant Protestant missionary based in San Francisco, wrote to relatives in Ohio that in California there were "no villages of any size" without prostitution. Enos Christman, a forty-niner from Pennsylvania, went even further: "I have scarcely met with half a dozen respectable women . . . since I left the Atlantic States. The women . . . , what few there are, are nearly all lewd harlots, who are drunk half the time, or sitting behind the gambling table dealing monte . . . . Indeed, the majority of our females are a disgrace to woman. All, all ruined!" These assertions were clearly exaggerated but, nonetheless, remained resonant for decades.

In 1853 San Francisco, the city had about fifty thousand residents, including roughly eight thousand women and three hundred children. A relative handful of women are listed in the census that year as spouses, domestic servants, or industry workers, which has led some historians to infer from the demographic records that many other women may have been employed in entertainment jobs, restaurants, or as prostitutes. Again, no official reckoning of the larger sex worker population exists, but by

1870, census manuscripts recorded that 61 percent of the 3,536 Chinese women in California officially listed their occupation as prostitute.

While the hub of the sex trade was San Francisco, prostitution was found throughout California. Allusions to the occupation came from locales up and down the state, and mentions of "female boarding houses," a common euphemism for brothels, were recorded throughout Gold Country. In 1840s Los Angeles, prostitutes were clustered in a segregated barrio known as Ranchería de Poblanos (Settlement of the People) that became, in the words of modern historian John Mack Faragher, "a favorite resort of dissolute Angelenos."

In an unsurprising example of how race intersected with the sex trade, many sources from the Gold Rush era were quick to link the immorality of prostitution to the inherent immorality of the races of the sex workers themselves (although this criticism would not be applied to sex workers of the same race as the critic, of course). Official documentation shows that the demographic mix of prostitutes during this era was reflective of the diversity of people in California. For example, in 1860 Sacramento, according to census manuscripts, 26 percent of prostitutes were Caucasian, 4 percent were black, 9 percent were Mexican, 6 percent were South American, and, shockingly, 55 percent were Chinese (at the time when Chinese immigrants made up only 9 percent of California's total population). Their ages ranged from as young as twelve to a few aged forty or above.

San Francisco in the 1850s was fascinated by French women in particular. French argonaut Albert Benard de Russailh commented:

> Nearly all the saloons and gambling-houses employ French women. They lean on the bars, talking and laughing with the men, or sit at the card tables and attract players .... She has to do nothing save honor the table with her presence .... Nearly all these women at home were street-walkers of the cheapest sort.

De Russailh was also one of the few observers who provided details as to the cost of doing business:

> All in all, the women of easy virtue here earn a tremendous amount of money. This is approximately the tariff. To sit with you near the bar or at a card table, a girl charges one ounce [of gold] ($16) an evening . . . . This holds true for the girls selling cigars, when they sit with you . . . . For anything more you have to pay a fabulous amount . . . . A whole night costs from $200 to $400.

The "fabulous amount" De Russailh quotes would be the equivalent of $6,000 to $12,000 today; even in the hyper-inflated economy of Gold Rush California, this was exorbitant. As years passed, however, the prices dropped dramatically, as evidenced by an 1876 court case in Los Angeles. Court transcripts of *People v. Ah Hoo, Ah Choy and Ah Lee* include testimony from an undercover police officer who, in crude and racist language, describes being propositioned by two Chinese sex workers (their pimp was the third defendant) who allegedly offered their services to the officer for "two bits" (or twenty-five cents then and about $6 in 2019). The defendants were found guilty and fined $85 ($2,050 today)—a high-priced and horrendous arithmetic for the two women.

o o o

The increasing presence of prostitution led to increasing civic concern statewide, and Old California saw calls for virtuous action and forceful policymaking regarding prostitution, especially when the sex trade was linked to political corruption. As city populations grew and crime increased, anxious, and sometimes angry, citizens throughout California called on their municipal governments to aggressively address problems associated with crime and corruption. When enough city residents felt that officialdom was not up to the task, however, this civic friction opened up to the possibility of vigilantism. In May 1856, such a flash point occurred and led to the turbulent rebirth of San Francisco's Committee of Vigilance.

Originally organized in 1851, the then seven-hundred-member committee sought to expel the criminal element and purge the city of vice and deceit. In 1851 alone, they hanged four and cast out many others. As years passed, the vigilance committee and its adherents claimed success after success, even while they recognized that crime, political and business corruption, and debauchery were still rampant. On November 15, 1855, tensions that had been churning for years finally exploded when a chance encounter that ignited an intense dispute over public tolerance of prostitution and vice ended in a street killing, an assassination, a public hanging, and the downfall of a once highly regarded madam.

On the fateful night, Charles Cora, a disreputable high-stakes gambler, took his mistress, Arabella Ryan, a madam known widely as Belle, to the American Theater for the dazzling premiere of *Nicodemus; or, The Unfortunate Fisherman*, a pantomime drama produced and performed by the Ravels, a renowned French ballet-pantomime troupe. Charles and Belle were in their usual seats in the expensive dress circle. United States Marshal William Richardson and his wife, Lavinia, were also in attendance. Lavinia Richardson was offended by the presence of these underworld characters, and Mr. Richardson asked the theater manager to remove Charles and Belle. Heated words were exchanged, and Cora refused to depart the theater. Two days later, Charles Cora and William Richardson met on the street, an argument erupted, and Cora shot and killed Richardson, possibly in self-defense.

Charles Cora was arrested for murder, and a few weeks later a sensational trial ensued that ended in a hung jury and allegations that the jurors had been bribed, probably by Belle. Belle's character and profession were as much on trial as Charles was, with one newspaper referring to her as "the harlot who instigated the murder of Richardson." On April 18, 1856, combative journalist James King of William wrote a sarcastic editorial for the *San Francisco Daily Evening Bulletin* mocking the characterization of Belle by Charles Cora's defense attorney, Colonel Edward Dickinson Baker: "The harlot is lauded to the skies in open court . . . and held up as a pattern of virtue and decency!"

Nearly a month later, on May 14, James King of William was assassinated by James P. Casey, a member of the San Francisco County Board of Supervisors, who was angry that King of William had called for the hanging of Charles Cora, who was a friend of Casey's. This act of retaliation spurred a resurgence of the Committee of Vigilance, which garnered twenty-five hundred new members within days. Cora was arrested by the committee on May 20, 1856, and retried under their auspices. After brief proceedings, Cora was pronounced guilty and sentenced to hang. On May 22, while awaiting execution, Charles and Belle married. Two hours later, Cora and his defender Casey were hanged before a cheering crowd of twenty thousand.

Both supporters and opponents of the vigilance committee sought to exploit the Cora hanging for political gain, and the city's newspapers were flooded with letters, a surprising number of them written by women. The most famous missive was published four days after Charles Cora's hanging and targeted the newly widowed Belle Ryan Cora.

TO THE VIGILANCE COMMITTEE: Allow me to express to your respected body our high appreciation of your valuable services so wisely and judiciously executed. You have exhibited a spirit of forbearance and kindness that even the accused and condemned cannot but approve. May Heaven continue to guide you.

But, gentlemen, one thing more must be done: Belle Cora must be requested to leave this city. The women of San Francisco have no bitterness toward her, nor do they ask it on her account, but for the good of those who remain, and as an example to others. Every virtuous woman asks that her influence and example be removed from us.

The truly virtuous of our sex will not feel that the Vigilance Committee have done their *whole* duty till they comply with the request of
MANY WOMEN OF SAN FRANCISCO

The request was ignored by the vigilance committee and by Belle Cora.

In the months that followed, Belle did not shrink from public view and sought to posthumously exonerate Charles Cora and to defend her vocation. Belle was seen everywhere, thumbing her nose at the disapproving by flaunting her finest clothes and grandly wheeling her elegant horse-drawn carriage down the swankiest San Francisco boulevards. Belle was also heard everywhere, reserving her most potent venom for the vigilantes who took her husband's life. She continued to operate her opulent Cora House—a combination social club, sanctuary, saloon, restaurant, and brothel known as a "parlor house"—but the business was not as profitable following the incident, and Belle began to exhaust her fortune. Finally, in the scandalous aftermath of the execution of Charles Cora, she was forced to sell her business, and within six years Belle Cora would be dead at the age of thirty-five.

o   o   o

While the San Francisco Committee of Vigilance was, in essence, a mob acting without official sanction from local authorities, there were plenty of ordinances and laws on the books aimed to address the flourishing business of prostitution. The rules were not always applied equally, however, and in this case the target was almost always Chinese prostitution. In 1865, the San Francisco Board of Supervisors issued the "Order to Remove Chinese Women of Ill-Fame from Certain Limits in the City"; in 1866, the state legislature passed "An Act for the Suppression of Chinese Houses of Ill-Fame"; and in 1870, the state authorized "An Act to Prevent the Kidnapping and Importation of Mongolian, Chinese, and Japanese Females for Criminal or Demoralizing

Purposes." All these actions decreased prostitution overall, but the records show that a sizeable proportion of Chinese women and girls in California were still part of the sex trade. According to the census, in 1870, 61 percent of Chinese women and girls living in the state were identified as prostitutes, and while that number had dropped significantly by 1880, it was still a noteworthy 24 percent.

The sex trade engaged in the brutish custom known as "yellow slavery," or the buying and selling of young Asian girls, some of whom were kidnapped or ensnared through deceit, while others had been sold by their impoverished families. When a shipment of girls arrived in the City by the Bay from China, they were put on the auction block in a secret location, and much like the practices of African slave trading in the American South, the victims were stripped, inspected, and physically appraised. When a price was agreed upon, payment was made, often with gold coins, and the girl signed a contract. The girls were exploited by many different people—including the Chinese men and women who marketed and sold them, and the white men who purchased them. A typical agreement stated:

> For the consideration of [amount], paid into my hands this day, I, [name] promise to prostitute my body for the term of _____ years. If, in that time, I am sick one day, two weeks will be added to my time; and if more than one, my prostitution shall continue an additional month. But if I run away, or escape from the custody of my keeper, then I am to be held as a slave for life.
>   [Signature] _____

There were also direct sales of sex slaves. In a stunning exposé of the casual and dispassionate nature of the practice, the *San Francisco Call* of April 2, 1899, printed a bill of sale for various goods in addition to a nine-year-old girl offered by seller Loo Wong to purchaser Loo Chee.

BILL OF SALE

Loo Wong to Loo Chee

April 16 – Rice, six mats, at $12
April 18 – Shrimps, 50 lbs., at 10¢ 5
April 20 – Girl 250
April 21 – Salt Fish, 60 lbs., at 10¢ 6

$$\overline{}$$
$273
Received payment
Loo Chee

Girls in their early teens were most desirable—a Chinese prostitute older than twenty was uncommon—and most died within five or six years from abuse or illness, which included venereal diseases, estimated to have affected 90 percent of the Chinese sex workers.

Prostitution stalls in San Francisco's Chinatown were commonly referred to as "cribs" or "bagnios" in the nineteenth century. Many women and girls were held as prisoners in these small cells. "A Chinese Bagnio, San Francisco B3018," photograph by I. W. Taber, c. 1880. Image courtesy of the California State Library, Sacramento; California History Section, Digital ID: 2008-1069.

As with prostitutes of other ethnicities, there was a range of circumstances in which a Chinese sex worker might find herself. Some were stationed in the more swanky and sumptuous "parlor houses" adorned with handsome furniture, brocade pillows, and tasteful paintings, and in these establishments they were provided the finest silks and satins, were made up to resemble dolls, and would be instructed in the "seductive arts." The patrons were mostly middle-class white and Chinese men.

Most Chinese sex workers, however, were relegated to grimy back-alley cribs. These brothels resembled a bay of horse stalls, each roughly twelve by fifteen feet and divided by curtains into two rooms occupied by two to six girls wearing the same distinctive uniform: blue or black silk blouses with greenish-blue embroidery. These Chinese cribs, or "bagnios," served customers of any age, nationality, or economic standing, as long as they could pay. The women and girls were subjected to countless indignities. They were often only allowed to leave their stalls for brief periods, they were whipped or branded for even the slightest infractions, and they commonly were not allowed to keep any portion of their earnings. It did not take long for the women to lose their physical, mental, and emotional health, and those who were deemed no longer viable as prostitutes were, in the 1860s and 1870s, forced into tiny, dark, and dreary quarters that the sex trade called "hospitals" to await a grisly fate. In an article entitled "Horrors of a Great City," the *San Francisco Chronicle* of December 5, 1869, described one of these "death cells":

> It is loathsome in the extreme . . . . There is not the first suggestion of furniture in the room, no table, no chairs or stools, nor any window . . . . Led . . . to this hole of a "hospital," she is forced within the door and made to lie down . . . . A cup of water, another of boiled rice, and a little metal lamp are placed by her side . . . . The assassins pass out of the death cell, the heavy door is locked and the unfortunate creature is left to die alone.

The *Chronicle*'s account of the blasé atmosphere outside the cell is chilling: "The smothered shrieks of despair, the dreadful moans with which weakened nature announces its sufferings may be heard by those who burrow in the immediate vicinity; but they either pay no attention to them or simply curse the victim in uncouth language as an annoyance." The women did not leave these hellholes alive, whether from starvation, suicide, or murder.

In the later years of the nineteenth century, the "hospitals" were used less regularly as Chinese prostitutes were more frequently able to escape to one of the sanctuaries operated by religious groups. The best known was San Francisco's Occidental Mission Home for Girls, founded in 1874 and operated by the Presbyterian Church. Its superintendent, Margaret Culbertson, was dedicated to rescuing Chinese girls and women from the clutches of slavery and prostitution. Until her retirement in 1897, Culbertson raided brothels and provided refuge for hundreds of people, some as young as ten, despite threats from Chinese criminal syndicates and brothel owners; in 1895, sticks of unignited dynamite were left as a threat on the porch and windowsills of the Occidental Mission Home.

Culbertson was succeeded by her assistant Donaldina Cameron, who became known as the "Angry Angel of Chinatown." Cameron would lead the Occidental Mission Home for the next thirty-nine years, and during her tenure she would be credited with rescuing as many as three thousand Chinese women from sex slavery.

In 1895, just a few weeks after Cameron arrived at the home as a new employee, she participated in her first raid. Margaret Culbertson, her staff, and local police raided a seedy bordello on Bartlett Alley in Chinatown, a notorious street featuring wall-to-wall bagnios. Using axes and sledgehammers, the police chopped through a window and encountered a terrified girl cowering in the corner. Asked if she wished to go to the Mission Home, the girl answered, "I come! I come!" but as she was being whisked away, the crib owner burst in screaming, "Stop it! Stop it! You break my house!" The rescued girl's "owner" assailed her with crude expletives and with the Chinese insult "May all

During the late nineteenth century, Donaldina Cameron was known as the "Angry Angel of Chinatown" for her work rescuing an estimated three thousand Chinese women and girls from prostitution and indentured servitude in San Francisco. Many saw Cameron as a heroic figure, while some considered her a disconcerting example of a white person imposing Victorian morality on people of color. Photograph by Louis J. Stellman, c. 1910. Image courtesy of the California State Library, Sacramento; California History Section, Digital ID: 2018-0594.

your ancestors curse you and turn you into a turtle." This rescue pattern was repeated hundreds of times, and thousands of women were freed from sex slavery.

The actions of Culbertson, Cameron, and their collaborators were not without controversy, however. Modern critics have looked back at the work of Donaldina Cameron and other similar missionaries and accused them of seeing the Chinese women as, in the words of historian Judy Yung, "the ultimate symbol of female powerlessness, as exemplified in their domestic confinement, sexual exploitation, and treatment as chattel." Yung continues:

> In their zeal to rescue and transform Chinese women into their own image, missionary women . . . not only infringed

on the civil rights of an already disenfranchised population, but also helped to perpetuate negative stereotypes of the Chinese, thus adding fuel to anti-Chinese sentiment and legislation.

Others have been troubled by the subsequent imposition of Victorian morality upon the women liberated from prostitution, as they were now merely living under another set of rules rather than allowed to make their own choices. Cameron became the legal guardian of the underage girls in her charge, and the girls were forced to reside at the Mission Home and convert to Christianity. A girl was not allowed to leave the home until she married a Christian man of whom Cameron approved. Some women ran away after being rescued, but many accepted the conditions Cameron laid down, whether because they were grateful for being liberated from horrible circumstances or because, most likely, they had few other options.

o o o

Conspicuously missing from accounts of the Old California sex trade are the voices of the prostitutes themselves. While numerous accounts of the activities, milieu, and corruption of prostitution were published in the newspapers and journals of the era, the vast majority of press on the subject was standard reportage, not personal interest stories. Supposed "firsthand" statements were sometimes concocted by reporters and reformers, but historians generally find these accounts sensationalized and suspect: the newspaper articles were most likely exaggerated to titillate and entice readers during the nineteenth-century newspaper wars, and the stories presented by reformers—often referred to as "missionary narratives"—were almost certainly designed to promote their specific agenda.

It was not until the early twentieth century that more reliable testimonies of sex workers became available. This was primarily due to the efforts of Fremont Older, crusading editor of the *San Francisco Bulletin*. In 1913, the *Bulletin* serialized "A

Voice from the Underworld," a ghostwritten autobiography of a prostitute who was called "Alice Smith." Scholars today debate whether Alice was one person, a fusion of several individuals or, as a handful argue, a completely fictional character made up by a reporter, but while some question the trustworthiness of the narrative, few dispute that, in comparison to other accounts of the period, Alice's story is a raw and candid portrait of prostitution that includes an unprecedented degree of detail. The series was both sensation and scandal, and critics assailed its publication as salacious and debauched. Typical was the response of the Reverend Leslie Briggs of the First Congregational Church of Santa Cruz. As the *Santa Cruz Evening News* reported in August 1913, Reverend Briggs denounced "A Voice from the Underworld" in no uncertain terms:

> The pastor declared that the effect of these articles was to demoralize and not improve and that all Christian people should place upon them their stamp of disapproval .... Briggs asserted that the articles are written in a way to make the recital [the lifestyle] alluring to young women .... He asserted that the *Bulletin* was the type of paper that would sell more papers [if it] would devote more space to religion than it devotes to the gutter.

The public response to "A Voice from the Underworld" was remarkable. More than four thousand letters flooded the *Bulletin*, many from current and former prostitutes sharing their experiences. Although these letters combined to form their own powerful narrative, the dispatches were almost exclusively from white women, meaning the corresponding stories from women of color, men, and people from across the sexual and gender spectrums are still absent from the conversation.

Working with what we do have, however, Alice's story and the letters it inspired are a window to the subject and cover a range of perspectives and purposes. The correspondence delivered to the *San Francisco Bulletin* was largely heartwrenching and horrifying, but it was also often bursting with passionate advocacy for reform and pleas for understanding. Both the original chronicle and the communications that followed expressed and reinforced the progressive idea that sex workers are not hopelessly immoral "fallen women" but real people with real struggles and needs. As a correspondent who called herself "One of Society's Victims" wrote to Fremont Older: "No, Mr. Editor, we are not prostitutes because we love the life. Most of us would love to be real wives and feel the clasp of baby arms about our necks." Another letter writer, Alma Greene, wrote to the *San Francisco Bulletin* that among the important considerations that led women to prostitution were personal catastrophe, vital family responsibilities, and the lack of any viable economic alternative:

> There are so many angles to this problem that you must not hope to solve it . . . . Some calamity puts the husband on the verge of insanity, and the wife, for love of him— perhaps for the sake of their children—makes the horrible sacrifice . . . . There are three women in this house . . . who are supporting their children. Four others send money home to their parents each week. One girl is caring for a crippled sister.

Other stories focused on the work itself, shining a light on the brutal physical and psychological nature of prostitution. Violet Brown recounted her experience as a sex slave: "I was locked in a room and kept for weeks—how many I do not know. While kept prisoner in this room I was compelled to submit to unspeakable outrages."

Alice Smith bitterly recalled the degrading catcalls and bestial behavior of the male patrons: "We were the men's big show; put there by men; kept there for the use of men, to be used as they chose and talked to as they chose, meant forever to be the satisfaction and the victims of their worst hours . . . . Our trade was not our own; . . . it was created by the men when they had a mind to be lower than animals . . . . And they were lower than animals."

Arguably the most moving passage from "A Voice from the Underworld" is from the section in which Alice Smith is an adult somberly reflecting on her past. Her memory is triggered by a brief visit to her childhood home in Chicago, where she lived with her grandparents. As Alice entered the vegetable garden, she came upon a forgotten and melancholy reminder of her youth. It was, she wrote, "my dolls' graveyard . . . . I had buried them there, and wept over each one, and had fixed up white stones at the head and foot of each little grave." As Alice gazed upon the spot, she "laughed and cried together" as she recalled years gone by. She pondered the tortured decisions, the loss of dignity, the shattered dreams, and the challenging consequences of the twisting path from her girlhood. "After all," Alice sorrowfully concluded, "hadn't I buried more things than dolls—buried them forever."

While many nineteenth-century California entertainments were rough-and-
tumble, there were calls for refinement and genteel amusements as well.
Here, on March 4, 1870, the Norwegian violin virtuoso Ole Bull is welcomed by
prominent figures to a concert in San Francisco. Image courtesy of the California
State Library, Sacramento; California History Section, Picture Collection: F-Map
Portraits: Bull, Ole. Digital ID: 1960-1607a.

CHAPTER SEVEN

Put's Golden Songster, The India
Rubber Man, and Pedestrianism

ECCENTRIC AND EXTRAORDINARY ENTERTAINMENTS

I t is July 1890 and a remarkable sight is unfolding in San Francisco. Ned Foster, the pudgy, boisterous impresario of the Bella Union Saloon and Music Hall, is making his daily appearance on the Barbary Coast. For regular denizens of the fabled district, his entrance is old hat, but for the new observer it is glitzy and distinctive. Daily, on his way to the Bella Union, Ned Foster parades down Pacific Street behind a garish dogcart pulled by a team of black Shetland ponies. At Foster's side is his massive, commanding bodyguard, an African American man named Deacon Jones. It is but another day at the office for Foster, but it is emblematic of the bawdy, happy-go-lucky, avant-garde, unrestrained entertainment of Old California. And if the boss's arrival at work was this theatrical, imagine the nature of the performances.

This carefree, randy attitude was memorably expressed in the ribald advertising produced for the Bella Union by Ned Foster. While enticing the patron, it also defined the culture of Old California entertainment. This typical example touting an upcoming event at the saloon was plastered on walls and streetlamps throughout San Francisco in 1890:

> If you want to "Make a Night of It."
> This Show is not of the Kindergarten Class,
> But Just Your Size, if You are In-
> Clined to be Frisky and Sporty.
> It is Rapid, Spicy and Speedy — As
> Sharp as a Razor, and as Blunt at Times
> As the Back of an Axe.

California has for decades been at the center of media entertainment—including radio, television, movies, and the Internet—and these modern phenomenon were directly born from the freewheeling productions—whether homegrown or professionally staged—of the nineteenth century. Showbiz in our day certainly reflects our modern sensibilities, but it also echoes the high-spirited mix of features common in Old California entertainment: classical fare, music-hall energy, Victorian sentimentality, lowbrow knockabout humor, improvisation, sensational curiosities, and singular, unclassifiable players. Nineteenth-century California saw an explosion of the eccentric and the extraordinary that excited the senses and provided a welcome distraction from the cares of everyday existence.

Entertainment took many forms, from a solitary harmonica player in the glow of a campfire to elaborate stage shows, and it was found everywhere from tiny hamlets to raucous boomtowns to sprawling cities. In Old California, most show business was centered in three areas: ports such as San Francisco and Sacramento, the network of larger mining camps, and the scattered hubs of commerce like trading posts and forts.

In the dawn of the epoch, almost all diversions were unso-
phisticated and frequently spontaneous, but even as they
evolved with the culture, some things remained constant. Singing and dancing was universal, and they often revealed much
about the social mosaic of their times. Richard Henry Dana,
Jr., recalled a gathering of fifty traders in 1835 San Diego comprised of

> almost every nation under the sun,—two Englishmen,
> three Yankees, two Scotchmen, two Welshmen, one Irish-
> man, three Frenchmen (two of whom were Normans, and
> the third from Gascony), one Dutchman, one Austrian,
> two or three Spaniards (from old Spain), half a dozen Span-
> ish-Americans and half-breeds, two native Indians from
> Chili and the Island of Chiloe, one negro, one mulatto,
> about twenty Italians, from all parts of Italy, as many more
> Sandwich-Islanders, one Tahitian, and one Kanaka from
> the Marquesas Islands.

The night before setting sail, this congregation met and, as
Dana continued, "we had songs of every nation and tongue":

> A German gave us "Ach! mein lieber Augustin!"[;] the
> three Frenchmen roared through the Marseilles Hymn;
> the English and Scotchmen gave us "Rule Britannia," and
> "Wha'll be King but Charlie?"[;] the Italians and Spaniards
> screamed through some national affairs, . . . and we three
> Yankees made an attempt at the "Star-spangled Banner."

Slightly more organized were sing-alongs using the familiar songbooks of the era, including, most famously, *Put's Golden
Songster*, written by John Stone, who was known professionally as "Old Put." Stone wrote or collected dozens of popular
songs of the Gold Rush, and he composed or arranged nearly
fifty tunes for his songbook. For his most famous work, he combined new lyrics and a traditional English folk tune to create the
song "Sweet Betsy from Pike," an anthem of the California Gold

Rush. The titles of his songs often spotlighted the reality the gold seekers faced: "The Fools of '49," "Prospecting Dreams," "There Is No Luck About the House," and "The Lively Flea." This representative lyric is from "The Miner's Lament":

> Cold, wet, and hungry, I've slept on the ground,
>   When those visions of happiness came,
> But sad and disheartened, awoke by the sound
>   Of the screech-owl that lit on my claim.

Put's Golden Songster could easily fit in the pocket of a city dweller, and it became a fixture in many miners' knapsacks. The collection sold thousands of copies. Old Put was not alone in his success, either. Among the other songwriters of his time were entertainers known as Dr. Robinson, J. Swett, Mart Taylor, the redoubtable Jack the Grumbler, and a comic singer known only as Johnson.

o   o   o

Dancing and music also brought communities together, as with the *fandangos* commonly held among Californios. The fandango was a social ritual that mixed hospitality, courting, and demonstrations of family wealth, and it integrated a cappella singing, band music, dancing, eating, and often liberal consumption of *aguardiente*, a term for alcohol that literally translates as "firewater." In the 1830s, Alfred Robinson, a leading hide and tallow merchant headquartered in Santa Barbara, attended many fandangos, especially after he married into a prominent Californio family. In his 1846 book *Life in California*, Robinson described a typical fandango:

> During the performance of the dances, three or four male voices occasionally take part in the music, and towards the end of the evening, from repeated applications of *aguardiente* they become quite boisterous and discordant.

The waltz was now introduced, and ten or a dozen couples whirled gaily around the room, and heightened the charms of the dance by the introduction of numerous and interesting figures. Between the dances, refreshments were handed to the ladies, whilst in an adjoining apartment, a table was prepared for the males, who partook without ceremony. The most interesting of all their dances is the *contra danza* and this, also, may be considered the most graceful. Its figures are intricate, and in connection with the waltz, form a charming combination. These *fandangos* usually hold out till daylight, and at intervals the people at the door are permitted to introduce their *jarabes* [folk dances] and *jotas* [a triple-time Spanish dance using castanets].

Gold rushers were also fond of social dancing, although in many cases the dances were impromptu and improvised. Alfred Doten, who is best known for his detailed diary spanning the 1840s into the early twentieth century, noted that one night he developed a dance he called the "Double Cow Turd Smasher." Frequently, the primary problem with goldfield dances was the lack of women to have as partners. In 1853, John David Borthwick visited Angels Camp, a thriving mining community in Calaveras County, and colorfully explained how the miners cleverly adapted to this circumstance:

In the evening, a ball took place . . . [and] though none of the fair sex were present, dancing was kept up with great spirit for several hours . . . . The absence of ladies was a difficulty which was very easily overcome, by a simple arrangement whereby it was understood that every gentleman who had a patch on a certain part of his inexpressibles should be considered a lady for the time being. These patches were rather fashionable, and were usually large squares of canvass, showing brightly on a dark ground, so that the "ladies" of the party were as conspicuous as if they had been surrounded by the usual quantity of white muslin.

The demographic explosion of the California Gold Rush not only changed the nature of entertainment in the region but also fundamentally altered its importance. With most gold seekers failing to strike it rich, a moment's respite from the drudgery and frustration was especially welcome and, as a result, Gold Country and its environs became a hotbed for a wide variety of diversions, including stage shows. One 1935 study of performances in 1850s San Francisco indicated that at least 1,000 different theatrical pieces had been offered during that decade; of those counted were 907 plays, 48 operas, 84 "spectacles" and ballets, and 66 unique minstrel companies. Historian George Stewart noted that in the eighteen months that ran from 1856 to 1858, the single mining camp of Nevada City presented almost fifty "serious" plays (i.e., tragedies, comedies, and tragicomedies) in addition to music-hall performances, concerts, and lectures.

Theatrical quality was as diverse as the genres. Performers ranged from downright amateurs to those at the pinnacle of theatrical expertise. The entertainers in the larger communities tended to be more artistically proficient, but even there it was hit-and-miss.

In San Francisco on June 22, 1849, the first professional performance of the Gold Rush was said to have been put on by a copper-haired Englishman who called himself "Jeems Pipes of Pipeseville." His real name was Stephen Massett, and he was a jack-of-all-trades. A poet, actor, singer, auctioneer, newspaper editor, humor writer, lawyer, clerk, composer, and incorrigible drifter, Massett referred to himself as a wandering minstrel, and he was a true enigma. He was ultimately unknowable, as no one could quite determine what he did or why, perhaps including Stephen Massett himself. His performance of June 22 was organized, advertised, written, and performed by Massett alone, and this ambitious one-man show included comic songs and recitations, impressions, humorous asides, and a skit in which he played seven different parts. Massett's performance paved the way for the torrent of theater that followed, but the man who jumpstarted it all was restless and soon took his show far afield.

More than three decades after his San Francisco premiere, and after performances throughout the mainland United States and in China, India, Japan, Australia, Hawaii, England, and South Africa, Massett resurfaced in Sacramento. The *Sacramento Daily Union* of August 5, 1882, commented that he was

> a character, and though his clustering locks have grown gray and the lines have deepened in his face, he has not changed his disposition or his habits . . . . He will sing, recite, give imitations, and make himself miscellaneously useful and ornamental, any afternoon or evening, without any consideration . . . . Just what his calling is it would be hard to say . . . . I doubt if anybody except himself knows how he lives.

The first regularly scheduled professional theatrical performance in Gold Rush California was in Sacramento's Eagle Theater on October 18, 1849. The theater could hold eight hundred patrons, but it had canvas sides and a tin roof, and the stage was constructed out of packing crates. Located on the banks of the Sacramento River, the theater was heavily attended by forty-niners desperately seeking anything that might deserve the label of "professional" production. The leading man on opening night was John Bowman, who had arrived in Sacramento a few weeks earlier barefoot and broke.

In late December and early January 1850, Sacramento suffered a massive flood, and although the Eagle Theater was inundated, the shows continued. As the floodwaters rose, the audience stood on the chairs, exiting only when the quickly rising water was lapping at their soles of their boots. Due to the Great Flood, the theatrical company abandoned Sacramento, but it reemerged in San Francisco and, at the end of January 1850, presented the melodrama *The Wife*, which was the first scheduled stage performance in the city. The engagement was abbreviated, however, when the company treasurer, a Mr. Mattinson, announced to the cast, who had assembled for their pay, that he had lost all the box office receipts playing monte.

∘   ∘   ∘

In addition to all the small-time performers who took the stage in Old California, there were also many famous names who dazzled audiences. Then as now, the local culture was also influenced by some luminaries who never set foot in the region but nonetheless made their mark. Songbird Jenny Lind, the celebrated "Swedish Nightingale," never visited California, but she was adored across much of the Western Hemisphere and was so renowned in Europe that "Great American Showman" P. T. Barnum signed her to perform in one hundred concerts in the United States before he heard her sing one note. When a Nevada County theater named after Jenny Lind was demolished by the flooding of nearby Deer Creek in March 1852, the reports that "Jenny Lind has disappeared" evoked deep sorrow among those who thought the actual Jenny Lind had died. Consumer products bearing Lind's name or likeness—cigars, chewing tobacco, gloves, hats, shoes, sofas, pianos, carriages, paper dolls, and hair gloss—were available throughout Old California, and there was even a mining camp in Calaveras County christened "Jenny Lind."

Old California also hosted a constellation of operatic divas—including the Irish soprano Kate Hayes, Madame Anna Bishop from England, the Italian-French prima donna Adelina Patti, coloratura soprano Luisa Tetrazzini, and Nellie Melba, the renowned Australian soprano—but for scandal no one could beat Lola Montez, the provocative Countess of Landsfeld and the infamous performer of the Spider Dance.

Born in 1821, she had numerous lovers and, most notably, was, beginning in 1846, the mistress of Ludwig I, King of Bavaria. Ludwig I bestowed the royal title of countess on Lola and gifted her with land, expensive personal property, and, controversially, influence in court. Many in Bavaria viewed Lola as a symbol of decadence and political corruption, and in 1848, the Year of Revolution in Europe, disgust over royal entitlements in general and Lola's governmental clout in particular became a flash point. Ludwig I abdicated, a move that led to years of social and political turmoil in Bavaria, and the public's reaction against Ludwig and Lola was considered a trigger for additional revolutions in Europe.

Lola fled both Ludwig and Bavaria, but her reputation followed her. Rather than go into hiding, Lola capitalized on her celebrity in Gold Rush California and for years was notorious for her suggestive Spider Dance. During her brief and voluntary retirement from the stage in 1853, she settled in the foothill mining camp of Grass Valley, where she once horsewhipped a local newspaper editor who had published disparaging comments about her. She was also remembered for mentoring a little red-haired neighbor girl named Lotta Crabtree.

Crabtree, in contrast to Montez, was a homegrown celebrity who enjoyed her success without scandal, quite an accomplishment for someone who started her entertainment career at six years old. Called "The Eternal Child," she was especially adored by the miners for her energetic singing and dancing, and by the 1880s she was famous throughout the nation and was the highest paid actress in the country. She used some of that money to support charities, and she also donated a series of fountains to various cities, including San Francisco. Today, at the intersection of Market, Geary, and Kearny, visitors can still see the fountain Crabtree donated as a watering hole for the city, and particularly its thirsty horses.

Many prominent thespians also trod California's boards during this era, including Edwin and Junius Booth, Mathilda Heron, Laura Keene, and Sarah Bernhardt. A pair of sisters, Kate and Ellen Bateman, were ages eleven and nine when their tour of the United States brought them to California in 1853. The duo performed, in full adult wardrobe, as Macbeth and Lady Macbeth, Shylock and Portia, and Richard III and Richmond, wearing mustaches as necessary.

The astonishing Adah Isaacs Menken achieved great fame while strapped to the back of a horse. Menken was the featured performer in an old chestnut of a melodrama entitled *Mazeppa*, and her entire role was to be belted to a horse that ran furiously on an inclined treadmill for fifteen minutes. Because she was portraying a young man, she had the unique opportunity to daringly crop her hair and, most importantly in the eyes of the male audience members, to wear flesh-colored tights. Adah Isaacs Menken was an inimitable personality, a talented writer, and a pioneer in the bohemian movement, which embraced performers and artists out of the mainstream. She was also, perhaps surprisingly, one of the most highly paid performers of her time.

In the field of music, Ole Bull, a Norwegian violin prodigy, received rapturous praise in California and beyond, including from eminent German composer Robert Schumann, who considered Bull the "greatest violinist of all." Ole Bull made several tours of California from the 1850s to the 1870s. In an 1854 *Daily Alta California* review of an Ole Bull recital, concertgoer L. Maria Child is breathless in her admiration:

> I have twice heard Ole Bull. I scarcely dare to tell the impression his music had upon me. But casting aside all fear of ridicule for excessive enthusiasm, I will say that it expressed to me more of the infinite than I ever saw or heard, or dreamed of, in the realms of Nature, Art, or Imagination . . . . He looks pure, natural and vigorous, as I imagine Adam in Paradise . . . . He comes to the New World, because genius craves the sympathy of the universe, and delights to pour itself abroad like the sunbeams.

Ole Bull was so beloved in California that on March 4, 1870, he received from the citizens of San Francisco "a slight token of their affectionate regards"—a golden wreath containing thirty-six pearls and the monogram "O. B." in diamonds. It cost $1,000 to produce, the equivalent of $19,270 today.

o   o   o

Through most of the nineteenth century, a popular light theatrical genre for Old California was minstrelsy; a survey of California newspapers from the 1840s to 1890 reveals more than
eight thousand advertisements for minstrel shows. Brought to
Old California from the East Coast, minstrel shows featured
white performers in "blackface"—a look achieved by using
burnt cork to darken the performers' skin. These programs
invariably comprised songs, dances, and comedic skits featuring
racist depictions of black people as immoral and ignorant fools.
The origins of minstrelsy in California are summed up in this
1939 note from the San Francisco Theater Research Project of
the Works Progress Administration:

> During its initial epoch, minstrelsy was restricted to the
> populous Eastern cities where the theatre has always flour-
> ished. New York had its resident companies, as did Brook-
> lyn, Philadelphia and Chicago. Nearly every season one or
> several of these troupes took to the road, but their circuits
> were confined to relatively small areas until 1849, when
> discovery of gold in California occasioned a vast exodus to
> the West. Then San Francisco became a minstrel town.

Most scholars today believe the shows were designed to
mock free blacks in the North and to reinforce racial stereotypes. "Blackface" shows were racist and cruel, then as now.
Among the most prominent of the minstrel companies were
Christy's Minstrels, the New York Serenaders, the Celebrated
and Original New Orleans Serenaders, Buckley's Serenaders, Max Zorer's Ethiopian Burlesque Troupe, and the Haverly
Mastodon Minstrel Company. Among the stars that emerged
were Billy Birch and Charley Backus—both white men in
blackface. There was only a smattering of women minstrels in
Old California, and the first production to include them was
the farce *Three Fast Men of San Francisco, or The Female Robinson Crusoes*, staged in 1862. Not until 1882 did the first all-black

minstrel troupe—the Callender Company—headline a top theater in California.

Passionate critics of minstrelsy were making their voices heard in California as early as 1848. On October 27 of that year, abolitionist Frederick Douglass, who had escaped slavery at age twenty, opined in the pages of his newspaper, the *North Star*, that blackface performers were "the filthy scum of white society, who have stolen from us a complexion denied them by nature, in which to make money, and pander to the corrupt taste of their white fellow citizens." In 1862, a correspondent to the *Pacific Appeal*, the most influential black-owned and -operated newspaper in Old California, decried the "moral ulcer" of minstrelsy and, further, called out the horrifying specter of black performers participating in these "exhibitions of ridicule." The author, identified only as J.M.B., wrote:

> [Blackface minstrel shows] with all their burlesquing caricatures . . . were gotten up by pernicious men, at the expense of the poverty and ignorance of an oppressed, long-outraged and downtrodden people . . . . We have represented the work of burlesquing and caricaturing as being performed by men with white bodies and blackened faces, and upon this feature we could look forever with a nettled brow of scorn, and treat its contemptuous perpetrators as vile, traducing dogs. But . . . we tremble for the fate of our people; for, recently, to our utter astonishment and disgust, we learn, that men, naturally black, . . . have been induced, through ignorance, lack of principle, or sheer cupidity, to be a party in representing, by public entertainment, their own degradation and that of their unfortunate race. This . . . is by far the "the unkindest cut of all" . . . . Think of it; a people reveling in their own disgrace.

This criticism directs much of the blame to the performers, instead of on the producers, theaters, and patrons who made minstrelsy feasible. As black performers had limited options within the theatrical world, and in society in general, it seems unfair to judge them for being products of circumstances beyond their control.

o   o   o

Over time, minstrelsy gave way to vaudeville, and by the end of the 1880s, the favored form of entertainment was this style of "variety show," in which a series of distinct acts appeared on the same bill. Some vaudeville bills carried on the toxic legacy of minstrelsy, but overall the shows were more eclectic, with a mix of musicians, singers, dancers, animal acts, acrobats, jugglers, and celebrity lecturers, all of it ranging from the classical to the comedic.

Another genre of stage entertainment that was all the rage throughout the period following the Gold Rush were the "leg shows," which the *San Francisco Bulletin* described in 1862 as "principally intended to introduce about two scores of female legs, nearly as good as naked, of all shapes, thicknesses and lengths, which parade on stage for half an hour, or so." Critics questioned their morality, but the overwhelmingly male audiences nonetheless flocked to see the "real live women" on stage. These performances frequently expanded into elaborate extravaganzas, also called "sensations" by the newspapers, and one memorable 1861 leg show featured the requisite number of women plus thirty-six horses, nine wagons, and a corps of singers, dancers, pantomimists, and acrobats.

The most famous leg show was such a sensation it spawned a lawsuit. In 1867, *The Black Crook* debuted in San Francisco. Already a hit in New York, the performance featured dozens of young women displaying their legs in creamy flesh-colored tights, and three separate theaters in San Francisco zealously competed to be the first to present the act in California. One, Maguire's Opera House, tried to leapfrog its competitors by purchasing a purloined copy of the script. Another theater, the Metropolitan, responded by staging a rip-off entitled *The Black Rook* that was almost identical to *The Black Crook*, including verbatim dialogue. A third theater, the Olympic, offered another barely altered version called *The Black Hook with a Crook*. The theaters auditioned scores of women for roles; the Maguire's Opera House version called for one hundred women on stage, surpassing the Metropolitan's call for eighty. With massive box office numbers at stake, the two theaters sought injunctions against each other and hurled accusations that included copyright infringement, even though they were both using stolen scripts. In an astounding decision in April 1867, Judge Matthew Deady of the United States Circuit Court of San Francisco went far afield from the realm of copyright infringement to pontificate (some said inappropriately) on the morality of the "leg shows" themselves, reflecting in his speech the concerns of the emergent conservative elements of California society. In his estimation, Judge Deady felt that *The Black Crook* and its variations were entirely unfit for the stage.

> The principal part and attraction of the spectacle seems to be the exhibition of women in novel dress or undress, or in striking attitudes or action. The closing scene is called Paradise and consists . . . of "women lying about loose" [in] imitation grottoes . . . . To call such a spectacle a "dramatic composition" is an abuse of language. An exhibition of . . . a menagerie of wild beasts might as well be called a dramatic composition and claim to be entitled to copyright. A menagerie is an interesting spectacle, and so may this be, but it is nothing more . . . . It cannot be denied that this spectacle of *The Black Crook* merely panders to the prurient curiosity of very questionable exhibitions of the female person.

Ruling that a pilfered, immoral script was unworthy of copyright protection, Judge Deady dismissed both complaints. Unsurprisingly, however, the legal opinion of the judge had little impact on the popularity of the leg shows overall, and they continued to be an audience favorite for years.

Meanwhile, these and similar shows had public critics in numbers as impressive as those of their sprawling casts. Old

California was home to a lively corps of theater reviewers, and San Francisco had a handful of newspapers that focused exclusively on show business news and criticism, such as the *Daily Critic*, *Figaro*, and the *Dramatic Review*. In 1865, a pair of teenage brothers, Charles and Michael DeYoung, founded the *Daily Dramatic Chronicle*, which eventually transformed into the more traditional *San Francisco Chronicle*, which today remains the only major daily paper in the city.

While most reviews served up the standard fare of begrudging approval, the most interesting critiques were the sarcastic and out-and-out caustic ones. On October 29, 1854, the *Golden Era*, another San Francisco newspaper primarily devoted to the arts, offered this potent assessment: "During the week, large audiences attended the disgustingly vulgar and demoralizing performances of a troupe of gentlemen (!) styling themselves 'Christy's Minstrels.' No truly moral community should patronize such people. Vulgarity is their forte."

The king of the acid reviewers was Ambrose Bierce, the trenchant editor of the satirical magazine *The Wasp* from 1881 to 1885. Bierce was a prolific short story writer, journalist, and poet, and a professional scold. For the *Wasp*, he wrote a column entitled "Prattle," which provided a forum for his fiery opinions on many subjects, including the theater.

In 1882, Bierce sharpened his knives to skewer the attitudes and lectures of Oscar Wilde, the outrageous English poet and playwright who, at twenty-eight years old, was already a cultural phenomenon in Europe. A leader in the aesthetic and decadence movements that fascinated the literati, Wilde was engaged to give a series of lectures in the United States during the first few months of 1882, and when he arrived in New York in January, his performances were met with a mixture of acclaim from his fans and curiosity and puzzlement from the newly aware.

Ambrose Bierce was not impressed. In the January 27, 1882, edition of the *Wasp*, Bierce sneered that Wilde was a "pigeon-breasted, spindle-shanked apostle of the nineteenth-century renaissance of bosh [nonsense]" whose writings and utterances were "intellectual pabulum particularly suited for weak and disordered minds." Wilde arrived in San Francisco in March 1882, and Bierce unleashed his harshest jibes following Oscar's lecture entitled "Art Decoration! Being the Practical Application of the Esthetic Theory to Everyday Home Life and Art Ornamentation!" In his "Prattle" column of March 31, Bierce unloaded on the man he called the "sovereign of insufferables": "The ineffable dunce has nothing to say and says it . . . . There never was an impostor so hateful, a blockhead so stupid, a crank so variously and offensively daft." Bierce lambasted what he saw as "the limpid and spiritless vacuity of this intellectual jelly-fish . . . with a knowledge that would equip an idiot to dispute with a cast-iron dog, an eloquence to qualify him for the duties of caller on a hog-ranch, and imagination adequate to the conception of a tomcat when fired by contemplation of a fiddle-string."

o   o   o

As it did many other aspects of California life, the general reform impulse that swept the state following the height of the Gold Rush targeted show business. As communities grew more conservative and family-oriented, some Californians attempted to cast off the state's no-holds-barred, laissez-faire reputation and become more socially constrained, as had been the pattern codified earlier on the East Coast. Old California had fewer rules and looser standards than other parts of the United States, but there was no denying that the winds of change had arrived. A prime example was an 1858 state statute, called "An Act for the Better Observance of the Sabbath," that mandated that

> no person, or persons, shall, on the Christian Sabbath, or Sunday, keep open any store, warehouse, mechanic shop, work-shop, banking-house, manufacturing establishment, or other business house, for business purposes; and no person or persons shall sell, or expose for sale, any goods, wares, or merchandise on the Christian Sabbath, or Sunday.

This legislation was commonly referred to as the "Sunday Closing Law" or the "Sunday Blue Law," and it reflected similar legislation that had been enacted in colonial British America and the early days of the Republic. The law was patently discriminatory, particularly toward Jewish merchants, who closed shop on Saturday, the Jewish sabbath, but remained open on Sunday, the Christian sabbath. The act also threatened theatrical productions that depended on Sunday audiences. In 1858, the California Supreme Court struck down the Sunday Closing Law in the decision of *Ex Parte Newman*. The ruling argued that the law violated the state constitution's commitment that "the free exercise and enjoyment of religious profession and worship, without discrimination or preference, shall be forever allowed in the state."

In 1861, the 1858 Sunday Closing Law reappeared in almost identical form with a slightly adjusted title. Now called "An Act for the Observance of the Sabbath," it provided some exceptions but was largely the same as the previous legislation. This time around, the 1861 law was repeatedly upheld in the courts, which concluded that it was not aimed at religious discrimination but was an appropriate and necessary civic regulation properly applying state police powers. It would remain on the books for the next twenty-one years, and although enforcement was spotty overall, some jurisdictions applied the law enthusiastically. In 1873, the rural farm town of Woodland, near Sacramento, noted that on Sunday "every saloon in town as well as every store (drugstores excepted) being closed . . . the streets presented a quiet and Christian like appearance and the churches were well filled." From the act's passage through 1882, the Central California coastal town of San Luis Obispo continually issued threats that anyone conducting business on Sunday would be subject to arrest and prosecution.

Other communities viewed the legislation as unwarranted interference with private religious beliefs and practices and simply ignored it. In 1882, reports from Bakersfield, in Kern County, and from San Andreas, the county seat of Calaveras

County, bluntly stated that no attempts had been made to enforce the law within their boundaries.

In San Francisco, the theatrical hub of California, "An Act for the Observance of the Sabbath" was not firmly enforced for years. Most residents echoed the sentiments expressed by an editorial published in the *Daily Dramatic Chronicle* of March 6, 1867:

> It does [San Franciscans] more good to go to Hayes Park, or the Cliff House, or Bay View, or to take a trip to Oakland, and enjoy themselves according to their tastes and inclinations than to go to church . . . . The church-goers enjoy the liberty of acting according to their own convictions and tastes; . . . let the theater-goer possess the same liberty.

San Francisco theater owners and managers routinely defied the law by presenting Sunday shows, and occasionally they were arrested. Usually, the owners were found guilty and, after promising not to break the law in the future, they were fined a few dollars and released. The law was not a serious deterrent to show business.

That said, the Sunday Closing Law had a larger role across California as a whole, and in 1882 General George Stoneman, the Democratic candidate for governor, won an overwhelming victory on a campaign platform that included abolishing the 1861 legislation. In 1883, the state legislature repealed the act, making California the first state to eliminate legal prohibitions on Sunday business.

Other laws attempted to disrupt the entertainment industry from other angles. In April 1879, the City of San Francisco issued an ordinance prohibiting "the personification of any scriptural character upon the stage of any theatre," a rule that would apply to Passion plays, oratorios, or any other Biblical exhibitions. Traditionalist San Franciscans and likeminded civic leaders considered these productions to be uncomfortably emotional at best and blasphemous at worst. What they might not have predicted was that this decree would lead to one of the more bizarre detentions in nineteenth-century California history.

In the spring of 1879, *The Passion Play* was offered at the Baldwin Theatre under the direction of impresario David Belasco. Written by Salmi Morse, the production was a straightforward depiction of the last days of Jesus. It had played previously in the City by the Bay and starred the Irish actor James O'Neill as Jesus. The play was, in the words of theater historian Edmond Gagey, "dull, devout, didactic, and completely innocuous," but it was troublesome for some influential citizens and was in fact part of the argument that led to the passage of the city ordinance in April 1879.

A few weeks after the law was instated, however, *The Passion Play* was revived for Easter, with O'Neill once again portraying Jesus. The play was now in direct defiance of the new city prohibition on religious productions, and James O'Neill, taking the fall as the leading actor, was arrested and fined $50 for violating the ordinance. (Other cast members were fined far less.) When O'Neill refused to pay the fine, he was sent to jail; since he had by that time become so closely identified with his role, some members of the public acted as if Jesus himself had been incarcerated. The validity of the prohibition was tested in court and upheld, and *The Passion Play* closed. James O'Neill appealed his fine and jail sentence but then had a change of heart and paid the penalty.

o   o   o

For all the fuss over performers, producers, and the content they put out into the world, let us not forget about the critical role audiences played in the growing entertainment industry. In some memorable instances, they caused as much drama as the people on stage. In certain venues, attending a performance became akin to a contact sport when raucous and drunken patrons felt inspired to let others known they were dissatisfied with an act. In 1853, Scottish visitor and artist John David Borthwick was staying in a Nevada City hotel that adjoined

a theater offering a production of Shakespeare's *Richard III.*
Through the thin walls of his hotel room, he "could hear every
word as distinctly as if [he] had been in the stage-box."

> After King Richard was disposed of, the orchestra, which
> seemed to consist of two fiddles, favoured us with a very
> miscellaneous piece of music. There was then an interlude
> performed by the audience, hooting, yelling, whistling,
> and stamping their feet; and that being over, the curtain
> rose [and the entertainment continued].

Disorderly behavior was far from the norm, however. Usually, theatergoers expected, even demanded, respect for the
players. While Old Californians jealously guarded their rights
to independently judge and criticize performers, there were
societal standards to be maintained. While they might hoot
and holler in delight or displeasure, most were not rough and
uncultured but products of Victorian upbringings and therefore expected a certain decorum in the theater, particularly in
the form of virtuous language and behavior both on stage and
from the audience.

One well-known account of acceptable comportment was presented in the 1856 book *Men and Memories of San Francisco* by
Theodore Barry and Benjamin Patten. It tells of a miner recently
arrived in San Francisco from the farmlands of the Midwest
who innocently removes his jacket in the theater. As Barry
and Patten reported, the other patrons "detected this breach
of etiquette before the offender had seated himself, and there
arose from the sky-critics such a yell of derision that the words
upon the stage were drowned. The actors ceased for a moment,
entirely unconscious of the cause, supposing the tumult would
subside; but . . . the bumpkin culprit . . . sat, gaping at the gallery, wondering why the show didn't go on." Finally, after many
catcalls and cries of "Shirtsleeves! Shirtsleeves!" the target realized his mistake and donned his jacket. "The yell of triumph
that arose from the [gallery] 'gods' in their joyful sense of victory," Barry and Patten continued, "was beyond the description

of tongue or pen. The play proceeded, and the dignity of San Francisco dress-circle etiquette was established."

o o o

Despite efforts to thwart Californians' pursuit of a good time, the state was developing into a veritable three-ring circus in the land of make-believe. Popular celebrities certainly held their sway, but it was the outliers—those showcasing unconventional stagecraft, distinctive talents, unusual gifts, and unpredictable actions—that provided the exquisite panache of Old Californian theatromania. The most exhilarating acts were the quirkiest—part vaudeville, part sideshow, part honky-tonk, part extravaganza—and together they forged California's reputation as a harbor for the weird and whimsical.

Dr. C. H. Bassett offered his Equestrian Circus, featuring the acrobatic daredevil Walter Aymar, who would leap from one galloping horse to another. The pageant included a young equestrienne marvel known only as Little Lottie; William Alexander, a contortionist on horseback; and Mrs. A. P. Durand, with her trick dogs, talking horses, and trained ponies. In 1862, Professor G. A. Belew advertised himself as the "Great American Hippozaneapprivoiser," or an expert in the "Science of Horsemanship." Belew would use his alleged telepathic powers to humble the wildest horses and bulls in the country, and in one performance in Sacramento he promised to "thoroughly tame one of the most vicious horses in the state, . . . a wild brute which created such consternation among the Vaqueros." After the admission prices were collected and Belew had solicited an additional $5 (about $150 today) from anyone who wished private lessons, a horse was trotted into the arena. As one observer noted, the animal was not a snorting stallion but a three- or four-year-old mare that "was not by any means a very wild animal" but that Professor Belew dramatically "subdued" nonetheless.

The "King of the Marathon Horse Riders" was Jack Powers. In 1858, Powers would attempt to ride 150 miles in under eight

hours on the Union Course racetrack in San Francisco, a feat
that was considered next to impossible, especially when using
supposedly inferior California horses. Bets were taken, and Powers was expected to receive at least $2,500 (about $75,000 in
today's economy) if successful. Twenty-four horses were made
available, and an eager crowd numbering in the thousands was
in attendance. When the race began, Powers rode at top speed
the entire distance; the farthest any single horse was ridden was
four miles, and the least was one mile. On dismounting, Powers
would stretch his legs for a few seconds and then vault onto the
saddle of a waiting horse.

All was going according to plan and Powers was well ahead
of schedule when something disturbing happened during
mile 130. Powers began spitting up blood and complaining of
abdominal distress and weakness in his legs. It appeared that the
rider was done for and would be unable to complete his journey.
Immediately, wagers against Powers skyrocketed. But it was all
subterfuge. The blood that observers had seen was from a small
sheep's bladder Powers had secreted in his mouth and bitten
into at the most opportune moment. Powers's friends, who were
in on the plot, urged him on in dramatic fashion, pleading with
him not to surrender to the pain, and seeing the concern on the
faces of these confederates, the unsuspecting dupes in the audience increased the volume and amount of their bets . . . only to
have Jack Powers complete the 150 miles with more than an
hour to spare. A *Sacramento Union* correspondent reported that
the rider came in "perfectly fresh" and "[made] an extra mile
in two minutes and twenty-eight seconds, to display his condition." With the last-minute side bets, Jack Powers pocketed a
cool $10,000 that day (or roughly $300,000).

Feats of strength and skill were always a hit with audiences,
and circus acts were a real crowd-pleaser. Tightrope walker Rosa
Celeste was a favorite in the goldfields in the mid-1860s, and
the highlight of her act came when she crossed the rope while
pushing a wooden wheelbarrow. For dramatic effect, she would
feign losing her balance and seem in imminent danger of falling. On one occasion, in the mining camp of Rough and Ready,

in Nevada County, a concerned audience member rushed forward to catch her should she fall. Rosa Celeste did not fall, but the wheelbarrow did, and it toppled onto the poor man waiting below. His head poked through the bottom, making it look like he was wearing the wheelbarrow as a collar. In 1880, historians and prolific book publishers Thomas Hinckley Thompson and Albert Augustus West recounted in their *History of Nevada County*, "The man suffered no injury but what ... a few drinks of whiskey could repair."

o   o   o

The melting pot of California attracted performers from all around the world. In San Francisco, a young Australian garnered a following due to his prowess with a boomerang. As Theodore Barry and Benjamin Patten recounted in their book *Men and Memories of San Francisco*, the youthful Aussie "became known as adept in casting the mysterious missile ... and he was often hired by people to see the *modus operandi*." A crowd would tail him as he walked to nearest wide-open space, and "his audience would increase until the number afforded a very nice little contribution, when, subsequent to the performance, the hat was passed around." Upon seeing the crowds that gathered in this spot semi-regularly, two tavern keepers named Langley and Griffiths opened an alehouse nearby. Naturally, they called their establishment "The Boomerang."

In 1860, a mysterious attraction appeared briefly in San Francisco. Called the "Gorgeous Mongolian Spectacle," the entertainers purported to be from the Celestial Company of Chinese Dramatists, who had "repeatedly performed before the Emperor of China," or so their advertisement claimed. They were passing through the city, they pronounced, on their way to Paris for a command performance before the Imperial Court of Louis Napoleon. No one was quite sure if this was true, but audiences leapt at the chance to see a show that promised "Scenes, Combats, the most Magnificent Processions, Battles, & c. (in which the mystic realities of the Chinese Mythology and Superstitions will be illustrated), Vaulting, Transformations, and all that is typical of the Chinese Character and Magnificence of Costume." Tickets were $10 (about $300 today). After the show completed its three-day run at Maguire's Opera House, it was widely agreed that the Gorgeous Mongolian Spectacle was neither gorgeous nor spectacular. According to author Lois M. Foster in *Annals of the San Francisco Stage, 1850–1880*, each second-rate performance was met with a combination of vulgar derision and uproarious laughter. It was generally assumed that the Chinese troupe were in fact "long-time local favorites with refurbished advertising."

A more impressive act, Monsieur D'Evani was a contortionist who billed himself as "The India Rubber Man" for performances throughout Northern California. The *Daily Alta California* reported that D'Evani "possesses the power of assuming with his body every imaginable shape and appearance . . . . He appears to have annihilated the regular and natural actions of the muscles, so that no posture is impossible for him to take at will." The newspaper speculated that Monsieur D'Evani was "half Frenchman and half eel." (He was, in fact, born John Evans in England.)

When it comes to stage names, not all were as innocuous as the change from Evans to D'Evani. In the early 1880s, P. T. Barnum brought to the United States a Russian sideshow performer named Fyodor Yevtishchev (sometimes spelled Fedor Jeftichew). Only sixteen years old at the time, Yevtishchev had a medical condition called hypertrichosis that led to excessive hair growth on his face. Barnum promoted Fyodor as "Jo-Jo, the Dog-Faced Boy," and within a few years, Jo-Jo was famous. He never performed in California, but the comic act known as "Lorraine and Jo-Jo, the Dog-Faced Dog" capitalized on his popularity in the state. As the *Los Angeles Herald* reported in 1896, "An element of fun is neatly brought into play when the little sky-terrier, Jo-Jo, or as Mr. Lorraine calls him, the dog-faced dog, barks loudly and interrupts a speech which his master is attempting to make to the audience. The entire act is full of life and fun."

Perhaps the most famous animal attraction to come through California was the "Mountaineer Museum," staged in a basement on Clay Street in San Francisco and operated by a hunter, trapper, and wild animal collector named John Adams. Adams, a forty-niner and transplanted Massachusetts shoemaker, was known by all as Grizzly Adams.

Adams used extensive advertising to attract visitors to his "rare collection of animals," and posters, broadsides, and newspaper notices were omnipresent, particularly near his Barbary Coast location throughout the museum's years of operation, from 1856 to 1860. Guests were promised bears of all species and sizes, plus elk, eagles, lions, tigers, cougars, an "enormous hog," and an extensive taxidermy display. Newspaper editor Theodore H. Hittell noticed one of the posters, visited the museum, and described the lair in the introduction to his 1860 hagiographic biography of Adams entitled *The Adventures of James Capen Adams, Mountaineer and Grizzly Bear Hunter of California*:

> Descending the stairway, I found a remarkable spectacle. The basement was a large one but with a low ceiling, and dark and dingy in appearance. In the middle, chained to the floor, were two large grizzly bears, which [were named] Benjamin Franklin and Lady Washington . . . . Not far off on one side, likewise fastened with chains, were seven other bears, several of them young grizzlies, three or four black bears, and one a cinnamon. Near the front of the apartment . . . were haltered two large elks. Further back was a row of cages, containing cougars and other California animals . . . . At the rear, in a very large iron cage, was the monster grizzly Samson. He was an immense creature weighing some three-quarters of a ton.

And at the center of the attraction was a middle-aged man "dressed in coat and pantaloons of buckskin, fringed at the edges and along the seams of arms and legs. On his head he wore a cap of deerskin, ornamented with a fox-tail, and on his feet buckskin

moccasins." As Hittell deduced, it was "Adams, the proprietor—
quite as strange as any of his animals."

Similar displays in other venues throughout the state offered
visitors a peek at even more exotic creatures. For one week in
1863, the Eureka Theater in San Francisco exhibited what they
trumpeted as "The Mammoth Crocodile, the Greatest Natural Living Curiosity Ever on the Pacific Coast." Charles Tibbetts, the theater manager, confirmed "this monster is over 17
feet, and its weight is over 2,000 pounds. He was captured by
Prof. Geo. Nutter, in the River Nile." As an extra attraction, the
gigantic beast would be accompanied by its "Youthful Progeny."
Price of admission: a mere twenty-five cents. Visitors with even a
passing acquaintance with natural history noted that the "mammoth crocodile" looked more like a large alligator, yet another
reminder of the old adage *Caveat emptor.*

o   o   o

Other deceptions were far more obvious, and it was, in fact,
the point of the act. Gender-bending routines were fashionable
during this time, and both female and male impersonators were
frequent fixtures on stage. The female impersonators often sang
and danced, but they were mostly judged on the verisimilitude of
their womanly behaviors. The most successful female impersonators replicated the sentimental and comfortable-to-Victorian-
sensibilities virtues of femininity, refinement, and coquettish-
ness. The leading female impersonator of the age was Eugene
D'Amilie, known on stage as Master Eugene; he was promi-
nently advertised as a featured performer for Christy's Minstrels
during the Gold Rush era and earned glowing reviews. Typical
was this appraisal from the *Sacramento Union* of July 29, 1858:
"Master Eugene did great execution as a dancer and vocalist.
The manner in which he sang [as a woman] brought down the
house, and was an excellent carricature imitation of that lady's
peculiarities."

On style of female impersonation that especially charmed
audiences in Old California was when a performer alternated

between female and male personas. In 1894, the *Sacramento Union* reported on Frank Belton, "a new female impersonator who is a surprise and has excited much interest. He 'makes up' cunningly, and sings a duet—so to speak—sustaining the parts of a baritone and a soprano in a manner amusing and surprising."

One the other side of the coin, two of the most highly regarded male impersonators were the English "vocal comedienne" Tina Corri and the energetic Zelma Rawlston, who had her own touring company. In 1900, the *San Francisco Call* noted the frenetic nature of Rawlston's act: "Her 'lightning changes' are made with unparalleled alacrity from morning dress to a yachtsman's afternoon neglige, and from that to what the lady novelists call 'faultless' evening dress. Her voice is good, her songs clever, her wardrobe, . . . her walk and 'business' manly to a turn."

Of course, the Bateman Children—sisters Kate and Ellen—also performed as grown men with mustaches and were two of the most popular child stars of the time. There were also many other acts featuring children, whether solo, as with Lotta Crabtree, or in troupes, some of which could be quite large. A favorite was Marsh's Juvenile Comedians, an ensemble of thirty children, mostly girls, ranging in age from five to fifteen. The performers sang, danced, and, most famously, formed *tableaux vivants*, recreating scenes from Shakespeare, classical literature, foreign cultures, and legend. An audience favorite was "Naiads in Their Retreat," in which "the Nymphs of the Blue Waters are discovered disporting themselves amid the waves in the Bath of Beauty, sheltered by grottoes and shell work, where the Naiads float around amid strains of enchanted music."

o   o   o

Switching gears entirely, from stage to sport, one of the most fascinating amusements of the period has been largely forgotten today: pedestrianism. Participants in this athletic endeavor were the superstar athletes of the mid-to-late nineteenth century, and

Pedestrianism—a mostly forgotten sport akin to today's race walking—was so ingrained in nineteenth-century California popular culture that it became a compelling subject for graphic artists who created works such as this lithograph entitled "The Pedestrian," produced by the San Francisco publishers Pettit and Russ, c. 1879. Library of Congress Prints and Photographs Division, Digital ID: LC-DIG-pga-07850.

they were the subjects of hagiographies and trading cards much like today's baseball cards.

The concept of pedestrianism was quite simple but featured several variants. The basic form is speed walking, with techniques ranging from the fancy heel-and-toe method of contemporary Olympic race walking to a more straightforward form of fast hiking across country. Some pedestrian matches were torturous marathons with racers battling each other until all but one had collapsed. In other contests, participants would attempt to walk a certain distance in a certain time, for instance, one hundred miles in three days. Wagers were made, and the competitor would be paid only upon successful completion of the undertaking. Sometimes, additional tasks would be required while walking, such as pushing a wheelbarrow, pulling a wagon, or, in one odd case, gathering stones in a basket.

The maestro of California pedestrians was James "Uncle Jimmy" Kennovan. He was lionized for his gumption, endurance, and persistence; one admirer described Uncle Jimmy as "a man of undying energy, wonderful powers of endurance, and unequalled in the world . . . . His presence of mind and coolness in times of peril seem to be admirably adapted to his physical abilities." The *San Francisco Daily National* of March 11, 1859, was less laudatory and more succinct: "Kennovan is a queer little fellow."

James Kennovan had many followers who were delighted when, in 1863, author J. A. Woodson published *Life and Adventures of James Kennovan, Champion Pedestrian of the World.* Part biography, part training manual, and part chronology of Kennovan's races, the book was esteemed by pedestrianism enthusiasts. It listed Kennovan's "22 Rules of Exercise," which included these helpful hints:

> Rule 9: *Above all things* in exercise never wear a *tight belt.*
> Rule 17: Learn to breathe with the mouth closed.
> Rule 20: Food and drink should not be taken very cold, neither very hot or warm . . . . Avoid rich spiced stews, greasy concoctions, [and] pot pies.

But the extraordinary aspect of *Life and Adventures of James Kennovan, Champion Pedestrian of the World* was its list of the results of the numerous and often dangerous pedestrianism competitions Uncle Jimmy had entered over his many years in the sport. For instance, from August 1856 to March 1857, the then forty-three-year-old Kennovan participated in the following:

> *August 1856 in Sacramento* – Kennovan won a race of 90 non-stop hours.
>
> *September 1856 in Marysville, Yuba County* – Kennovan prevailed in a contest of 101 consecutive hours.
>
> *November 1856 in Oroville, Butte County* – Uncle Jimmy raced 100 hours "without rest or sleep."
>
> *December 1856 in San Francisco* – James Kennovan clashed in a large indoor auditorium against other pedestrians in a marathon race—Kennovan won after 106 ¼ hours. One of his competitors "sunk" after 42 hours and was carted to the hospital with his feet bleeding profusely.
>
> *December 1856 in Sacramento* – Kennovan was victorious in a marathon race after 106 ½ hours.
>
> *January 1857 in Sonora, Tuolumne County* – James Kennovan won after 101 non-stop hours. He was presented a large gold medal which was promptly stolen.
>
> *February 1857 in Columbia, Tuolumne County* – triumphed in a 106 hours race.
>
> *March 1857 in Mokelumne Hill, Calaveras County* – Kennovan competed in but was not the victor of a 62 hours competition. Uncle Jimmy was suffering from a cold and rheumatism and he completed the last eighteen miles on crutches.

In 1859, in a moment that perfectly encapsulates the intersection of the eccentric and extraordinary in Old California entertainment, Uncle Jimmy Kennovan proposed staging a public spectacle in association with Grizzly Adams. Kennovan suggested that Adams put him in a cage with a live and unrestrained mountain lion and bear, and the cage would then be paraded through the streets of San Francisco to promote Adams's Mountaineer Museum. In return, Uncle Jimmy, who was at that point essentially destitute, would receive handsome compensation for the deed. Grizzly Adams wholeheartedly agreed to the promotion, and with this "piece of recklessness," as it was called in *Life and Adventures of James Kennovan, Champion Pedestrian of the World*, Uncle Jimmy "accomplished much, to his own pecuniary assistance and to Adams' delight."

At the conclusion of the stunt, and only a few seconds after Kennovan left the cage, the bear attacked one of Adams's helpers and tore off the man's right arm.

"Spirit photography" was one popular humbug that netted the naive during the latter half of the nineteenth century. These photographs purporting to show the ghosts or spirits of the deceased were created with the easily executed techniques of double exposure and superimposition. Even obviously staged photos, such as "The Haunted Lane" from 1889, shown above, were often enough to hook the gullible and the grieving. "The Haunted Lane," Chicago: Merlander, 1889. Library of Congress Prints and Photographs Division, Digital ID: cph 3a49425u.

CHAPTER EIGHT

Hornswogglers, Honey-Foglers,
and Humbugs

SCOUNDRELS AND CHARLATANS

Ozing smarmy self-confidence, radiating counterfeit
sincerity, and tendering bogus guarantees can be very
lucrative. Fleecing the naive has been omnipresent in
California since the days of Mexican dominion, and even today
it remains a worrying and seemingly unrelenting threat. In
2018, a survey ranked California as the state most vulnerable
to fraud and first in the highest dollar amount lost per capita to
online deception.

Such statistics may not be pleasant, but they shouldn't be surprising; hucksters, con artists, and grifters have always wandered
amongst us, although perhaps using different techniques and
going by different names. In the nineteenth century, they were
branded "hornswogglers," "slumguzzlers," "mountebanks,"
and "honey-foglers," and their deceits, hoaxes, and scams were
routinely dubbed "humbugs." These swindlers did not dis-
criminate, as everyone could be a target, from the humblest

forty-niners struggling to pan just enough gold to return home to the wealthiest barons of a skyrocketing economy, whose extravagance and hubris made them ripe for the picking. Willing victims seemed remarkably easy to find. As Ambrose Bierce, the sarcastically inventive author of *The Devil's Dictionary*, wrote in the 1880s of one popular scheme, the definition of "clairvoyant" was "a person ... who has the power of seeing that which is invisible to the patron, namely, that he is a blockhead." In 1894, English physician and editor Ernest Abraham Hart memorably labeled these dupes "The Eternal Gullible."

Seeking to gain a personal edge or simply to rip off an impressionable sucker was a tendency ingrained in Old California. So widespread was conning that the first state constitution in 1849 attempted to identify and punish fraud, deception, and misrepresentation. However, the 1849 charter was notorious for being unclear and imprecise, and the document in fact housed only one narrow remedy to fraud. The earliest state legislatures attempted to rectify this shortcoming with many statutes defining and redefining fraud, but uncertainty (and loopholes) remained until, in 1872, mirroring the persuasive New York model, California enacted more serviceable and comprehensive versions of its Penal Code, Civil Code, Code of Civil Procedure, and Political Code. In 1879, the new state constitution was predicated on the concept of "the more detail, the better," and in the years that followed, California expanded to 29 codes, ranging from the Business and Professions Code to the Welfare and Institutions Code. All told, there are now 1,883 sections in the current codes dealing with fraud, deception, misrepresentation, and misinformation. But even the most savvy government cannot legislate against gullibility.

In 1850, two brazen charlatans descended upon Gold Country, offering trusting souls the fantasies of easily obtaining two precious resources: gold and water. The first trickster was the redoubtable Robert Fletcher, who arrived in Sonora, Tuolumne County, in September to demonstrate his wonderful "Goldometer," an impressive device that was purported to flawlessly indicate the presence of gold where none was expected. Several spectators testified to the effectiveness of the device, and two men from the crowd agreed to test the Goldometer further. Six days later, they reported that the apparatus worked perfectly, and, as the *Daily Alta California* reported, the two deeply impressed product testers stated that "the Goldometer has generally been relied upon," and they "passe[d] a high compliment on the inventor, Mr. Fletcher."

Within days, many of the expensive Goldometers had been sold, most after Fletcher had hurriedly left town, but as the purchasers soon discovered, the Goldometer did not work. Some of the victims yearned to confront the two solemn witnesses who had endorsed the doodad, eager to ask them why the gadget was now suddenly inoperable, but of course the two men, Fletcher's confederates, had skedaddled.

The second visitor arrived in Sonora less than a month after Robert Fletcher had departed. His name was Professor Alberto Gabrialdo Turonski and he claimed to have fashioned an improved version of Fletcher's Goldometer. The good professor called his upgrade the "Patent Hydro Electro Magnetic Goldometer," and he said it would not only find gold but also produce copious amounts of water, even rainstorms, from the same location. As the *Sacramento Transcript* described, the Patent Hydro Electro Magnetic Goldometer "requires no manual labor to put it in motion or to aid it in its operations; it has but to be carried from one place to another until the indication of gold is had—then placing it, level six inches from the ground, it commences its wonderful operations, and ceases from it not until its labor is completed."

Despite their recent unfortunate history with Goldometers, Sonora residents purchased several of Professor Turonski's gizmos, and he continued to tour throughout the mining districts offering his magical contraption to willing buyers. The *Sacramento Transcript* was not captivated, calling it a "grand humbug," which it soon became obvious it was.

Still other hopeful forty-niners secured "gold-saving machines" before heading to California. The devices—possessing such curious names as "Bruce's Hydro-Centrifugal Chrysolyte" and "Buffum's Eldorado and Scientific Gold Sifter, Separator, and Safe Depositor"—were of various sizes and extravagance, but all had the same purpose: to extract gold, with as little labor as possible, from sand, dirt, and gravel. In theory, a miner would shovel dirt and rock into the bulky contrivance, add water, and turn a crank, and then the machine would do all the work of obtaining and packaging the gold into bottles. The only problem was that these expensive "gold-saving" thingamabobs were useless. The end result? No gold, just a messy box full of sludge.

o　o　o

The California Gold Rush was a particularly fruitful time for scoundrels, when dreams of instant wealth meant people were more vulnerable to being bamboozled. The swindles and tricks assumed many different forms in Old California, each designed for the time and place. One scam popular in the goldfields was called "claim salting," in which a person would deliberately and fraudulently alter a mining claim to make it appear richer than it was, and then sell the claim to a clueless victim. In most cases, a shotgun was the preferred method of "salting" the soil; one blast could effectively broadcast gold dust throughout a patch of unproductive ground, and since shotguns were common in the area, the sound would not arouse suspicion—or at least it didn't at first.

As more miners became aware of this subterfuge technique, the fraudsters came up with more sophisticated and stealthy techniques. Hornswogglers would use sleight of hand and distraction to deposit gold in all forms, including loose flakes or filings from gold coins dropped to the ground via a hole in a pants pocket, gold dust mixed with tobacco ashes that fell to the dirt as the con artist emptied his pipe bowl, or nuggets enveloped in mud that could be surreptitiously daubed onto a shovel blade. The unscrupulous would place a few flecks into their hatband and, while doffing said cap in respect (and with a few subtle shakes), allow the gold dust to fall.

In his 1872 classic *Roughing It*, Mark Twain chronicled a salting scam he had observed throughout California and Nevada.

> Every man you met had his new mine to boast of, and his "specimens" ready; and if the opportunity offered, he would infallibly back you into a corner and offer as a favor to you, not to him, to part with just a few feet in the "Golden Age," or the "Sarah Jane," or some other unknown stack of croppings . . . . Then he would fish a piece of rock out of his pocket, and after looking mysteriously around as if he feared he might be waylaid and robbed if caught with such wealth in his possession, he would dab the rock against his tongue, clap an eyeglass to it, and exclaim: "Look at that! Right there in that red dirt! See it? See the specks of gold? . . . There's a hundred thousand tons like that in sight! Right in sight, mind you!"

Twain noted that the exuberant miner would then pull out a ragged assay sheet showing the rock was very high grade indeed. Urging the purchaser to act fast, the con artist quite frequently succeeded in getting the wide-eyed innocent to purchase a piece of the big bonanza, sight unseen. The seller would then disappear with his ill-gotten gains, never to be seen again. As Twain recalled: "I little knew, then, that the custom was to hunt out the richest piece of rock and get it assayed! Very often, that piece, the size of a filbert, was the only fragment in a ton that had a particle of metal in it—and yet the assay made it pretend to represent the average value of the ton of rubbish it came from!"

Occasionally, an entire mining camp would be involved in the salting sting, especially when a claim was "played out." Buyers were understandably skeptical when presented with an offer too good to be true, and so the camp residents, in anticipation of such resistance, would arrange for an impartial expert to evaluate the claim. Little did the prey know that the "expert" had already been salted with a bribe. The unwise men who fell for this dodge were, as the mining historian Otis Young observed, "unworthy of pity," as they should have known better. In considering the pervasiveness of claim salting in Old California, Thomas A. Rickard, a California mine superintendent in the 1880s and later the editor of the three most influential mining journals published in the nineteenth century, put it best, recommending that a prospective gold seeker, "when about to examine a mine [to purchase,] should write *caveat emptor* on the first page of his notebook."

Another familiar confidence trick was called "selling the gold brick." Throughout California in the nineteenth century, it was common to hear of some fool who had purchased a "solid gold brick" that turned out to be mostly lead or brass. In March 1890, the *Los Angeles Herald* chronicled the following "gold brick swindle" in Nevada County:

David Parks, an elderly resident of the hydraulic mining town of Bloomfield, was approached one day by a stranger named Erwin, who claimed to know one of Parks's sons and presented himself as the former chaplain of the Arizona Territorial Prison. Erwin related how he had been called to the bedside of a dying convict named Eastman. Eastman, with his last breath, confessed that he had robbed a stagecoach in Nevada County three years earlier and had buried part of the loot, a gold bar, near Bloomfield. Erwin told Parks that Eastman's brother wanted to find the gold bar and sell it to the United States Mint, as he (Eastman's brother) needed $1,500 (about $42,000 in today's money) immediately for a business venture. To facilitate that, Eastman's brother had authorized Erwin to engage someone who could find the bar *and also* loan him $1,500 as soon as it was found. That person was respected community elder David Parks. Erwin outlined the plan: Once Parks found the gold bar, he (Parks) would send $1,500 to Eastman's brother—while still holding the gold bar as security—and then he (Parks) would be repaid, with interest, upon selling the gold bar to the Mint.

Parks agreed to the terms and searched for the buried bar. Following clues provided to Erwin by Eastman's brother, he found the bar after considerable effort and took it to Erwin. Erwin chopped off a corner of the bar and gave it to Parks, who had the chunk tested by a jeweler. The sample was verified to be gold, and David Parks advanced Eastman's brother $1,500. Erwin told Parks that he (Erwin) had to leave to take Eastman's brother to meet a train in Petaluma, but he promised to return the next day. Once Erwin was back in Bloomfield, he said, he and Parks would immediately travel to San Francisco and sell the gold bar to the Mint. But Erwin never returned, and Parks became suspicious. He had the entire bar tested then, and it was revealed to be solid brass. Parks lodged a criminal complaint, but Erwin and Eastman's brother had disappeared. In reporting on the fiasco, the *Los Angeles Herald* passed harsh judgment on David Parks's gullibility in the most unflattering terms possible; the headline of the article read: "A Senile Sucker."

It was startling how quickly the term "selling a gold brick" entered the lexicon as a metaphor for being deceived. In 1898, the *San Francisco Call* reported on a brick-selling case involving Thomas Garrett, city editor for the competing *San Francisco Examiner*. In this case, the "gold brick" was a confession by an accused murderer named Albert Hoff. Garrett's motive was to secure a scoop in the sensational story. The transaction, secretly arranged by Hoff's attorney Benjamin W. McIntosh, was simple: pay up front and we will provide the confession. Of course, once the money changed hands and the confession was provided, the attorney would later deny the transaction ever took place. Albert Hoff was unaware of this plot and continued to proclaim his innocence.

The *Examiner* editor paid McIntosh $35 in company funds as a down payment for the "brick," and as the *Call* gleefully reported, "[The editor] not only squandered good money, but he made the man who swindled him his guest, entertaining him at expensive midnight dinners and paying the bills for costly wines that were consumed while the gold brick swindle was being consummated." Although McIntosh later denied it in court, he had sought an additional payday by claiming that Hoff was having second thoughts about the supposed confession, and so to convince his client to go ahead with the plan, the lawyer had demanded an additional $2,000 (about $62,000 today) or he and his client would reveal the scheme to the public.

In response to this threat, Thomas Garrett brought other *San Francisco Examiner* reporters and editors into his plan and they wined and dined this slippery customer. As Benjamin McIntosh later testified in court, the newspaper staff also offered liberal amounts of bad whiskey and possibly doped cigars to cloud McIntosh's judgment in hopes of keeping him on board with the charade but for a smaller payout.

As it happened, after the *Examiner* had expended countless hours and hundreds of dollars on banquets and bribes, Benjamin McIntosh would not deliver. As McIntosh put it, "I refused to talk about a confession with them and got away from them as quickly as I could." But that was not the end of the story for Hoff and McIntosh. Albert Hoff was eventually put on trial for murder anyway, convicted, and sentenced to death. When the bribery plot was exposed, Hoff received a second trial, was again found guilty, and was sentenced to life in Folsom Prison. For his role in the scheme, Benjamin McIntosh was disbarred and publicly labeled a "legal scalawag." The *San Francisco Examiner* brazenly asked the court to order reimbursement of their bribes, but the request was denied. Otherwise, it suffered no punishment beyond the embarrassment of having been stung by a modified version of the "gold brick swindle."

o   o   o

While some scams garner no sympathy on either side, others, at least from a distance, can be appreciated for their cleverness and cunning. Among the most widely enjoyed stories are those in which the worst offense is parting a wealthy fool from his money.

In California during the Gold Rush and the Gilded Age that followed, fast money was not only made in large amounts but encouraged to be spent in flamboyant fashion, and the conspicuous consumption was often shameless. Fortunes from gold, silver, railroads, stagecoaches, timber, finance, real estate, and cattle spawned the births of many *nouveau riche* hell bent on exhibiting their newfound affluence, and this arrogance and decadence made the wealthy classes a very attractive quarry for con artists who salivated at the chance to fleece those who would avoid public embarrassment at all costs, and hopefully very high costs. The moneyed targets were blackmailed or sold counterfeit goods or roped into huge investments or donations, sight unseen, or simply duped for whatever was in their pocketbooks. The parade of well-heeled suckers who were humiliated, hustled, or hoisted on their own petards was long and lively.

Some might say that the unabashed exhibitions of California Gilded Age riches were as criminal as the attempts to defraud them. As a few examples of the excesses of the very wealthy, we can look to the solid gold tea service (priced at $50,000 in 1853, or $1.5 million today) upon which Mary Garrison, wife of financier and San Francisco mayor Cornelius K. Garrison, served her guests at a civic reception. Or the pillowcases, which cost $70 each ($1,600 today) at the magnificent San Francisco mansion of William Sharon, president of the Bank of California. Or the fireplace mantle crafted from gold-bearing quartz that was installed in the new bank founded by the Bonanza Kings of the Comstock Lode. (The amount of money with which they started the venture remains the largest initial capital investment of a financial institution to date: $10 million in their time and $230 million in ours.) After the death of Central Pacific Railroad founder Collis P. Huntington in 1900, his widow, Arabella, lost in grief, decided to buy some art as a way of soothing her spirit, but upon leaving the art dealer with her purchase, she was quickly followed by a gallery employee racing to catch her departing carriage, for Mrs. Huntington had forgotten her handbag, which contained eleven pearl necklaces valued at more than $3.5 million, the equivalent of $108 million today.

Among the most dazzling and enduring displays of good fortune were the ornate Victorian mansions of the last quarter of the century. Historian Kenneth Naversen has called these elaborate residences the "unselfconscious élan of *Victoriana Pacifica*" and described the mammoth structures as "architectural expressions of the giddy, turbulent times in which they were born"— archetypes of "extraordinary effervescence."

The palaces of the extremely wealthy were potent symbols of the class divide in California, and as such they were also expressions of self-indulgent, unabashed personal power. Nowhere was this more evident than on the San Francisco hillside block bounded by California, Jones, Sacramento, and Taylor Streets. In 1855, Nicholas Yung, a mortuary proprietor who had come to California from his native Germany, purchased a then reasonably priced corner lot at the intersection of Sacramento and Taylor and built an unpretentious residence with stunning views of the Golden Gate, boomtown San Francisco, and the Berkeley Hills across the bay. For over twenty years, the Yungs lived quietly in their modest home, until the mid-1870s, when the neighborhood was discovered by the freshly minted railroad millionaires of Old California. Virtually overnight, the breathtaking location became San Francisco's most fashionable and desirable real estate, and the Central Pacific Railroad's "Big Four"—Leland Stanford, Mark Hopkins, Collis P. Huntington, and Charles Crocker—built lavish mansions on what soon was dubbed Nob Hill ("nob" being a shortened form of "nabob," a borrowed term used for the excessively wealthy).

It wasn't long before the Railroad Robber Barons were competing to construct the grandest palace. Charles Crocker bought the most elevated lot with the most splendid aspect. It covered most of the city block at the intersection of California and Taylor, save for the northeast corner, which was the property of Nicholas Yung. Crocker wanted Yung to sell, giving Crocker control of the entire block, and made several lowball offers to purchase Yung's property, but Yung refused. Crocker didn't take it lightly. It is rumored that when the Crocker land was being leveled in advance of construction, Crocker himself directed his workers to aim the airborne debris from the explosions toward Yung's house. Still, Nicholas Yung did not surrender.

In 1876, as the completion date drew near for Crocker's massive domicile—which featured a seventy-five-foot tower that lorded over the mansions of his business partners down the hill—Charles made one last unsuccessful offer to his neighbor. Rebuffed yet again, Crocker petulantly retaliated by constructing a forty-foot-tall wooden "spite fence" between his property and Yung's, effectively blocking Yung in on three sides and effectively obstructing the Yungs' view, sun, and sea breezes, turning the property into a stagnant, dark enclosure. The *San Francisco Chronicle* called Crocker's fence "the most famous memorial of malignity and malevolence in the city." Yung passed away in 1880, and Crocker died eight years after that, but the "ugliness of the lofty barricade" remained for another sixteen years, until 1904, when the Yung family finally sold their property to Crocker's heirs.

The palatial mansions of San Francisco's Nob Hill include those of Charles Crocker (labeled #3) and Collis P. Huntington (#4). Crocker's infamous "spite fence" is marked #7. "Panorama of San Francisco from California Street," photograph by Eadweard Muybridge, c. 1877. Library of Congress Prints and Photographs Division, Digital ID: LC-DIG-ppmsca-23775.

o   o   o

Among all this excess and entitlement, it is not surprising that the free-spending wealthy were favorite targets of tricksters of all types, including those of an "unearthly" variety.

The spiritualism movement of the nineteenth century was founded on the belief that spirits of the dead have not just the capacity but the penchant to communicate with the living, usually through a human intermediary called a "medium." Séances became a popular way for people to reunite with the dead, and some scholars of nineteenth-century social movements have concluded that, while not authentic in the way they advertised themselves to be, mediums provided a valuable service to their clientele via their unique way of linking religion, entertainment, and psychological therapy. Some early suffragists even found spiritualism to be advantageous to their own agendas, using the popularity of these spectacles to draw in audiences that might not otherwise be solely interested in information on voting rights for women. Spiritualism had its fair share of prominent supporters and converts, including Mary Todd Lincoln, Sir Arthur Conan Doyle, and Nobel laureate Pierre Curie, but many thought the movement, and séances in particular, were the purest humbug.

As proof of a bridge between the living and the dead, practitioners of spiritualism developed an assortment of tricks they presented as evidence; such "materializations" either stirred the true disciples or amused the cynics, who insisted it was all just so much claptrap. "Spirit photography" purported to capture the ghostly images of the dearly departed (often the photos were simply double exposures), and for those looking for tactile evidence of the afterlife, some mediums were known to expel, or "exteriorize," from their bodies a gauze-like substance they called "ectoplasm," which supposedly represented the "spiritual energy" of a dead relative. (Skeptics discovered it was nothing more than a well-rehearsed illusion, a magic trick, commonly created with cheesecloth.)

There was also "table-turning," in which furniture would move in different directions, or even hover, to indicate "yes" or "no" answers to questions asked by those gathered to speak to the dead. (Debunkers noted that this effect could be easily accomplished by mediums using their feet as levers under the legs of furniture pieces.)

In 1857, *Hutchings' Illustrated California Magazine* published the satirical article "Snudgger's Investigations into Table-turning," which lampooned the baroque and highly convoluted explanations spiritualists offered for these wonders. In the article, clueless sleuth Caleb Snudgger uses tortured logic to conclude that table-turning is the result of the mysterious and powerful "Odic Force," an unproven "life principle" that prominent chemist, geologist, and fellow of the Prussian Academy of Sciences Baron Carl von Reichenbach fruitlessly studied and named after the Norse god Odin. To accentuate the absurdity of spiritualism, the author of the piece has Caleb Snudgger continually refer to the power as the "Odious Force," which Snudgger insisted was "a more properer word."

Spiritualism provided endless fodder for cynics, but perhaps the most obvious ruse was the "full-form materialization" of the "spirit lover," an attraction that became very popular in late-nineteenth-century San Francisco. In his 1907 book *The Physical Phenomena of Spiritualism, Fraudulent and Genuine*, psychic-incident researcher Hereward Carrington recounted how the deception unfolded. After a wealthy man, usually married, shows interest in spiritualism, "plans are laid to relieve him of his wealth, or a goodly portion of it." Once ensnared, the well-to-do dupe is informed by the crooked medium that he will soon meet his "spirit lover," his true soul mate, at a séance. There is no razzle-dazzle, no extraordinary showmanship to create a mystical apparition—it is just a young woman in an interesting set of clothes.

As Carrington explained, the woman—the medium's accomplice—is "supplied with an elegant costume that will glitter with tinsel and gems. She will wear a white crown (signifying purity) on the front of which blazes a star, indicative of the advanced sphere in which she exists in spirit life." The target is told that the spirit lover will appear whenever the medium receives a payment of twenty-five or more dollars for each encounter (equivalent to about $675 today). In return, the princess will spend thirty minutes with her ill-fated paramour, kissing him and sitting on his lap. She will tell him of "the beauties of spirit life, and the home they are to occupy together when he comes to her side." Hereward Carrington notes that these meetings were usually held in private, "but the writer has been present when a gentleman met his royal spirit lover, and kisses and embraces were indulged in in the presence of a public circle of as many as twenty persons."

It is at this moment of pleasure that the medium and the bogus soul mate spring their trap. The Affinity Princess informs the hapless suitor that she requires "certain things," a great many things, in fact, that she is unable to purchase herself, as she is living in the "spirit world," after all. She whispers in his ear that these "modest" gifts will make their "communing" more perfect. Many checks are written and conveyed to the medium, with amounts ranging from ten to several hundred dollars. As Carrington continues, "When [the unfortunate] has been bled until he will stand it no longer, or has no more money, his princess tells him she must return to her heavenly sphere again, not to return for a number of years . . . [and] he is . . . speedily shown the door, and possibly kicked through it."

Carrington was acquainted with one of the mediums who executed this scam, and he himself witnessed several "spirit lover" séances. He told how these trickeries sometimes led to divorce but, more commonly, to profound embarrassment when the target regained his senses and grasped his loss of hundreds, if not thousands, of dollars. But, as Carrington tellingly concludes, "Does he ever prosecute the medium or attempt to recover any of the money? Not one time in ten thousand. Why? Simply because he has a reputation to sustain" and "would rather give up twice the amount he has been swindled out of than to have his friends and business associates know what an ass he has made of himself."

o   o   o

Making an ass of lonely, affluent men was a specialty of Bertha Heyman—known far and wide as "Big Bertha" or "The Confidence Queen," among other aliases—who arrived in San Francisco in 1888 and immediately set up shop. Big Bertha was preceded by an extensive criminal record that was chronicled in an 1886 book entitled *Professional Criminals of America* by Thomas F. Byrnes, who described Bertha as an "excellent talker" who came from a family of professional lawbreakers. (Bertha's father had spent five years in a Prussian prison for check forgery.) In 1880, twenty-nine-year-old Bertha was arrested for defrauding a Chicago railroad conductor, whom she had known only a few hours, of $1,035 (the equivalent of $25,571 today). In Canada the next year, she was charged with hustling hundreds of dollars from a Montreal merchant, and in June of 1881, back in the United States, she was arrested again for stealing $250 and two gold watches from an old lady she had just met on the Staten Island Ferry. She was acquitted for that crime, but, on the way out of the courtroom, she was arrested *again* for sweet-talking two New York businessmen out of $1,460. Found guilty, Bertha Heyman spent two years in prison, but while incarcerated she somehow befriended a man and conned *him* out of his life savings.

In a July 1881 interview with the *New York Times*, Big Bertha Heyman boasted, "I delight in getting into the confidence and pockets of men who think they can't be 'skinned.' It ministers to my intellectual pride." On October 27 of that year the *New York Times* reported in another story that "Mrs. Heyman has swindled people all over the country," including evading payment on a dentist bill she ran up while in jail. When the dentist asked for payment, Bertha responded that the doctor need not be worried as she had $14 million on deposit with a trust company. Of course, Big Bertha did not have the funds and she simply never paid the dentist bill.

Bertha Heyman, known far and wide as "Big Bertha," was proclaimed the
"Confidence Queen" by San Francisco newspapers in the late 1880s. This
photograph is from the 1886 book *Professional Criminals of America,* which was
published *prior* to Heyman's arrival in California but did nothing to curb her
criminal schemes for years. From Thomas F. Byrnes, *Professional Criminals of
America.* New York: Cassell, 1886. Image #122 – Bertha Heyman, p. 201. Image
from a volume in the author's personal collection.

In 1883, soon after leaving the penitentiary, Heyman was arrested and convicted for forging securities, and she was sentenced to another five years in prison. As Thomas Byrnes noted in 1886, "[Heyman] has been concerned in a number of swindling transactions, and has the reputation of being one of the smartest confidence women in America." Byrnes also published her photograph. All of this background information was publicly available *prior* to Bertha's arrival in San Francisco, but she didn't let that stop her.

In the City by the Bay in 1888, Bertha Heyman, recently released from prison and now calling herself Bertha Stanley, posed as a grieving Jewish widow searching for an honest and true man—perhaps a new husband?—to help her manage the $500,000 bequeathed by her late husband. Dozens of eager gentlemen with visions of tapping this bounty volunteered to assist her. But Bertha had a test to which the prospective advisor/spouse must consent in order to determine his worthiness. Each suitor was required to transfer a large sum of money directly to her and her twenty-four-year-old stepson Willie. This commitment would be matched by Bertha's own funds and then invested in a "project," the details of which she would not reveal. Trusting the sorrowful and wealthy widow, nearly twenty men delivered thousands of dollars to Bertha. They never saw their money again. Bertha and Willie fled to Texas.

When Big Bertha was at last identified based on the photograph in *Professional Criminals of America*, both she and Willie were arrested in San Antonio and brought to trial in San Francisco in June 1888. The trial was a sensation, and the *Daily Alta California* wrote of the throng "pushing forward to get a glimpse of the notorious Confidence Queen. Judge Murphy could hardly force his way through the crowd, and he ordered the floor to be cleared when he had after great difficulty reached the bench." A witness declared that Bertha, in addition to her "matching fund" scam, had also finagled a diamond ring from a willing investor as a gift for a sympathetic local rabbi, but of course Bertha had kept the ring for herself. Other testimony told of Bertha ordering an expensive dress, but she never paid up. Yet another victim reported that Big Bertha had secured lodgings purely on her status as a supposedly wealthy woman, but, as the *Alta California* stated, "The charming and accomplished lady also forgot to pay her board bill."

The trial ended in acquittal for Bertha, but Willie was found guilty of obtaining goods under false pretenses and sentenced to six months in jail. After that, Bertha parlayed her notoriety into appearances on stage, usually in dives in San Francisco's Barbary Coast district. By all accounts, she was simply a no-talent curiosity, but patrons flocked to see her nonetheless. For the rest of her life, Big Bertha Heyman traveled throughout the West to "perform," with occasional stops during which she took up managing shabby saloons in Bakersfield, Spokane, and Butte. It was also rumored that she managed to participate in a few extra swindles as she went. Bertha passed away in May 1901 in Chicago, at age fifty-one. The Queen was dead.

o   o   o

While there's no consensus as to who is the most notorious figure in nineteenth-century California Scoundreldom (although Big Bertha Heyman is certainly in the running), most would agree that the most notorious crime was the one the *San Francisco Chronicle* dubbed "the most gigantic and barefaced swindle of the age"—the Great Diamond Hoax of 1872, an infamous affair that entrapped and humiliated prominent bankers, financiers, merchants, a high-ranking army officer, renowned lawyers, and the founder of America's most elegant jewelry company.

As the 1870s dawned, Californians were still discovering the extent of the mineral wealth beneath their feet. That there was an abundance of gold and silver had long been established, but even during the Gold Rush there were reports of diamonds, rubies, and sapphires appearing in the diggings. When a smattering of diamonds was found near Placerville in 1871, Watson A. Goodyear, an assistant with the California State Geological Survey, wrote a letter to the *Placerville Mountain Democrat* to helpfully suggest to gold miners that, "though it may not pay to hunt for diamonds, yet it always pays to pick them up when you do happen to see them." Each new find further whipped up the excitement of fortune seekers and investors, and also made them that much more liable to be plucked by adept charlatans.

In 1871, two cousins named Philip Arnold and John Slack deposited a sack of diamonds in San Francisco's Bank of California. The precious stones were found, they said, in a rich deposit on the Colorado-Wyoming border, but, in fact, they were industrial-grade uncut diamonds that the duo had purchased, or perhaps stolen, in San Francisco, with the intention of running a con. Seeking funds to "develop their find," Arnold and Slack approached investor George D. Roberts. Roberts was interested, very interested. The bait was cast, Roberts bit, and the scam commenced.

The Great Diamond Hoax of 1872 was one of the boldest and most audacious con games in California history. Clarence King (left) was the geologist who discovered the swindle; William Ralston (right) was the president of the Bank of California and one of many ensnared by the hoax. King image courtesy of the United States Geological Survey, Digital ID: Port0001-King USGS. Ralston image courtesy of the California State Library, Sacramento; California History Section, Digital ID: 2016-0120.

In a letter to Kentucky's *Louisville Courier-Journal* on December 16, 1872, after the hoax had been uncovered, Arnold recalled that "Roberts was very much elated by our discovery and promised Slack and myself to keep it a profound secret." The two grifters knew that Roberts would probably not keep it hush-hush, however, and they were right. Roberts soon roped other investors into the scheme, including Horace Greeley, the famous newspaper publisher; George McClellan, a commander of the Union Army during the Civil War; William C. Ralston, a prominent financier and founder of the Bank of California; Baron Ferdinand de Rothschild, a British banker and member of Parliament; and jeweler Charles Lewis Tiffany, founder of Tiffany and Company. Roberts also contacted frequent business associate and shifty operator Asbury Harpending, who, as he recalled in his breathtakingly self-absorbed memoir, *The Great Diamond Hoax and Other Stirring Incidents in the Life of Asbury Harpending* (1913), rushed back to San Francisco "as fast as steamships and railroads would carry us."

Once the investors had advanced money to Arnold and Slack, the pair of con artists used the funds to surreptitiously purchase thousands of poor-quality uncut diamonds and rubies in England. Then, they took their goods to the Colorado-Wyoming border to salt their allegedly rich fields with the low-grade stones.

They met Harpending upon their return to Oakland, having shrewdly affected a grimy appearance to accentuate their ploy. Harpending was fooled, recalling that "both were travel stained and weather beaten and had the general appearance of having gone through much hardship and privation." They then showed Harpending a container filled with stones from the extraordinary site that they claimed had already yielded an estimated $2 million in priceless gems.

Harpending took possession of the precious cargo and dashed across the bay to San Francisco to meet with the other stakeholders. "We did not waste time with ceremonies," he explained. "A sheet was spread on my billiard table; I cut the elaborate fastenings of the sack and, taking hold of the lower corners, dumped the contents. It seemed like a dazzling, many-colored cataract of light." Despite his ignorance of how to grade uncut diamonds, Charles Lewis Tiffany examined the stones and declared them genuine and of high quality. Further tests by Tiffany employees, who were also unschooled in examining raw diamonds, verified the erroneous opinion of their boss.

The investment group persuaded Philip Arnold and John Slack to sell their interest for $660,000 (equivalent to $13.5 million today). The new owners then formed a mining corporation and sent mining engineer Henry Janin to evaluate the diamond field. He submitted a highly optimistic and widely published report on the find, immediately spiking the stock price of the new Lent-Harpending Diamond Mining Company. Millions of dollars were raised.

The bad news came when the investors learned that geologist Clarence King of the United States Geological Exploration of the Fortieth Parallel had *also* inspected the fields and reported that "some designing hand had 'salted' them with deliberate fraudulent intent." Samuel F. Emmons, an associate of King's, confirmed his colleague's assessment in this dismissive statement from his diary of October 6, 1872: "Henry [Janin] shows us some of the diamonds—pretty crystals."

General David Colton, general manager of the mining company, also corroborated the deception, informing the board of directors that he had observed rubies atop bare rock where "it would have been as impossible for Nature to have deposited them as for a person standing in San Francisco to toss a marble in the air and have it fall on Bunker Hill monument."

The jig was up. After a short delay to verify his findings, Clarence King urged the investors to suspend operations and discourage any further speculation by the public, but it was already too late. The victims of the Great Diamond Hoax had lost not only their shirts but their pants, shoes, hats, and good reputations as well. The estimated aggregate loss among the private speculators was $8 million (equivalent to $157 million today).

The story was soon revealed to the public. It was a national sensation. The headlines screamed:

"Salted!" — The Diamond Bubble Bursts — The Most Gigantic Swindle on Record — The Money Kings of California Taken In and Done For
San Francisco Chronicle, November 25, 1872

A Swindle. — Exposure of the Diamond Fraud. — The Vicinity of Table Rock "Salted" with Diamonds and Rubies.
Daily Alta California, November 29, 1872

Unmasked! — The Great Diamond Fiasco — The Mammoth Fraud Exposed — How the Millionaires were Victimized
San Francisco Chronicle, November 26, 1872

The Diamond Fraud. — The Greatest Swindle Ever Exposed in America — The Sharpest Men in California Lose Nearly $2,000,000
New York Sun, December 5, 1872

J. B. Cooper, a bookkeeper for the Lent-Harpending Diamond Mining Company, offered a pitiful excuse for the owners' gullibility in a letter to the *New York Times* on December 8, 1872: "The project . . . swept away all prudence. There is something so fascinating in picking up diamonds, rubies, and emeralds . . . . We see gold and silver by the ton; and it is an old story, but diamonds, emeralds, rubies! The idea was too much for us, and we were all wild. Of course, [the] reader will say, how the deuce did you allow yourselves to be so duped?"

San Francisco newspapers were flush with admiration for Clarence King's exposure of the fraud and his efforts to halt investment in the hustle. On November 26, 1872, the *San Francisco Daily Evening Bulletin* rhapsodized, "Fortunately for the good name of San Francisco and the State, there was one cool-headed man of scientific education who esteemed it his duty to investigate the matter in the only right way." Two days later, the *San Francisco Chronicle* exclaimed, "We have escaped, thanks to GOD and CLARENCE KING, a great financial calamity." That same day, November 28, Thanksgiving Day, King was even praised from the pulpit. Reverend Horatio Stebbins, the *Sacramento Daily Union* reported, "exalted Clarence King for his scientific knowledge and high moral courage." As modern historian Robert Wilson has stated in his excellent retelling of the incident, "[Clarence] King's role in exploding the diamond hoax made him an international celebrity . . . and he dined out on his deed for the rest of his days."

As for the two schemers who perpetrated this swindle, John Slack seemingly vanished, but Philip Arnold was easy to find, and victimized investor William Lent sued Arnold for $350,000. Arnold replied that he had retained his own legal representation—"a good Henry rifle." Philip Arnold would end up settling out of court for $150,000, leaving him a net profit of at least $150,000 (or about $3 million today).

On December 6, 1872, a *New York Times* editorial supplied this coda for the dishonorable and embarrassing incident: "It is now settled beyond question that the whole thing was a gigantic swindle . . . and shows how easy it is to gull a community made up in large part of adventurers and speculators, whose whole dream of life is the sudden acquisition of riches."

o o o

This humbug was but one shard in the distinctive mosaic that was California in the nineteenth century. It was a heaven where fantasies could come true in an instant but also a hell where dreams could be unraveled in a long con. California was a seemingly sturdy ship, steadily sailing toward good prospects, but also a roiling maelstrom of perils, teeming with sharpers and hucksters eager to bring down the vulnerable. Old California was a place to be on guard, to remain constantly aware, on your toes and on the lookout for, on the one hand, excellent opportunities and, on the other, the possibility that someone will try to scam you. In short, it was a place where anything goes. It still is.

Sources

Introduction

Bancroft, Hubert Howe. *The Works of Hubert Howe Bancroft: History of California, Volume 6 (1848–1859)*. San Francisco: The History Company, 1888.

Birmingham, Stephen. *California Rich: The Lives, the Times, the Scandals and the Fortunes of the Men and Women Who Made and Kept California's Wealth*. New York: Simon and Schuster, 1980.

Brown, David. *Southern Outcast: Hinton Rowan Helper and the Impending Crisis of the South*. Baton Rouge: Louisiana State University, 2006.

Caughey, John. *Gold Is the Cornerstone*. Berkeley: University of California Press, 1948.

Connelley, William Elsey. *A Standard History of Kansas and Kansans*. 5 vols. Chicago: Lewis Publishing Company, 1918.

Daily Alta California [San Francisco]. May 4, 1851. Fire of May 3–4, 1851.

———. May 26, 1851. Windy San Francisco.

Fogelson, Robert M. *Fragmented Metropolis: Los Angeles 1850–1930*. Cambridge: Harvard University Press, 1967.

Gregory, James N. "The Shaping of California History." In *Encyclopedia of American Social History*. New York: Scribner, 1993.

Hall, J. Linville. *Journal of the Hartford [Connecticut] Union Mining and Trading Company, 1849*. Printed by J. L. Hall on board the *Henry Lee*, 1849.

Helper, Hinton Rowan. *The Land of Gold: Reality versus Fiction*. Baltimore: Hinton Helper, 1855.

Holliday, J. S. *Rush for Riches: Gold Fever and the Making of California*. Berkeley: University of California Press, 1999.

Rosenus, Alan. *General Vallejo and the Advent of the Americans*. Berkeley: Heyday, 1995. Quoting a January 11, 1877, letter from Mariano Vallejo to his son Platón.

Starr, Kevin, and Richard J. Orsi. *Rooted in Barbarous Soil: People, Culture, and Community in Gold Rush California*. Berkeley: University of California Press, 2000.

Walton, Daniel. *Wonderful Facts from the Gold Regions; Also Valuable Information Desirable To Those Who Intend Going To California.* Boston: Stacy, Richardson and Co., 1849. *Wonderful Facts from the Gold Regions* is the title printed on the outer wrapper; the title printed on the title page is *The Book Needed for the Times, containing the latest well-authenticated facts from the gold regions.*

Chapter One
Black-Legs, California Prayer Books, and Twisting the Tiger's Tail: Games of Chance

Barry, Theodore A., and Benjamin A. Patten. *Men and Memories of San Francisco, in the "Spring of '50."* San Francisco: A. L. Bancroft, 1856.

Bell, Horace. *Reminiscences of a Ranger; or, Early Times in Southern California. By Major Horace Bell.* Los Angeles: Yarnell, Caystile and Mathes, 1881.

Bodie Morning News. September 9, 1879. On the death of Madame Moustache.

Borthwick, John David. *Three Years in California.* Edinburgh: William Blackwood and Sons, 1857.

Brent, Joseph Lancaster. *The Lugo Case: A Personal Experience.* New Orleans: Seavey and Pfaff, 1926.

City of San Francisco. "Schedule J: Summary of Action Taken by the Board of Police Commissioners in the Retail Liquor Dealers' Licenses for the Fiscal Year Ending on the 30th Day of June, 1890," *San Francisco Municipal Reports for the Fiscal Year ending June 30, 1890,* p. 220. Published by Order of the Board of Supervisors. San Francisco: W. M. Hinton and Co., Printers, 536 Clay St., 1890.

Colville, Samuel. *Colville's Marysville Directory for the Year Commencing November 1, 1855.* San Francisco: Monson and Valentine, 1855.

Cook, Jesse B. *San Francisco Police and Peace Officers' Journal,* June 1931.

De Russailh, Albert Benard. *Last Adventure: San Francisco in 1851.* Translated by Clarkson Crane. San Francisco: Westgate Press, 1931.

Duhaut-Cilly, Auguste Bernard. *A Voyage to California, the Sandwich Islands, and Around the World in the Years 1826–1829.* Translated and edited by August Frugé and Neal Harlow. Berkeley: University of California Press, 1997. Originally published in Italian as *Viaggio Intorno al Globo: Principalmente alla California ed alle Isole Sandwich Negli Anni 1826, 1827, 1828 e 1829.* Napoli: Stamperia E Cartiere del Fibreno, 1842. Duhaut-Cilly is extensively quoted in Richard

Pourade's *Time of the Bells: The History of San Diego*. San Diego: Union-Tribune Publishing Company, 1961.

Evans, Albert S. *À la California: Sketch of Life in the Golden State, by Col. Albert S. Evans*. San Francisco: A. L. Bancroft and Company, 1873.

Fabian, Ann Vincent. *Rascals and Gentlemen: The Meaning of American Gambling, 1820–1890*. Ph.D. diss., Yale University, 1983.

Faragher, John Mack. *Eternity Street: Violence and Justice in Frontier Los Angeles*. New York: W. W. Norton, 2016.

Fey, Marshall A. "Charles Fey and San Francisco's Liberty Bell." *California Historical Quarterly*, vol. 54, no. 1 (Spring 1975): 57–62.

Gunn, Lewis C., and Elizabeth Le Breton Gunn. *Records of a California Family: Journals and Letters of Lewis C. Gunn and Elizabeth Le Breton Gunn*. Edited by Anna Lee Marston. San Diego, 1928.

Hall, J. Linville. *Journal of the Hartford [Connecticut] Union Mining and Trading Company, 1849*. Printed by J. L. Hall on board the *Henry Lee*, 1849.

Letts, John. *California Illustrated, including a description of the Panama and Nicaragua routes*. New York: R. T. Young, 1853.

Longstreet, Stephen. *Win or Lose: A Social History of Gambling in America*. Indianapolis: Bobbs-Merrill, 1977.

Lord, Israel. *A Doctor's Gold Rush Journey to California. By Israel Shipman Pelton Lord*. Edited by Necia Dixon Niles. Lincoln: University of Nebraska Press, 1995. Original diary covering 1849–1851 in Collections of the Huntington Library, San Marino, California.

National Police Gazette. October 4, 1879. Quoted in Michael H. Piatt, "The Death of Madame Moustache: Bodie's Most Celebrated Inhabitant," March 2009, www.bodiehistory.com. Piatt's website provides additional information on the varied mining and social history of Bodie, California.

Peters, William B. "Gold Rush Letter, 1851, Jan. 1." Letter to Miss Emily Howard, January 1, 1851. Original letter in the California History Room, California State Library, Sacramento, SMCII: Box 13: Folder 12.

Reid, Hugo. "Hugo Reid's Account of the Indians of Los Angeles County, California." *Bulletin of the Essex Institute* (Salem, Massachusetts), vol. 3, nos. 1–3 (March 1885): 17.

San Francisco Call. "Odious to Mothers," March 19, 1898. Editorial about the dangers of "pool-rooms" for women.

Shandel, Pamela. "Inside Straight: A History of Poker from Bones to the Internet." Master's thesis, University of Southern California, 1995.

Sherman, William Tecumseh. Letter to Henry S. Turner, April 2, 1857. Quoted in J. S. Holliday, *Rush for Riches*. Berkeley: University of California Press, 1999, p. 181.

"Slot Machines and Pinball Games." *Annals of the American Academy of Political and Social Science*, vol. 269, "Gambling" (May 1950): 62–70.

Soulé, Frank, John H. Gihon, and James Nisbet. *The Annals of San Francisco*. New York: D. Appleton, 1855.

Standard Pioneer Journal of Mono County. May 29, 1878. On the arrival of Madame Moustache in Bodie, California.

Starr, Kevin. *California: A History*. New York: Modern Library, Random House, 2005.

Starr, Kevin, and Richard J. Orsi. *Rooted in Barbarous Soil: People, Culture, and Community in Gold Rush California*. Berkeley: University of California Press, 2000.

State of California. "Constitution of the State of California, Adopted in Convention at Sacramento, March 3, 1879, Ratified by Vote of the People, May 7, 1879." San Francisco: Bancroft-Whitney, 1902. Page 242 provides a summary of the decision in *Ex Parte Tuttle*, 91 CAL 589, 27 PAC 933.

———. *The Penal Code of California*, Part 1, Title 9, Chapter 10, Section 330 (Gaming). Sacramento: State of California Office of Legislative Counsel. https://legislativecounsel.ca.gov.

Tamony, Peter. "The One-Armed Bandit." *Western Folklore*, vol. 27, no. 2 (April 1968): 117–124.

Taylor, Bayard. *Eldorado: Adventures in the Path of Empire*. New York: G. P. Putnam; and London: R. Bentley, 1850.

United States Bureau of the Census. "Population Estimates, as of July 1, 2019 V2019." U.S. Census Bureau, Population Estimates Program (PEP), updated annually.

Vallejo, Mariano Guadalupe. Letter from Cosme Peña to Mariano Guadalupe Vallejo, June 6, 1839. In Hubert Howe Bancroft, *The Works of Hubert Howe Bancroft, Volume 20*. San Francisco: The History Company, 1888.

Waldie, D. J. "Draw, Stud and Hold'em: A Brief History of Poker in LA." Published by *Lost LA*, March 15, 2017. www.kcet.org.

Weeks, George F. *California Copy*. Washington, D.C.: Washington College Press, 1928.

Will, Frederick, and Julius Finck. *Will and Finck's 1896 Gamblers' Cheating Equipment Catalog*. Reprint, San Francisco: Levine, 1977.

Yan, Geling. Quoted in the transcript of "Becoming American: The Chinese Experience," Program One, p. 5, produced by PBS, 2003.

Chapter Two
Anti-Fogmatics, Coffin Varnish, and Oh-Be-Joyful: The Demon Drink

Avery, Benjamin Parke. *Californian Pictures in Prose and Verse.* New York: Hurd and Houghton, 1878.

Ayers, James J. *Gold and Sunshine: Reminiscences of Early California.* Boston: R. G. Badger, 1922.

Balls, Edward K. *Early Uses of California Plants.* California Natural History Guides 10. Berkeley: University of California Press, 1962.

Bancroft, Hubert Howe. *The Works of Hubert Howe Bancroft: History of California, Volume 6 (1848–1859).* San Francisco: The History Company, 1888.

Blocker, Jack S., Jr., David M. Fahey, and Jan R. Tyrrell, eds. *Alcohol and Temperance in Modern History: A Global Encyclopedia.* Santa Barbara: ABC-CLIO, 2003. Information on the Dashaway Association and the American Association for the Study and Cure of Inebriety.

Borthwick, John David. *Three Years in California.* Edinburgh: William Blackwood and Sons, 1857.

Brewers Association (Boulder, Colorado). *Report: Beer Industry Production Survey (BIPS), 2016–2017.*

Bull, Donald, Manfred Friedrich, and Robert Gottschalk. *American Breweries.* Trumbull, CT: Bullworks, 1984.

Davis, William Heath. *Seventy-five Years in California.* San Francisco: J. Howell, 1929.

Doten, Alfred. *The Journals of Alfred Doten, 1849–1903.* 3 vols. Reno: University of Nevada Press, 1973.

Evans, Albert S. *À la California: Sketch of Life in the Golden State, by Col. Albert S. Evans.* San Francisco: A. L. Bancroft and Company, 1873.

Haraszthy, Agoston. *Grape Culture, Wines, and Wine-Making: With Notes Upon Agriculture and Horticulture.* New York: Harper and Brothers, 1862.

Híjar, Carlos N., Eulalia Pérez, and Agustín Escobar. *Three Memoirs of Mexican California.* Recorded in 1877 by Thomas Savage. Berkeley: University of California, Berkeley, Friends of the Bancroft Library, 1988.

Hingston, Edward Peron. *The Genial Showman: Reminiscences of the Life of Artemus Ward.* London: John Camden Hotten, c. 1870.

Knox, Thomas W. *Underground, or Life Below the Surface.* Hartford, CT: J. B. Burr, 1874.

Leland, Joy. *Firewater Myths: North American Indian Drinking and Alcohol Addiction*. New Brunswick, NJ: Rutgers Center of Alcohol Studies, 1976.

Los Angeles Herald. "A Novel Bath," June 27, 1897.

Marryat, Frank. *Mountains and Molehills; or, Recollections of a Burnt Journal*. New York: Harper and Brothers, 1855.

Newmark, Harris. *Sixty Years in Southern California, 1853–1913*. New York: The Knickerbocker Press, 1926.

Perkins, William. *Three Years in California*. Edited by Dale L. Morgan and James R. Scobie. Berkeley: University of California Press, 1964.

Pinney, Thomas. *A History of Wine in America: From the Beginnings to Prohibition*. Berkeley: University of California Press, 1989.

———. *City of Vines: A History of Wine in Los Angeles*. Berkeley: Heyday, 2017.

Sacramento Bee. December 29, 1952. Article on Native Californians from the Modoc tribe not being able to purchase aftershave lotion.

San Francisco Board of Supervisors. *San Francisco Municipal Reports for Fiscal Year Ending June 30, 1890*. San Francisco: W. M. Hinton, Printers, 1890. On the number of saloons with liquor licenses as of July 1889.

"Sixty Years of Leadership and Service." *Report of National Council on Alcoholism and Drug Dependence*. New York, 2004.

State of California. "An Act for the Government and Protection of Indians." *Statutes of California*, April 22, 1850, chapter 133.

———. Senate Bill 344. *Statutes of California*, April 8, 1953, chapter 146, p. 918.

Statista 2018—the Statistics Portal (Hamburg, Germany). *Report: Producing Wineries in 2018*. www.statista.com.

Taylor, Bayard. *Eldorado: Adventures in the Path of Empire*. New York: G. P. Putnam; and London: R. Bentley, 1850.

Thomas, Jerry, and Christian Schultz. *How to Mix Drinks, or The Bon-Vivant's Companion*. New York: Dik and Fitzgerald, 1862.

United States Congress. "An Act to Regulate Trade and Intercourse with the Indian Tribes, and to Preserve Peace on the Frontiers." *Congressional Globe*, 33rd Congress, Session 1 (1834), Chapter 161, pp. 729–735.

———. H.R. 1055. *Congressional Record*, 83rd Congress, Session 1 (1953), vol. 67, 67 Stat. 587, Public Law 83-277, pp. 586–587.

Weeks, George F. *California Copy*. Washington, D.C.: Washington College Press, 1928.

Yenne, Bill. *San Francisco Beer: A History of Brewing by the Bay.* Charleston, SC: American Palate, imprint of The History Press, 2016.

Chapter Three
Grizzly Bear Steak, Sourdough Slapjacks, and Whole Jackass Rabbit: Gracious Dining and Gluttony

Bailey, H. C. "California in 1853." Memoir. University of California, Berkeley, Bancroft Library.

Balch, William Ralston, compiler. *The Mines, Miners and Mining Interests on the United States in 1882.* Philadelphia: The Mining Industrial Publishing House, 1882.

Berger, Frances de Talavera, and John Parke Custis. *Sumptuous Dining in Gaslight San Francisco, 1875–1915.* New York: Doubleday, 1985.

Borthwick, John David. *Three Years in California.* Edinburgh: William Blackwood and Sons, 1857.

Browne, J. Ross. "A Peep at Washoe." *Harper's Monthly,* vol. 22, no. 127 (December 1860): 1–17.

Buffum, Edward Gould. *Six Months in the Gold Mines.* Philadelphia: Lea and Blanchard, 1850.

Carey, Joseph. *By the Golden Gate: Or, San Francisco, the Queen City of the Pacific Coast.* Albany, NY: Albany Diocesan Press, 1902.

Caughey, John W. *Rushing for Gold.* Berkeley: University of California Press, 1949.

Chen, Jack. *The Chinese of America.* New York: Harper and Row, 1980.

Chez Panisse website. "About Chez Panisse." www.chezpanisse.com.

Clifford, Josephine. "Chinatown." *Potter's American Monthly,* vol. 14 (May 1880): 354–364.

Cogswell, James L. "Autobiography and Reminiscence of Dr. James L. Cogswell." *Autobiographies and Reminiscences of California Pioneers,* vol. 1, pp. 41–44. San Francisco: Society of California Pioneers, 1901.

Conlin, Joseph. R. *Bacon, Beans and Galantines: Food and Foodways on the Western Mining Frontier.* Reno: University of Nevada Press, 1986.

Delano, Alonzo. *Life on the Plains and Among the Diggings.* Auburn and Buffalo, NY: Miller, Orton and Mulligan, 1856.

Doten, Alfred. *The Journals of Alfred Doten, 1849–1903.* 3 vols. Reno: University of Nevada Press, 1973.

Duhaut-Cilly, Auguste Bernard. *A Voyage to California, the Sandwich Islands, and Around the World in the Years 1826–1829.* Translated and edited by August Frugé and Neal Harlow. Berkeley: University of California Press, 1997.

Fisher, Vardis, and Opal Laurel Holmes. *Gold Rushes and Mining Camps of the Early American West*. Caldwell, ID: Caxton Printers, 1968.

Freedman, Georgia. "The Secrets of California's Oldest Recipes," May 22, 2018. *Taste Magazine* website. www.tastecooking.com.

Gibson, Otis. *Chinese in America*. Cincinnati: Hitchcock and Walden, 1877.

Gillespie, Charles B. "A Miner's Sunday in Coloma." *Century Illustrated Monthly Magazine*, New Series vol. 20 (May–October 1891): 259–269.

Hall, Frederic. *The History of San José and Surroundings*. San Francisco: A. L. Bancroft, 1871. For a review of and commentary on the above, see also [San Francisco] *Pacific Rural Press*, vol. 1, no. 3 (January 21, 1871).

Harrison, H. A. Letter sent from San Francisco by Harrison to the *Baltimore Clipper* newspaper, February 3, 1849. Quoted in David Rohrer Leeper, *Argonauts of '49*. South Bend, IN: J. B. Stoll, 1894. Letter listing commodity prices in 1849 San Francisco.

Hastings, Lansford W. *The Emigrant's Guide to California and Oregon*. Cincinnati: George Conclin, 1845. Reprint, Princeton, NJ: Princeton University Press, 1932.

Haun, Catherine. "A Woman's Trip Across the Plains, 1849." Manuscript diary. San Marino: Huntington Library. Reprinted in part in Lillian Schlissel, *Women's Diaries of the Westward Journey*. New York: Schocken Books, 1992.

Helper, Hinton Rowan. *The Land of Gold: Reality versus Fiction*. Baltimore: Hinton Helper, 1855.

Historical Statistics of the United States. Washington, D.C.: Government Printing Office, 1975.

Kelly, William. *A Stroll through the Diggings of California*. London: Bonwit, 1852.

Lord, Eliot. *Comstock Mining and Miners*. Washington, D.C.: Government Printing Office, 1883.

Lord, Israel. *A Doctor's Gold Rush Journey to California. By Israel Shipman Pelton Lord*. Edited by Necia Dixon Niles. Lincoln: University of Nebraska Press, 1995. Original diary covering 1849–1851 in Collections of the Huntington Library, San Marino, California.

Manuwal, David Allen, Harry R. Carter, Tara Zimmerman, and Dennis L. Orthmeyer, eds. *Biology and Conservation of the Common Murre in California, Oregon, Washington, and British Columbia: Vol. 1, Natural History and Population Trends*. Information and Technology Report 2000-0012. Washington, D.C.: U.S. Fish and Wildlife Service, 2001. Also available through United States Geological Survey, USGS-BRD/ ITR 2000-2012.

Margo, Joan. "The Food Supply Problem of the California Gold Miners, 1848–1855." Master's thesis, University of California, Berkeley, 1947.

Marryat, Frank. *Mountains and Molehills; or, Recollections of a Burnt Journal.* New York: Harper and Brothers, 1855.

Miller, John H. *St. Joseph Valley [Indiana] Register,* October 6, 1849. Quoted in David Rohrer Leeper, *Argonauts of '49.* South Bend, IN: J. B. Stoll, 1894. Letter listing commodity prices in 1849 Weberville, near Placerville.

Mulford, Prentice. "California Culinary Experiences." *Overland Monthly,* vol. 2, no. 6 (June 1869): 556–562.

Newmark, Harris. *Sixty Years in Southern California, 1853–1913.* New York: The Knickerbocker Press, 1926.

New York Times. "Old Days in California," January 20, 1885. Description of the annual meeting of the Associated Pioneers of the Territorial Days of California, in New York City.

Nordhoff, Charles. "The Farallon Islands." *Harper's New Monthly Magazine,* vol. 48 (April 1874): 617–625.

Pinedo, Encarnación. *El Cocinero Español.* San Francisco: E. C. Hughes, 1898.

Robinson, Phillip Stewart. *Sinners and Saints.* London: Sampson, Low, Marston and Company, 1892.

Root, Waverly, and Richard De Rochemont. *Eating in America: A History.* New York: William Morrow, 1976.

Sacramento Daily Union. June 16, 1858. Size of wagonload shipments of provisions.

Shaw, William. *Golden Dreams and Waking Realities: Being the Adventures of a Gold-seeker in California and the Pacific Islands.* London: Smith, Elder and Co., 1851.

Shinn, Charles. *Mining Camps: A Study in American Frontier Government.* New York: Charles Scribner's Sons, 1885.

Snow, Horace. *Dear Charlie Letters.* Fresno: Mariposa County Historical Society, 1979.

Spence, Mary Lee. "They Also Serve Who Wait." *Western Historical Quarterly,* vol. 14 (January 1983).

Stevenson, J. D. Letter to his son-in-law James H. Brady, in New York City, April 1849. Quoted in Walker Wyman, *California Emigrant Letters.* New York: Bookman Associates, 1952. Originally published in the *St. Joseph [Missouri] Adventurer,* July 27, 1849.

United States Bureau of the Census. Documents 1850–1910.

Walker, W. S. *Glimpses of Hungryland, or California Sketches.* Cloverdale, CA: Reveille Publishing, 1880.

Warzybok, P., M. Johns, and R. W. Bradley. "Status of Seabirds on Southeast Farallon Island during the 2014 Breeding Season." Report to the U.S. Fish and Wildlife Service, Farallon National Wildlife Refuge. Petaluma, CA: Point Blue Conservation Science, December 2014.

Weekly Alta California [San Francisco]. "Wholesale Prices Current, San Francisco, Oct. 30, 1849, Prepared and Revised for the *Alta California* by Woodworth & Morris," November 1, 1849. Article on wholesale commodity prices in 1849 San Francisco.

Wilson, William D. *St. Joseph Valley [Indiana] Register*, February 21, 1849. Quoted in David Rohrer Leeper, *Argonauts of '49*. South Bend, IN: J. B. Stoll, 1894. Letter listing commodity prices in 1849 Sacramento.

Winther, Oscar O. *Express and Stagecoach Days in California*. Palo Alto: Stanford University Press, 1936.

Woods, Daniel Bates. *Sixteen Months at the Gold Diggings*. New York: Harper and Brothers, 1851.

Chapter Four
Spittoons, Quids, and Cigarillos: Tobacco Culture

Apollonio, Dorie E., and Stanton A. Glantz. "Minimum Ages of Legal Access for Tobacco in the United States from 1863 to 2015." *American Journal of Public Health*, vol. 106, no. 7 (July 2016): 1200–1207.

Balls, Edward K. *Early Uses of California Plants*. California Natural History Guides 10. Berkeley: University of California Press, 1962.

Borthwick, John David. *Three Years in California*. Edinburgh: William Blackwood and Sons, 1857.

Chiu, Ping. *Chinese Labor in California, 1850–1880: An Economic Study*. Madison: The State Historical Society of Wisconsin, 1967.

Daily Alta California [San Francisco]. "Things Theatrical Which Should Be Amended," January 6, 1851. Description of tobacco smoking and chewing habits in San Francisco theaters.

Davis, William Heath. *Seventy-five Years in California*. San Francisco: J. Howell, 1929.

Derby, George Horatio. *Phoenixiana; or, Sketches and Burlesques*. New York: D. Appleton, 1856. Reprint, 1902. Derby's pseudonyms were John Phoenix and the Veritable Squibob.

Farnham, Eliza W. *California, In-doors and Out; or, How We Farm, Mine, and Live Generally in the Golden State*. New York: Dix, Edwards and Co., 1856.

Huntley, Henry Vere. *California: Its Gold and Its Inhabitants*. London: T. C. Newby, 1856.

King James I of England. "A Counterblaste to Tobacco," 1604. Originally
   published in 1604; reprinted in the *The Workes of King James* in 1616,
   and again as "A Counterblaste to Tobacco" in 1905 (London: G.
   Putnam and Sons).

Krieger, Lisa M. "Tobacco Smoked in Ancient California, Researchers
   Find," *San Jose Mercury News*, March 1, 2013. Article on recent
   archaeological studies regarding tobacco smoking in Native California.

Los Angeles Times. "Protect the Innocents," July 26, 1900. Article on the
   failure to enforce laws prohibiting tobacco sales to minors age sixteen
   and younger.

McIlhany, Edward Washington. *Recollections of a '49er.* Kansas City, MO:
   Hailman Printing Company, 1849.

Meyer, Carl. *Bound for Sacramento: Travel-pictures of a Returned Wanderer.*
   Claremont, CA: Saunders Studio Press, 1938. *Bound for Sacramento* is
   the English translation of Meyer's *Nach dem Sacramento*, published in
   Aarau, Switzerland, in 1855.

Mulford, Prentice. *Life by Land and Sea.* New York: F. J. Needham, 1889.

Peters, Charles. *The Autobiography of Charles Peters, in 1915 the oldest
   pioneer living in California, who mined in . . . the days of '49. . . . Also
   historical happenings, interesting incidents and illustrations of the old mining
   towns in the good luck era, the placer mining days of the '50s.* Sacramento:
   The LaGrave Company, c. 1915.

Red Bluff Independent. July 25, 1862. Anti-tobacco remark.

Russian River Flag. "Going Off in Smoke," May 28, 1874. Anti-cigarette
   editorial.

Sacramento Daily Union. "The Chinese in California," November
   27, 1869. Article containing San Francisco occupation statistics
   (including employment in cigar manufacturing) gathered by "The
   Six Companies," a group of six individual Chinese firms operating
   in California as express companies, banks, and information
   clearinghouses.

San Francisco Board of Supervisors. *San Francisco Municipal Reports,
   1867–1881.* Statistics on Chinese workers compiled and published in
   Ping Chiu, *Chinese Labor in California, 1850–1880: An Economic Study.*
   Madison: The State Historical Society of Wisconsin, 1967.

San Francisco Call. "Boy's Anti-Cigarette League," January 12, 1894.
   Description of the anti-smoking league sponsored by the *San
   Francisco Call.*

———. "Will Not Smoke Cigarettes," January 22, 1894. Listing of
   schoolboys who signed the anti-cigarette smoking pledge of the Boy's
   Anti-Cigarette League.

————. "Make It Lasting," February 16, 1894. Article claiming that nearly ten thousand schoolboys had signed the anti cigarette smoking pledge.

————. "Dog That Chews Tobacco and Is Now Taking Cure," March 17, 1901. Article on Sport, the tobacco-addicted dog.

Shaw, William. *Golden Dreams and Waking Realities: Being the Adventures of a Gold-seeker in California and the Pacific Islands.* London: Smith, Elder and Co., 1851.

Sonoma Democrat. December 10, 1881. Death of James Reilly, a 101-year-old smoker.

Spedden, Ernest Radcliffe. "The Trade Union Label." *Johns Hopkins University Studies in Historical and Political Science*, vol. 28, no. 2 (1910). Baltimore: Johns Hopkins, 1910.

State of California. *The Penal Code of the State of California: Adopted February 14, 1872, with amendments up to and including those of the thirty-eighth session of the Legislature, 1909, with citation digest up to and including volume 154 California reports, and volume 8 Appellate reports,* p. 144. Edited by James H. Deering. San Francisco: Bancroft-Whitney, 1909.

Swan, John Alfred. *A Trip to the Gold Mines of California in 1848.* San Francisco: Book Club of California, 1960.

Taylor, Bayard. *Eldorado: Adventures in the Path of Empire.* New York: G. P. Putnam; and London: R. Bentley, 1850.

Twain, Mark. *Sketches: New and Old.* Hartford, CT: American Publishing Company, 1893.

United States Bureau of the Census. *Report on the Manufactures of the United States at the Tenth Census (June 1, 1880).* Washington, D.C.: Government Printing Office, 1879, 1880, 1882, 1883. Cigar manufacturing statistics.

————. *Statistics of the Population of the United States at the Tenth Census (June 1, 1880).* Washington, D.C.: Government Printing Office, 1879, 1880, 1882. Major occupations of Chinese immigrants in 1880.

Chapter Five
Demanding Satisfaction, Frogstickers, and the Slogging Fraternity: Dueling, Knife Fights, Fisticuffs, and Animal Baiting

Asbury, Herbert. *The Barbary Coast: An Informal History of the San Francisco Underworld.* New York: Alfred A. Knopf, 1933.

Australian National Maritime Museum website. https://www.sea. museum/2018/05/02/the-sydney-ducks-and-the-san-francisco-49ers. Article about the Sydney Ducks.

Bell, Horace. *Reminiscences of a Ranger; or, Early Times in Southern California. By Major Horace Bell.* Los Angeles: Yarnell, Caystile and Mathes, 1881.

Bidwell, John. *Addresses, Reminiscences, etc. of General John Bidwell.* Compiled by Charles C. Royce. Chico, CA: Royce, 1906.

Boessenecker, John. *Gold Dust and Gunsmoke: Tales of Gold Rush Outlaws, Gunfighters, Lawmen, and Vigilantes.* New York: John Wiley and Sons, 2000.

Borthwick, John David. *Three Years in California.* Edinburgh: William Blackwood and Sons, 1857.

Browne, J. Ross. *Report of the Debates in the Convention of California, on the Formation of the State Constitution, in September and October, 1849.* Washington, D.C.: Printed by J. T. Towers, 1850.

Bryant, Edwin. *What I Saw in California.* New York: D. Appleton, 1848.

Buck, Franklin A. *A Yankee Trader in the Gold Rush: The Letters of Franklin A. Buck.* Compiled by Katherine A. White. Boston and New York: Houghton Mifflin Company, 1930.

Daily Alta California [San Francisco].

"City Intelligence," June 29, 1851. Description of "Sydney Valley" in San Francisco.

"Not the 'Chicken,'" March 4, 1866. A man named Johnny Devine is offended, as he was not the same Johnny Devine who was arrested for highway robbery.

"Got Them At Last," November 23, 1866. Johnny Devine and Johnny Nyland arrested for beating the captain of the *Mary Ann Wilson*.

"Devine, alias 'The Chicken' Maimed," June 14, 1868. A graphic description of the violent "spree" in which Devine lost his hand.

"Slogging Matches," May 21, 1885. Efforts to ban boxing exhibitions.

"Ended in a Draw," May 22, 1891. Jackson-Corbett fight.

Dana, Richard Henry, Jr. *Two Years Before the Mast: A Personal Narrative.* Boston: Houghton Mifflin, 1911. Originally published in 1840.

Ellis, William Turner. *Memories; My Seventy-two Years in the Romantic County of Yuba, California.* Eugene: University of Oregon, Printed by J. H. Nash, 1939.

Farnham, Eliza. Quoted in the *Santa Cruz News*, September 21, 1859. On dueling.

Frisbee, Meg. *Counterpunch: The Cultural Battles over Heavyweight Prizefighting in the American West.* Seattle: University of Washington Press, 2016.

Grass Valley Daily Union. May 9, 1873. Notice that Johnny Devine will be hanged "next Friday." Devine was actually hanged in San Francisco on Wednesday, May 14.

Harlan, Jacob Wright. *California '46 to '88.* San Francisco: Bancroft Company, 1888.

Hittell, Theodore H. *General Laws of the State of California, From 1850 to 1864, Inclusive.* San Francisco: A. L. Bancroft, 1872. Dueling legislation, No. 1446, Section 44; and No. 1447, Section 45, p. 238.

Lang, Arne K. *Prizefighting: An American History.* Jefferson, NC: McFarland, 2008.

Los Angeles Herald. July 1, 1879. Rat catching in Los Angeles.

Los Angeles Times. "7000 Birds Seized in Largest Cockfighting Bust in U.S. History, L.A. County Authorities Say," May 16, 2017. Cockfighting bust in 2017.

Marin Journal. March 16, 1872. Article reporting that Johnny Devine was expected to hang in April for the murder of August Kemp. (He was not hanged until May 1873.)

Marryat, Frank. *Mountains and Molehills; or, Recollections of a Burnt Journal.* New York: Harper and Brothers, 1855.

Meyer, Carl. *Bound for Sacramento: Travel-pictures of a Returned Wanderer.* Claremont, CA: Saunders Studio Press, 1938. *Bound for Sacramento* is the English translation of Meyer's *Nach dem Sacramento,* published in Aarau, Switzerland, in 1855.

Monkkonen, Erik H. "Homicide in Los Angeles, 1827–2002." *Journal of Interdisciplinary History,* vol. 36, no. 2 (Autumn 2005): 167–183.

Pfaelzer, Jean. *Driven Out: The Forgotten War against Chinese Americans.* Berkeley: University of California Press, 2008.

Pittsburgh [Pennsylvania] Daily Post. "California Sports," August 15, 1854. Description of a bull-and-bear fight in Iowa Hill, California.

Richards, Leonard. *California Gold Rush and the Coming of the Civil War.* New York: Vintage, 2008.

Sacramento Daily Union.
    November 3, 1851. Fatal duel at Industry Bar.
    August 3, 1852. Description of Denver-Gilbert duel.
    November 11, 1853. Rat catching in Sacramento.
    July 29, 1854. Bear escapes from a bull-and-bear fight.
    December 16, 1858. Description of badger baiting.
    August 13, 1859. City of Sacramento animal baiting ordinance.
    April 29, 1863. City of Sacramento animal baiting ordinance.
    May 23, 1864. Johnny Devine shoots Tom Chandler.

December 23, 1864. Description of a boxing match featuring Johnny Devine.

February 18, 1869. Johnny Devine arrested for burglary.

March 23, 1869. Johnny Devine arrested in drunken brawl.

March 23, 1869. Johnny Devine arrested for $20 "murder for hire" of August Kemp. Devine killed Kemp with a rock.

"Beselena's Letter," May 19, 1892. Interview with pugilist "Gentleman Jim" Corbett.

San Francisco Evening Picayune. June 14, 1850. Quoted in Kenneth Johnson, ed., *San Francisco As It Is: Gleanings from the "Picayune."* Georgetown, CA: Talisman Press, 1964.

Smith, Stacy. "Remaking Slavery in a Free State: Masters and Slaves in Gold Rush California." *Pacific Historical Review,* vol. 80, no. 1 (February 2011): 28–63.

Soulé, Frank, John H. Gihon, and James Nisbet. *The Annals of San Francisco.* New York: D. Appleton, 1855.

Spangenberger, Phil. "Fighting Blades of the Frontier." *True West,* September 2014. https://truewestmagazine.com/ bowie-knife-fighting-blades-of-the-frontier.

Starr, Kevin, and Richard J. Orsi. *Rooted in Barbarous Soil: People, Culture, and Community in Gold Rush California.* Berkeley: University of California Press, 2000.

State of California.

Journal of the Senate of the State of California at their First Session, Begun and Held at the Puebla de San José on the Fifteenth Day of December 1849. San José: J. Winchester, State Printer, 1850. Dismissal of doorkeeper John Warrington.

"Message from Governor John B. Weller." *Journal of the House of Assembly of California,* 11th Session, January 1860–April 1860, p. 59. Sacramento: C. T. Botts, State Printer, 1860.

The Penal Code of California, enacted in 1872; as amended up to and including 1905, with statutory history and citation digest up to and including volume 147, California reports. Edited by James H. Deering. Statutory history and citation digest by Walter S. Brann; consolidated and edited to include extra session of 1906, Title 8, Chapter 7, Sections 225–232, pp. 107–109 (Dueling); and Title 11, Section 412, p. 174 (Prize Fights). San Francisco: Bancroft-Whitney, 1906.

The Statutes of California, passed at the Nineteenth Session of the Legislature, 1871–1872. Sacramento: J. A. Springer, State Printer, 1872. Statutes regarding prizefighting.

The Statutes of California, passed at the Thirty-Third Session of the Legislature, 1899. Sacramento: A. J. Johnston, Superintendent State Printing, 1899. Statutes regarding prizefighting.

Waldie, D. J. "Murder in Old Los Angeles." Published by *Lost LA*, October 17, 2017. www.kcet.org.

West's Annotated California Codes. Penal Code, Part 1 (Of Crimes and Punishment), Title 14 (Malicious Mischief), Section 597 (Cruelty to Animals). St. Paul, MN: West Publishing Group, 1954–present.

Wright, William (Dan DeQuille). "Mark Twain Takes a Lesson in the Manly Art," *Virginia City [California] Territorial Enterprise*, April 28, 1864. Mark Twain boxing match. Also quoted in Franklin Walker, ed., *The Washoe Giant in San Francisco: Being Heretofore Uncollected Sketches by Mark Twain Published in the Golden Era in the Sixties.* San Francisco: George Fields, 1938.

Chapter Six
Sparking, Philanthropic Importation, and the Hospital: Courtship, Divorce, and Prostitution

Anderson, Ivy, and Devon Angus, eds. *Alice: Memoirs of a Barbary Coast Prostitute.* Berkeley: Heyday, 2016. A reprint of the six-part series "A Voice from the Underworld" (*San Francisco Bulletin*, June 23–August 12, 1913), and including examples of the correspondence associated with the series, including the letters of Alma Greene, Violet Brown, and "One of Society's Victims."

Bancroft, Hubert Howe. *Literary Industries.* San Francisco: The History Company Publishers, 1890.

Barnhart, Jacqueline Baker. *The Fair but Frail: Prostitution in San Francisco, 1849–1900.* Reno: University of Nevada Press, 1986.

Barry, Theodore A., and Benjamin A. Patten. *Men and Memories of San Francisco, in the "Spring of '50."* San Francisco: A. L. Bancroft, 1856.

Beans, Rowena. *Inasmuch: The One-Hundred-Year History of the San Francisco Ladies Protection and Relief Society, 1853–1953.* San Francisco: James J. Gillick, 1953.

Bell, Horace. *Reminiscences of a Ranger; or, Early Times in Southern California. By Major Horace Bell.* Los Angeles: Yarnell, Caystile and Mathes, 1881.

Blackburn, Thomas, ed. *December's Child: A Book of Chumash Oral Narratives.* Berkeley: University of California Press, 1975.

Borthwick, John David. *Three Years in California.* Edinburgh: William Blackwood and Sons, 1857.

Butler, Anne M. *Daughters of Joy, Sisters of Mercy: Prostitutes in the American West, 1865–1890.* Urbana: University of Illinois Press, 1985.

Christman, Enos. *One Man's Gold: The Letters and Journals of a Forty-Niner, Enos Christman.* New York: Whittlesey House-McGraw-Hill, 1930.

City of San Francisco. "Order to Remove Chinese Women of Ill-Fame from Certain Limits in the City," *San Francisco Municipal Reports for Fiscal Year 1865–1866,* Order 666, October 17, 1865, p. 125. San Francisco: Towne and Bacon, 1866.

Coffin, Isaac Tibbetts. *The Story of a Placer County Gold Miner.* Brea, CA: Creative Continuum, 2004. Diary of Issac Tibbetts Coffin, edited by his great-granddaughter, Phyllis Gillogly Young.

Cox, Isaac. *Annals of Trinity County.* Eugene: John Henry of the University of Oregon, 1940.

Daily Alta California [San Francisco].

   January 26, 1851. Editorial on California divorce law.

   June 29, 1864. Advertisement for Madame Byron, spiritualist advisor to the lovelorn.

   February 22, 1891. The poem "Courtship or Marriage?"

Dana, Richard Henry, Jr. *Two Years Before the Mast: A Personal Narrative.* Boston: Houghton Mifflin, 1911. Originally published in 1840.

Del Castillo, Richard Griswold. *The Los Angeles Barrio, 1850–1890: A Social History.* Berkeley: University of California Press, 1979.

Delano, Alonzo. *California Correspondence.* Sacramento: Sacramento Book Collectors Club, 1952. Letter to the *New Orleans True Delta,* October 31, 1850, about "philanthropic importation," or prostitution.

De Russailh, Albert Benard. *Last Adventure: San Francisco in 1851.* Translated by Clarkson Crane. San Francisco: Westgate Press, 1931.

Faragher, John Mack. *Eternity Street: Violence and Justice in Frontier Los Angeles.* New York: W. W. Norton, 2016.

Farnham, Eliza W. *California, In-doors and Out; or, How We Farm, Mine, and Live Generally in the Golden State.* New York: Dix, Edwards and Co., 1856.

Federal Manuscript Census, 1860. California State Archives, Sacramento. Unpublished manuscript census quoted in Albert L. Hurtado, *Intimate Frontiers: Sex, Gender and Culture in Old California.* Albuquerque: University of New Mexico Press, 1999, pp. 94–95.

Gentry, Curt. *Madams of San Francisco.* New York: Doubleday, 1964.

Heizer, Robert, ed. *Handbook of North American Indians, Volume 8, California.* Washington, D.C.: Smithsonian, 1978.

Hopkins, Casper T. "Our Divorce Law." *The Pioneer, or California Monthly Magazine,* April 1854: 213. Hopkins signed the article "C.T.H."

Hurtado, Albert L. *Intimate Frontiers: Sex, Gender and Culture in Old California*. Albuquerque: University of New Mexico Press, 1999.

People v. Ah Hoo, Ah Choy and Ah Lee. Case No. 201, May 5, 1876, Los Angeles Justices Court Records, Los Angeles Area Court Records (LAACR). San Marino: Huntington Library.

Pérez, Erika. *Colonial Intimacies: Interethnic Kinship, Sexuality and Marriage in Southern California, 1769–1885*. PhD diss., University of California, Los Angeles, 2010.

Pond, William C. *Gospel Pioneering: Reminiscences of Early Congregationalism in California, 1833–1920*. Oberlin, OH: The News Printing Company, 1921.

Royce, Josiah. *California: A Study of American Character: From the Conquest in 1846 to the Second Vigilance Committee in San Francisco*. Boston: Houghton Mifflin, 1886.

Sacramento Daily Democratic State Journal. September 1, 1855. On revenge against the miner Big Tom. Quoted in Robert Heizer, ed., *They Were Only Diggers: A Collection of Articles from California Newspapers 1851–1866, on Indian and White Relations*. Ramona, CA: Ballena Press, 1974.

Sacramento Daily Union. October 1, 1858. On the cycle of violence in Klamath County.

———. June 21, 1875. On the short courtship of two Livermore residents.

San Francisco [Daily Evening] Bulletin.

"The U.S. Marshalship," April 18, 1856. Sarcastic editorial on the turbulent state of affairs in San Francisco and the Charles Cora trial, by *Bulletin* editor James King of William.

May 26, 1856. Belle Cora vigilance committee notice.

September 13, 1856. Sexual assaults by government agents, or "civilized monsters."

November 14, 1859. Native woman kills white man who sexually assaulted her.

"Charges Woman Conspired to Bring About Downfall," August 2, 1913. Letter from Violet Brown about her entry into prostitution. Quoted in Ivy Anderson and Devon Angus, eds., *Alice: Memoirs of a Barbary Coast Prostitute*. Berkeley: Heyday, 2016.

San Francisco Call. "Confession of a Chinese Slave-Dealer," April 2, 1899. Article on Suey Hin, a Chinese slave dealer based in San Francisco. The report details the practices of trafficking in young Chinese girls.

San Francisco Chronicle. "Horrors of a Great City," December 5, 1869. On Chinese prostitution and the "hospital."

Santa Cruz Evening News. "Rev. Briggs Talks of Alice Smith and Underworld Voice," August 12, 1913.

Sheldon, Henry Bradley. Letters 1851–1858. California State Library, Sacramento, California History Section, Stacks Manuscripts, manuscript box 306.

Shumsky, Neil Larry, and Larry M. Springer. "San Francisco's Zone of Prostitution, 1880–1934." *Journal of Historical Geography,* vol. 7, no. 1 (1981): 73–77.

Soulé, Frank, John H. Gihon, and James Nisbet. *The Annals of San Francisco.* New York: D. Appleton, 1855.

Sridharan, Mohini. "Prostitution in the Early Chinese Community, 1850–1900." Course materials, History 32, "Life, Death and Rebirth of Great American Cities," Dartmouth University, 2017.

State of California.

"An Act Concerning Divorce." *Statutes of California, passed at the 2nd Session of the Legislature, 1851,* chapter 20, March 25, 1851, pp. 186–187. San Jose: Eugene Casserley, State Printer, 1851.

"An Act to Prevent the Kidnapping and Importation of Mongolian, Chinese, and Japanese Females for Criminal and Demoralizing Purposes." *General Laws of the State of California from 1864–1871 Inclusive.* Bill #8525, March 18, 1870, pp. 253–254. San Francisco: A. L. Bancroft, 1871.

"An Act for the Suppression of Chinese Houses of Ill-Fame." *Henning's General Laws of California,* vol. 1, Senate Bill 352, Act 830, March 31, 1866, chapter 505, pp. 641–642. San Francisco: Bender-Moss, 1921, p. 348. Bill amended February 7, 1874.

Stewart, William Morris. *Reminiscences of Senator William M. Stewart of Nevada.* New York: Neale Publishing Company, 1908.

Tibesar, Antonine, ed. *Writings of Junípero Serra.* 4 vols. Washington, D.C.: Academy of American Franciscan History, 1955–1956.

Tong, Benson. *Unsubmissive Women: Chinese Prostitutes in Nineteenth-Century San Francisco.* Norman: University of Oklahoma Press, 1994.

United States Bureau of the Census. "Sacramento City Prostitutes by Age and Ethnicity in 1860." In *Population of the United States in 1860,* complied by Joseph G. C. Kennedy. Washington, D.C.: Government Printing Office, 1864.

———. Documents 1850–1900. The 1850 census includes an appendix with the special 1852 California census.

Wierzbicki, Felix. *California As It Is, and As It May Be.* San Francisco: Washington Bartlett, 1849.

Yung, Judy. *Unbound Feet: A Social History of Chinese Women in San Francisco.* Berkeley: University of California Press, 1995.

Zesch, Scott. *The Chinatown War: Chinese Los Angeles and the Massacre of 1871.* London: Oxford University Press, 2012.

Chapter Seven
Put's Golden Songster, The India Rubber Man, and Pedestrianism: Eccentric and Extraordinary Entertainments

Asbury, Herbert. *The Barbary Coast: An Informal History of the San Francisco Underworld.* New York: Alfred A. Knopf, 1933.

Barry, Theodore A., and Benjamin A. Patten. *Men and Memories of San Francisco, in the "Spring of '50."* San Francisco: A. L. Bancroft, 1856.

Bierce, Ambrose. "Prattle." *The Wasp*, vol. 8, no. 287 (January 27, 1882): 198. Commentary on Oscar Wilde.

———. "Prattle." *The Wasp*, vol. 8, no. 296 (March 31, 1882): 198. Review of Oscar Wilde lecture.

Borthwick, John David. *Three Years in California.* Edinburgh: William Blackwood and Sons, 1857.

Child, L. Marie. "Impressions of Ole Bull," *Daily Alta California* [San Francisco], July 17, 1854. A rapturous review of a performance by celebrated violinist Ole Bull.

Daily Alta California [San Francisco].
  August 14, 1851. Description of the twenty-five-yard footrace.
  September 14, 1851. Description of the ten-mile footrace.
  "Impressions of Ole Bull," July 17, 1854. See Child, L. Marie.
  October 24, 1856. Advertisement for the Mountaineer Museum operated by Grizzly Adams.
  February 19, 1857. Description of Monsieur D'Evani, the "India Rubber Man."
  May 16, 1860. Advertisement for the "Gorgeous Mongolian Spectacle."
  August 8, 1860. Advertisement for Marsh's Juvenile Comedians.
  July 3, 1862. Description of Dr. G. A. Belew, the Great American Hippozaneapprivoiser.
  April 26, 1863. Advertisement for the "Mammoth Crocodile."
  March 5, 1870. Wreath presentation to Ole Bull.
  April 22, 1879. Article on *The Passion Play* and James' O'Neill.

Dana, Richard Henry, Jr. *Two Years Before the Mast: A Personal Narrative.* Boston: Houghton Mifflin, 1911. Originally published in 1840.

Delano, Alonzo. *Old Block's Sketch-Book; or, Tales of California Life. Illustrated with Numerous Elegant Designs, by [Charles] Nahl, the Cruikshank of California.* Sacramento: James Anthony and Co., 1856.

Doten, Alfred. *The Journals of Alfred Doten, 1849–1903.* 3 vols. Reno: University of Nevada Press, 1973.

Douglass, Frederick. *The North Star.* October 27, 1848. On minstrelsy.

Estavan, Lawrence, ed. *San Francisco Theater Research: Minstrelsy.* Vol. 13. San Francisco: 1939.

Ex Parte Newman, 9 Cal. 502 (1858).

Foster, Lois M. *Annals of the San Francisco Stage, 1850–1880.* San Francisco: Federal Theatre Projects, 1936.

Gaer, Joseph, ed. "The Theater of the Gold Rush Decade in San Francisco." Monograph #5, California Literary Research, State Emergency Relief Administration Project, 1935.

Gagey, Edmond. *The San Francisco Stage: A History.* New York: Columbia University Press, 1950.

Golden Era [San Francisco]. October 29, 1854. Review of Christy's Minstrels at San Francisco's Musical Hall.

Gregory, James N. "The Shaping of California." In *Encyclopedia of American Social History.* New York: Scribner, 1993.

Hittell, Theodore H. *The Adventures of James Capen Adams, Mountaineer and Grizzly Bear Hunter of California.* New York: Charles Scribner's Sons, 1911. Originally published in 1860 by Towne and Bacon of San Francisco. Illustrations by Charles Christian Nahl.

Hudson, Lynn M. "Entertaining Citizenship: Masculinity and Minstrelsy in Post-Emancipation San Francisco." *Journal of African American History,* vol. 93, no. 2, Discourses on Race, Sex, and African American Citizenship (Spring 2008): 174–197.

Los Angeles Herald. February 25, 1896. Article on Jo-Jo, the Dog-faced Dog, and Tina Corri.

MacMinn, George A. *The Theater of the Golden Era in California.* Caldwell, ID: Caxton, 1941.

Masonic Standard [New York]. "Washington Lodge Entertains," December 5, 1903. Article listing Tina Corri as a "vocal comedienne."

Massett, Stephen. *Drifting About, or, What Jeems Pipes of Pipesville Saw-and-Did: An Autobiography of Stephen C. Massett.* New York: Carleton, 1858.

New York Clipper. December 15, 1860. Description of Dr. C. H. Bassett's Equestrian Circus. The *New York Clipper* was later renamed *Variety,* the name it uses today.

Pacific Appeal. May 24, 1862. Letter about minstrels from correspondent J.M.B.

Pacific Song Book, The. San Francisco: D. E. Appleton, 1861.

Placerville Mountain Democrat. August 25, 1855. Description of Monsieur
D'Evani, the "India Rubber Man."

Robinson, Alfred. *Life in California*. New York: Wiley and Putnam, 1846.

Sacramento Daily Union.

   "Mr. Grigsby's Pedestrian Feat," September 20, 1854.

   May 5, 1858. Description of Jack Powers's marathon horserace.

   July 29, 1858. Article on Eugene D'Amilie, or "Master Eugene."

   August 15, 1862. Description of Dr. G. A. Belew, the Great American
      Hippozaneapprivoiser.

   "Reminiscences of the Earliest Theatrical Times in California,"
      April 5, 1865. A short history of theatrical presentations in the
      nineteenth century, focusing mostly on Sacramento.

   April 22, 1867. Decision of Judge Matthew Deady.

   April 19, 1879; April 24, 1879; and May 24, 1879. Articles on *The
      Passion Play* and James' O'Neill.

   August 5, 1882. Description of Stephen Massett, also known as "Jeems
      Pipes of Pipesville."

   February 1, 1894. Article on Frank Belton.

San Francisco Bulletin. "The Female Forty Thieves; or, The Fairy Legion
   of the Golden Region," March 20, 1862. Review of *The Female Forty
   Thieves* stage show.

San Francisco Call. July 30, 1900. Article on Zelma Rawlston.

———. "Early Theatricals on the Pacific Coast," March 17, 1901. A
   short history of theatrical presentations in the nineteenth century,
   focusing mostly on San Francisco.

San Francisco Chronicle. "The Issue of the Day: Saloon Keepers As a Rule,
   Bid Defiance to the Sunday Law," March 20, 1882.

———. "The Sunday Law: Its Observance in Different Parts of the State,"
   January 16, 1873.

San Francisco Daily Dramatic Chronicle. "The Sunday Law," March 6,
   1867. Reaction against the "Sunday Closing Law."

San Francisco Daily National. March 11, 1859. Description of James
   Kennovan.

Schodt, Frederik L. *Professor Ridley and the Imperial Japanese Troupe*.
   Berkeley: Stone Bridge Press, 2012.

Starr, Kevin, and Richard J. Orsi. *Rooted in Barbarous Soil: People, Culture,
   and Community in Gold Rush California*. Berkeley: University of
   California Press, 2000.

State of California. "An Act for the Better Observance of the Sabbath."
   The Statutes of California, Passed at 9th session of the California Legislature,

1858, chapter 171, April 10, 1858, pp. 124–125. Sacramento: John O'Meara, State Printer, 1858.

———. "An Act for the Observance of the Sabbath." *The Statutes of California, Passed at 12th session of the California Legislature, 1861,* chapter 535, May 20, 1861, p. 655. Sacramento: Charles T. Botts, State Printer, 1861.

Stewart, George R. "The Drama in a Frontier Theater." In *The Parrott Presentation Volume.* New Jersey: Princeton, 1935.

Stone, John A. *Put's Original California Songster.* San Francisco: D. E. Appleton, 1858.

Thompson and West. *History of Nevada County.* Oakland: Thompson and West, 1880.

Woodson, J. A., comp. *Life and Adventures of James Kennovan, Champion Pedestrian of the World.* San Francisco: J. W. Sullivan, 1863.

Zeitlin, Jeremy. "What's Sunday All About? The Rise and Fall of California's Sunday Closing Law." *California Legal History,* vol. 7 (2012): 355–380.

Chapter Eight
Hornswogglers, Honey-Foglers, and Humbugs: Scoundrels and Charlatans

Asbury, Herbert. *The Barbary Coast: An Informal History of the San Francisco Underworld.* New York: Alfred A. Knopf, 1933.

Beebe, Lucius, and Charles Clegg. *San Francisco's Golden Era.* Berkeley: Howell-North, 1960.

Bierce, Ambrose. *The Devil's Dictionary.* New York, and Washington, D.C.: Neal Publishing, 1911, as part of *The Collected Works of Ambrose Bierce: Volume VII.* The first appearance of Bierce's definition of "clairvoyant" was in *The Wasp* [San Francisco], vol. 7, no. 259 (July 15, 1881): 37.

Byrnes, Thomas F. *Professional Criminals of America.* New York: Cassell, 1886.

Builder: An Illustrated Weekly Magazine [London]. June 23, 1877. Article about how wealthy San Franciscans build their mansions.

California State Legislature. *California Legislative Information.* https://leginfo.legislature.ca.gov. California code search website provided by the California State Legislature.

Carrington, Hereward. *The Physical Phenomena of Spiritualism, Fraudulent and Genuine.* Boston: Small, Maynard, and Company, 1907.

Carson, James H. *Early Recollections of the Mines, and a Description of the Great Tulare Valley.* Reprint, Tarrytown, NY: W. Abbatt, 1931. Carson's recollections originally appeared as a supplement in the [Stockton] *San Joaquin Republican* in 1852.

Daily Alta California [San Francisco].

> "San Joaquin Intelligence," September 8, 1850. Robert Fletcher's Goldometer.

> "From the Southern Mines," September 22, 1850. Robert Fletcher's Goldometer.

> "Report of Clarence King, United States Geologist," November 26, 1872. Article about the Great Diamond Hoax of 1872.

> "General Colton's Exhaustive Report," November 26, 1872. Article about the Great Diamond Hoax of 1872.

> "Mining Engineer Janin's Report," November 26, 1872. Article about the Great Diamond Hoax of 1872.

> "A Swindle—Exposure of the Diamond Fraud," November 29, 1872. Extensive reporting on the Great Diamond Hoax of 1872.

> "The Confidence Queen," June 10, 1888. Article about "Big Bertha" Heyman.

> June 15, 1888. Article about the trial of "Big Bertha" Heyman.

Emmons, Samuel F. Unpublished diary entry of October 6, 1872. Samuel F. Emmons Papers, Box 32, Manuscript Division, Library of Congress.

Goodyear, W. A. [Watson Andrews]. Letter to the *Placerville Mountain Democrat*, 1871. Quoted in "Statistics and Technology of the Precious Metals," Department of the Interior, Census Office, Report of S. [Samuel] F. Emmons and G. F. Becker. Washington, D.C.: Government Printing Office, 1885.

Harpending, Asbury. *The Great Diamond Hoax and Other Stirring Episodes in the Life of Asbury Harpending—An Epic of Early California.* Edited by James H. Wilkins. San Francisco: James H. Barry Press, 1913.

Hart, Ernest. "The Eternal Gullible." *Century Magazine*, vol. 48 (October 1894): 833–839.

Haskins, Charles Warren. *The Argonauts of California, being the reminiscences of scenes and incidents that occurred in California in early mining days.* New York: Fords, Howard and Hulbert, 1890.

Los Angeles Herald. "A Senile Sucker," March 3, 1890. Article on the "gold brick swindle" of David Parks.

Louisville [Kentucky] Courier-Journal. December 16, 1872. Quoted in Robert Wilson, *The Explorer King: Adventure, Science and the Great Diamond Hoax.* New York: Scribner, 2006.

Naversen, Kenneth. *California Victorians*. Woodburn, OR: Beautiful America Publishing Company, 1998.

New York Sun. "The Diamond Fraud," December 5, 1872. Article about the Great Diamond Hoax of 1872.

New York Times.
"The Diamond Hoax," December 6, 1872. Editorial about lessons to be learned from the Great Diamond Hoax of 1872.
December 8, 1872. Bookkeeper J. B. Cooper's statement to the executive committee of the Lent-Harpending Company.
"Bertha Heyman's Pride," July 11, 1881. Article about Big Bertha Heyman's criminal philosophy and actions.
"A Smart Female Swindler," October 27, 1881. Article about Big Bertha Heyman.
"Crocker Estate Buys Property That Caused a Bitter Feud," January 20, 1904. Article describing the removal of Charles Crocker's "spite fence."

Rickard, Thomas A. "Salting: The Nefarious 'Art' and Its Age-old Results as Practiced on the Mining Fraternity." *Engineering and Mining Journal*, vol. 142 (March 1941): 42–52.

Sacramento Daily Union. "The Diamond Frauds," November 26, 1872. Article about the Great Diamond Hoax of 1872.
———. November 29, 1872. Reverend Stebbens praises Clarence King.

Sacramento Transcript. "Progress of the Time," October 18, 1850. Professor Alberto Gabrialdo Turonski's Patent Hydro Electro Magnetic Goldometer.

San Francisco Call. "Connor's Cigar Made Hoff Sick," March 18, 1898. Description of a "gold brick swindle."
———. "McIntosh and Haymond," April 14, 1898. Benjamin McIntosh disbarred and labeled a "legal scalawag."

San Francisco Chronicle.
"Salted!," November 25, 1872. Article about the Great Diamond Hoax of 1872.
"Unmasked!," November 26, 1872. Article about the Great Diamond Hoax of 1872.
November 28, 1872. Article about the Great Diamond Hoax of 1872.
November 1, 1902. Article about Charles Crocker's "spite fence."

San Francisco Daily Evening Bulletin. November 26, 1872. Editorial about the Great Diamond Hoax of 1872.

"Snudgger's Investigations into Table-turning." *Hutchings' Illustrated California Magazine*, vol. 2, no. 2 (August 1857): 65–70.

"States Most Vulnerable to Identity Theft and Fraud,"
Wallethub.com, 2019. https://wallethub.com/edu/
states-where-identity-theft-and-fraud-are-worst/17549/.

Twain, Mark. *Roughing It*. Hartford, CT: American Publishing Company,
1872. Reprint, New York: Harper and Brothers, 1906.

Wilson, Robert. "The Great Diamond Hoax of 1872." *Smithsonian
Magazine*, June 2004.

———. *The Explorer King: Adventure, Science and the Great Diamond Hoax*.
New York: Scribner, 2006.

Young, Otis E., Jr. *Western Mining: An Informal Account of Precious-Metals
Prospecting, Placering, Lode Mining, and Milling on the American Frontier
from Spanish Times to 1893*. Norman: University of Oklahoma Press,
1970.

Acknowledgments

My heartfelt appreciation and greatest respect to my comrades and friends, the extraordinary crew at Heyday: Steve Wasserman, Executive Director/Publisher; Gayle Wattawa, Editorial Director; Editor Lisa K. Marietta; Marketing and Publicity Director Mariko Conner; Sales Manager Christopher Miya; Designer Ashley Ingram; Art Director Diane Lee; and all the remarkable personnel that comprise the amazing Team Heyday.

Extra-special thanks to my colleagues at the California History Room of the California State Library, Sacramento. I spent many, many hours in the library researching *Hellacious California* and being endlessly amazed by the variety and excellence of the collections. I was also blessed to enjoy the extensive guidance of my friend Gary F. Kurutz, retired Principal Librarian/Director of Special Collections and namesake of the California History Section Reading Room, and the incredible staff of the State Library. They are jewels beyond compare.

My thanks and appreciation to my Sierra College Press family. I am especially grateful to editor-in-chief Joe Medeiros and the outstanding Board of Directors. I have spent many pleasurable and fascinating hours in their company. I cannot adequately express my gratitude for their boundless support and friendship.

Finally, my love and thanks to my grandmother Mary Ethel Lewis Winkle (1888–1980), who told me fascinating stories of her childhood during the nineteenth century and helped spark my personal and professional interest in the history of the era. It is with great pride that I dedicate this book to my grandma.

About Sierra College Press

The Sierra College Press endeavors to reach beyond the library, laboratory, and classroom to promote and examine the Sierra Nevada. For more information, please visit www.sierracollege.edu/press.

Board of Directors: Chris Benn, Rebecca Bocchicchio, Sean Booth, Keely Carroll, Kerrie Cassidy, Mandy Davies, Dan DeFoe, David Dickson, Tom Fillebrown, Christine Freeman, Rebecca Gregg, Brian Haley, Rick Heide, Jay Hester, David Kuchera, Joe Medeiros (Editor-in-Chief), Lynn Medeiros, Sue Michaels, Gary Noy, Bart O'Brien, Sabrina Pape (Board Chair), Mike Price, Jennifer Skillen, Barbara Vineyard, Lynette Vrooman, and Randy White.

SIERRA COLLEGE PRESS

About the Author

A Sierra Nevada native and the son and grandson of Cornish hardrock gold miners, Gary Noy has taught history at Sierra Community College in Rocklin, California, since 1987. A graduate of UC Berkeley and CSU Sacramento, he is the founder and former director of the Sierra College Center for Sierra Nevada Studies and the editor-in-chief emeritus of the Sierra College Press. In 2006, the Oregon-California Trails Association (OCTA), a national historical society, selected Noy as Educator of the Year. He is the author of *Distant Horizon: Documents from the Nineteenth-Century American West* (1999); the coeditor, with Rick Heide, of *The Illuminated Landscape: A Sierra Nevada Anthology* (2010); the author of *Sierra Stories: Tales of Dreamers, Schemers, Bigots, and Rogues* (2014); and the author of *Gold Rush Stories: 49 Tales of Seekers, Scoundrels, Loss, and Luck* (2017). In 2016, *Sierra Stories* received the Gold Medal for Best Regional Non-Fiction from the Next Generation Indie Book Awards.

Photo by Mike Price

227